Building Your Career in Psychology

D1710888

Building Your Career in Psychology is a new practical, aspirational, and experiential book designed to help readers make informed decisions about their college, career, and life success.

The primary theme in this book is that *psychological knowledge makes a difference in people's lives*. Building on this theme, this book provides an empowered process for making the most of college and other career preparation experience, helping the reader to set the stage for academic, career, and life success. This book emphasizes academic skills, unwritten rules, career planning, and developing relationships – both professional and personal. Moreover, this book includes evidence-based career development content and exercises, as well as other resources to assist readers in discovering their own path to a meaningful career and life.

Highlights of this book include:

- Discussion of career options at the bachelor's, master's, and doctoral levels
- Forms, handouts, and exercises (both basic and advanced) to facilitate deeper processing and application of content
- References and resources for further information
- Website with additional information, including instructor resources
- Recognition and respect for the diversity of people, their experiences, and paths

Featuring the best practices in facilitating career decision-making and planning, this book is a must read for undergraduate and graduate students in psychology courses as well as anyone interested in a career in psychology.

Marie S. Hammond, Ph.D., is Professor of Psychology at Tennessee State University, Fellow in the American Psychological Association (Division 17), and licensed psychologist (HSP). She has over 30 years' experience teaching, researching, and practicing vocational psychology. Her research focuses on improving career development theory and practice related to diverse populations.

Peggy Brady-Amoon, Ph.D., Associate Professor at Seton Hall University, is a Fellow of the American Psychological Association, licensed psychologist, counselor, and certified school counselor. Building on decades of experience, her work is broadly focused on educational and career development with a particular emphasis on access and opportunity for under-respected people.

'*Building Your Career in Psychology* is a unique and comprehensive resource for psychology students who want to plan and manage their careers, understand career decision-making, and understand career paths in psychology. This book is an equally important resource for faculty researchers, practitioners, mentors, and teachers who are interested in equity, diversity, and inclusion, as well as those who need a roadmap of concrete, proactive actions and processes to support ethnic and minority students to reach their career goals. Historically Black Colleges and Universities (HBCUs) have been very successful at increasing the number of African American students in STEM and Psychology to persist and graduate from college, graduate school, and enter successful careers. The authors outline specific strategies that have made these HBCUs successful. These include teaching students the unwritten rules for success, and creating a welcoming, educational learning environment for academic excellence and experiential learning. Especially important are the chapters that focus on understanding the importance of personal and professional relationships for developing supportive networks and a positive sense of community. This book addresses critical topics that will provide support to students of color and increase representation and participation of these students in psychology as a field of study.'

Ruth L. Greene, *Ed.D., O'Herron Distinguished Professor of Psychology, Johnson C. Smith University*

'As someone who has taught an introduction to counseling course for many years, this is exactly the book I have been needing! It will help me in my efforts to guide students through the process of exploring the helping professions and charting their future course.'

Kimberly Howard, *Ph.D., Associate Professor, Boston University*

'How can a wise psychology student best plan ahead, to succeed in a competitive graduate school and career in psychology or a related field? In this new volume, Professors Marie Hammond and Margaret (Peggy) Brady-Amoon offer their expert "insider" advice that can be so invaluable to career-oriented students. This volume includes a trove of useful exercises, practical websites, important resources, and informative "side-bars" – all based on the large but elusive literature on career-preparation. This volume clearly gives a valuable "edge" to psychology students planning ahead for a successful career.'

Harold Takooshian, *Ph.D., Professor Fordham University*

Building Your Career in Psychology

Marie S. Hammond and
Peggy Brady-Amoon

2022

Dear Thomas,

Congratulations &
best wishes on your
new adventure!

Love,
Peggy

Peggy Brady-Amoon

Routledge
Taylor & Francis Group

LONDON AND NEW YORK

Cover image: © Getty Images

First published 2022
by Routledge
2 Park Square, Milton Park, Abingdon, Oxon OX14 4RN

and by Routledge
605 Third Avenue, New York, NY 10158

Routledge is an imprint of the Taylor & Francis Group, an informa business

© 2022 Marie S. Hammond & Peggy Brady-Amoon

British Library Cataloguing-in-Publication Data
A catalogue record for this book is available from the British Library

Library of Congress Cataloging-in-Publication Data
Names: Hammond, Marie S., 1955– author. | Brady-Amoon, Peggy, 1956– author.
Title: Building your career in psychology / Marie S. Hammond & Peggy Brady-Amoon.
Description: Abingdon, Oxon ; New York, NY : Routledge, 2022. | Includes bibliographical references and index.
Identifiers: LCCN 2021025665 (print) | LCCN 2021025666 (ebook) | ISBN 9780367274986 (hbk) | ISBN 9780367274993 (pbk) | ISBN 9780429296413 (ebk)
Subjects: LCSH: Psychology—Vocational guidance. | Career development.
Classification: LCC BF76 .H36 2022 (print) | LCC BF76 (ebook) | DDC 150.23—dc23
LC record available at https://lccn.loc.gov/2021025665
LC ebook record available at https://lccn.loc.gov/2021025666

ISBN: 9780367274986 (hbk)
ISBN: 9780367274993 (pbk)
ISBN: 9780429296413 (ebk)

DOI: 10.4324/9780429296413

Typeset in Times New Roman
by Apex CoVantage, LLC

Access the Support Material: www.routledge.com/9780367274993

Contents

11   Doctoral degrees: Educational options and career paths   178

12   Specializations, allied professions, and using psychology in the world   192

Boxes

Figures

Tables

Vignettes

Preface

HOW THIS BOOK CAME INTO BEING

We have a unique perspective as counseling psychologists and, more specifically, vocational psychologists. We pursued these specialties because we are interested in and committed to healthy human development in context; the dignity of work, broadly defined; and social justice. Moreover, we wrote this book because, in decades of working with diverse students and others exploring and engaging in career development, we've observed that most people benefit from additional information and guidance as they build their careers. Sure, some people seem to know exactly what they want to do and go out and reach those goals. Others get and sometimes even stay stuck. The majority, however, fall somewhere in the middle of these two extremes. As such, this book recognizes the differences in students' and others' decision-making status, knowledge, and skills (Hammond, 2017) – and is designed to address the broad range of career development skill sets, life/work experiences, and goals.

AUTHOR'S BIOGRAPHICAL SKETCHES

Marie S. Hammond, Ph.D., is currently a Professor of Psychology at Tennessee State University in Nashville, Tennessee. She currently teaches research methods, statistics, psychometrics, and testing courses in the APA-accredited doctoral program in Counseling Psychology at this Historically Black, Land Grant University. She has worked in HBCUs and other minority-serving institutions for more than 30 years and has used her education and experiences to address issues of career, as well as mental and psychological health in government, industry, and higher education. She is a Licensed Psychologist with Health Service Provider certification, was elected Fellow of the Society of Counseling Psychology in the American Psychological Association and was recently named the first Distinguished Researcher in Psychology at Tennessee State University.

Peggy Brady-Amoon, Ph.D., currently serves as an associate professor in the Department of Professional Psychology and Family Therapy at Seton Hall University. Building on decades of community, political, and counseling experience, her teaching, scholarship, and service are broadly focused on educational and career development, with a particular emphasis on access and opportunity for under-respected people. Dr. Brady-Amoon is a Fellow of the American Psychological Association through the Society of Counseling Psychology and a graduate of APA's Leadership Institute for Women in Psychology. She is licensed as a psychologist (NY), professional counselor (LPC; NJ), and certified as a school counselor (NJ). She earned a BA in Political Science and Spanish from SUNY Oswego, a MS in Counseling from Long Island University, and a Professional Diploma in Counseling and Personnel Services and Ph.D. in Counseling Psychology from Fordham University.

REFERENCE

Hammond, M. S. (2017). Differences in career development among first-year students: A proposed typology for intervention planning. *Journal of The First-Year Experience & Students in Transition, 29*(2), 45–64.

Introduction

Are you excited about a career or potential career in psychology? Do you understand how and why to engage with psychology? To know how to find and make the most of your opportunities to succeed in this field? This new practical, aspirational, and experiential book is designed to help readers make informed decisions about their college, career, and life success. Emphasizing best practices in facilitating career decision-making and planning for broadly diverse populations, this book offers an empowered process for achieving career and relevant life goals.

RATIONALE FOR THIS BOOK

Psychology is one of the most popular undergraduate majors in the U.S. (National Center for Education Statistics [NCES], 2011, 2017, 2019) and a career with wide ranging opportunities. With all that possibility, how do you figure out what works for you? This book serves as a practical guide and resource for people interested in psychology careers. It emphasizes making informed decisions to maximize engagement in college, career decision-making, preparation, and management. It includes relevant career development content and exercises, college success content and practice, as well as reflection exercises and other resources to assist readers in discovering their own path to a meaningful life and meaningful life's work.

The primary theme in this book is that *psychological knowledge makes a difference in people's lives*. As such, we emphasize the role of psychology in promoting well-being and solving real-world issues. Building on this theme, this book serves as an empowered process guide for making the most of your college and other career preparation experience, with a distinctive emphasis on 1) career/life planning and decision-making and 2) healthy professional and personal relationships. This text is also unique in respecting and addressing the experiences and interests and career development needs of an increasingly diverse population, including nontraditional students.

ORGANIZATION OF THE BOOK

There are many ways to use this book. This book is organized into parts in order to support both student learning and teaching faculty. The parts focus on major aspects of both career development and success in navigating the process of becoming successful in a psychology-oriented career path. As there are many excellent resources available to support you along the way, we have included references or mentions to valuable information sources, as well as people and offices that can support you as you develop more sophisticated techniques and methods for managing your career. These may change, so we apologize in advance if some are not available when you encounter this book. We encourage you to utilize these and other resources you find as you navigate your life and career journey.

Part I – *Psychology and How It Helps You Reach Your Goals*, frames the career development process as one of finding the best fit for who you are – your values, interests, personality, and skills. We do this by providing an overview of psychology career paths at different levels in Chapter 1. In Chapter 2, our goal is to help you see how the different aspects of work in psychology relate to your major and to graduate training in psychology so that you are empowered to think about and plan for your future. Chapter 3 introduces career decision-making and career management and related processes. This chapter provides some basics to help you recognize and use your developing critical thinking skills to identify what role you want to play in your psychology career.

Part II – *Practical Guidance, Unwritten Rules, and Planning to Reach Your Goals*, shifts to addressing many of the questions that students and career changers have asked us over the years. Chapter 4 addresses not only the basics of academic skills, but hopefully communicates the *why* about confusing aspects of being successful in your educational endeavors. As there is much more to know than can be adequately covered in this text, we include references to other sources that have worked well for our students and clients. Chapter 5 is a compilation of ideas and thoughts that have resonated with others with whom we've had the honor to advise, counsel, mentor, and support in their career development. Chapter 6 is focused on one of the foundational skills for managing the opportunities and demands of a career in psychology – that is, the ability to plan, prioritize, and be strategic in working towards your success. This chapter provides detailed instructions on developing goals and various types of plans that will allow you to more effectively balance your life and career.

Part III – *The Role of Relationships in Your Educational and Career Success*, is a unique and, we believe, very important section of this book. This topic is one that we have not seen in other books in this area and believe that it has become more important than ever to directly address these topics. The two chapters in this part of the text are designed to help you see beneath the surface of the educational process to better understand how relationships may impact your development and success. Our goal with these chapters is for you to be more comfortable understanding the role of interpersonal processes in educational and professional development. Chapter 7 focuses on relationships that directly impact your professional development and attempts to support you in learning to work with and manage those relationships in a positive manner. Chapter 8 highlights the role of personal relationships in maintaining as balanced a life as possible as you develop into the professional that you desire to be.

Part IV – *Career Paths and Options at Different Educational Levels*, is designed to provide you with additional information to help you choose the path that you will take to implementing your personalized career trajectory. Each chapter is focused on highlighting options and issues relevant to career paths for individuals completing the specified level of education. As a result, each chapter is uniquely focused – with the exception of Chapter 9. Chapter 9 is focused on career paths with a bachelor's degree in psychology. It also includes a reflection process that allows you to look back at the work that you completed in earlier chapters of this book and synthesize it so that you can move forward with your planning more intentionally and confidently. Thus, this chapter is a good chapter to read for anyone reading this text. Chapter 10 covers educational and career options at the master's level, while Chapter 11 addresses the same topics for those desiring to complete a doctorate. Please note that we discuss issues of licensure for those individuals wanting to do therapy and/or practice, as licensure is critical for individuals moving in these directions. Rather than a summary chapter, we chose to include a chapter on particular parts of psychology (specializations) as well as on related professions. The goal here is to help you better understand the diversity of psychology, as well as related professions so you can make the best choice for yourself. In sum, our goal is that by reading and working with this book, you gain perspective, confidence, and skills to more effectively manage your career.

ASSUMPTIONS ABOUT THE READER

We expect readers will be people interested in careers in psychology. Most will be undergraduate students however, others may be prospective students, recent or not-so-recent graduates, or college/university faculty. We also expect readers will benefit from the guided skill development process to make informed life/career decisions across the lifespan. In addition, readers, including returning and other older adults with varying life and work experience, will find this text focuses on building an appropriate level of confidence and skills and/or updating them for success in college, career, and life development.

This text also provides readily accessible guidance to promote college success as well as career and occupational information. We also focus on the practical matter of what to do with a bachelor's or master's degree in psychology, including graduate training in psychology as well as graduate training and careers in sister professions (e.g., counseling and social work). Therefore, this experiential, practical text is valuable for all readers, regardless of their intended or actual career path.

PEDAGOGY FOR FACULTY TEACHING COURSES ON CAREERS IN PSYCHOLOGY

We approached this text with a social justice orientation and developmental approach. Respecting the diversity of students, including older students, this book intentionally builds on readers' experiences, other knowledge, values, and goals. It takes the perspective that students – and faculty – know their lives best, and therefore are best suited to make their own choices (Brady-Amoon, 2011). At the same time, this text takes the position that college success, career and life preparation, and decision-making is not necessarily intuitive, particularly for people who are among the first in their families and/or communities to pursue an advanced degree (Brown & Krane, 2000; Hammond, 2017). It therefore takes the approach that structured guidance from seasoned professionals (i.e., the authors and faculty who adopt this book) will serve as an excellent resource for the specific course for which it is adopted – and as a resource beyond that course.

This orientation is grounded in current best practices in the scholarship of teaching and learning (SOTL) and the more recent findings in the area known as "productive persistence" (Silva & White, 2013). Facilitating deep learning requires ensuring that students are able to approach learning from a "growth mindset" (e.g., Dweck, 2016). The use of current examples, relevant websites, informational interviewing, and small group discussion will facilitate the processing necessary to solidify one's choices and planning. Please note that all individuals described in this book are composites designed to illustrate specific points and do not represent any specific person. Furthermore, drawing from the students' own experiences of problem solving, decision-making, and future planning, the text will guide students to generalize their skillsets in order to prepare them for a lifetime of career management and adaptability.

This text is unique in its provision of practical, experiential, and individualized guidance about career preparation, decision-making, and career and life success. It is also distinct in its inclusive approach including intentional recognition of the uniqueness and strengths of people who identify with groups that are historically underrepresented in higher education and the professions. Furthermore, this text and related website will provide support to Psychology Faculty who desire to increase their students' success, understanding of the field, and informed decision-making. It's informed by best practices in teaching and learning and helps faculty meet American Psychological Association (APA) Guidelines for undergraduate and graduate psychology.

REFERENCES

Brady-Amoon, P. (2011). Humanism, feminism, and multiculturalism: Essential elements of social justice in counseling, education, and advocacy. *Journal of Humanistic Counseling, 50*(2), 135–148. https://doi.org/10.1002/j.2161-1939.2011.tb00113.x

Brown, S. D., & Krane, N. E. R. (2000). Four (or five) sessions and a cloud of dust: Old assumptions and new observations about career counseling. In S. D. Brown & R. W. Lent (Eds.), *Handbook of counseling psychology* (3rd ed., pp. 740–766). John Wiley & Sons.

Dweck, C. S. (2016). *Mindset: The new psychology of success* (Updated). Random House.

Hammond, M. S. (2017). Differences in career development among first-year students: A proposed typology for intervention planning. *Journal of the First-Year Experience & Students in Transition, 29*(2), 45–64.

National Center for Education Statistics. (2011). *Digest of education statistics*. Table 290. Bachelor's, master's, and doctor's degrees conferred by degree-granting institutions, by sex of student and discipline division: 2009–10. http://nces.ed.gov/programs/digest/d11/tables/dt11_290.asp

National Center for Education Statistics. (2017). *Digest of education statistics*. Table 318.30. Bachelor's, master's, and doctor's degrees conferred by postsecondary institutions, by sex of student and discipline division: 2014–15. https://nces.ed.gov/programs/digest/d16/tables/dt16_318.30.asp

National Center for Education Statistics. (2019). Table 318.30. Bachelor's, master's, and doctor's degrees conferred by postsecondary institutions, by sex of student and discipline division: 2017-18. https://nces.ed.gov/programs/digest/d19/tables/dt19_318.30.asp

Silva, E., & White, T. (2013). Pathways to improvement: Using psychological strategies to help college students master developmental math. *Carnegie Foundation for the Advancement of Teaching*. www.carnegiefoundation.org

Acknowledgments

It is important for us to acknowledge the help, support, and assistance of those who have been walking with us through the process of producing the book. We would first like to thank the editors and staff at Routledge for making this book possible, particularly Lucy McClune, Sadé Lee, and Nicole Salazar, who provided helpful guidance and suggestions throughout the process. Our thanks to you. We appreciate the comments and feedback from the anonymous reviewers who gave of their time – to all of you, many thanks. We hope you like what we did with your feedback. We are also grateful for the many people, too numerous to mention by name, who nurtured and supported our interest and work in vocational psychology and career development, especially those who supported the development of the ideas that have coalesced into this book. To our teachers, mentors, and our colleagues in the Society for Counseling Psychology, the Society for Vocational Psychology, and the National Career Development Association, we say *thank you* for your colleagueship over the years.

This book grew out of our experiences – the communities in which we were raised and those we've chosen to live and work in as adults. Thus, there are many people who deserve thanks for helping to shape our worldviews, priorities, and values who may not realize their impact. To them, we extend our humble appreciation for helping us deepen our understanding of the dignity of work, broadly defined, and the associations among meaningful work, well-being, and social justice. We would also like to thank the clients, workshop and research participants as well as students and research team members who have challenged our thinking about the complex issues of life, career, and work, as well as allowing us to assist and support them on their journey toward their own careers.

Marie: I would like to thank the faculty and staff at Lincoln University (MO), William Woods University, the University of Tulsa, and Tennessee State University for the opportunity to practice, teach, and research career development, as well as the National Science Foundation for their support of research on African American and women STEM students. These experiences and research have done much to refine my thinking about helping students to build effective careers. My thanks to Dr. Norman Gysbers, who stimulated my interest in careers and who served as a role model for excellence in teaching. Finally, my thanks to my research team, the Career Commitment and Retention in STEM research team, and all the colleagues, students, family, and friends who have shared their stories and/or support throughout the years. I appreciate you all and express my gratitude.

Peggy: I am grateful for the many teachers, mentors, colleagues, friends, and family members who have supported me and my dreams, including writing this book. I would also like to thank my colleagues at Seton Hall University for my 2017–2018 sabbatical and Spring 2020 Provost's course release, both of which facilitated the development and writing of this book. Special thanks to Hind Fouad Albana, Ph.D., who, as a volunteer doctoral student at Seton Hall, wrote the first draft of a key part of Chapter 7. Dr. Albana, I am proud to cite your dissertation in this book. The process of writing a book about career decision-making and management in psychology prompted a great deal of personal reflection on my own career development and a renewed appreciation for the many people who opened doors for me, which is something I aspire to do for others. Special thanks and love to my husband and best friend, Joseph Brady-Amoon, our adult children, and wonderful grandchildren, all of whom bring love – and so much more – to my life.

PART I

Psychology and how it helps you reach your goals

CHAPTER 1

How does psychology change the world?

ORIENTING QUESTIONS

1. How has psychology contributed to understanding ourselves and others?
2. What are the most popular career directions for people with bachelor's degrees in psychology?
3. Will the skills and knowledge you learn in psychology help you in other fields? After graduation?
4. Does understanding yourself help you understand and work better with others?
5. How can you leverage psychology to improve your life? To change the world?

DOI: 10.4324/9780429296413-2

HOW PSYCHOLOGY HAS CHANGED THE WORLD

Psychology, as a relatively young profession, has made a positive difference for individuals, families, other groups, and society as a whole. Before the emergence of psychology – and since that time – people all over the world, particularly philosophers, clergy, and other spiritual people deeply considered, reflected upon, and shared their thoughts and beliefs about human development, including the causes of and amelioration of human suffering. Some of those ideas continue to influence us today. Psychology has also contributed to understanding ourselves and others through advances in the science, art, and the delivery of psychological services, including psychotherapy. Psychotherapy is not only popular, it's also effective. Psychotherapy is significantly more effective than medication for anxiety, depression, and other disorders. It is also more effective than some generally accepted medical procedures (Wampold, 2011). More specific to this book, vocational interventions, including career counseling, are also effective. Moreover, research shows that college students who successfully complete a career planning course are more likely than their peers who didn't take the course to make good choices about their major and career – and complete their degree (Whiston & Blustein, 2013)!

In the past century plus, psychology has also contributed to health care, for example, through increased understanding of subjects such as pain management (Jensen & Turk, 2014), law, education, politics, science, religion, international relations, and more. In fact, it's difficult to think of any area of human functioning or interaction that has not been positively impacted by psychology. Psychologists and psychological science have also made – and are making – a difference through advocacy and policy work (APA, 2019a). To illustrate, psychologists have and continue to be influential in work to promote and protect human rights, improve health care, advance educational and career opportunities, and much more (Stamm & Fowler, 2019; APS, n.d.).

Let's look at an example. Imagine a world where people with mental illness were assumed to have a "bad character" (a moral judgment) and were thrown into prison. Sounds terrible, doesn't it? However, this was the situation back in the 1800s. Fortunately, most human societies have progressed from believing that mental (and other) illnesses were religious/moralistic failures or punishments, to one in which mental illness was considered evidence of a character flaw, to the current psychologically informed, complex view of psychological functioning. In the future, we will likely develop an even clearer picture of this process – especially with your help.

How did society move from the former belief systems to the current belief system? The growth of the field of psychological science has provided a variety of information ranging from the functioning of the brain and its structures to theories and research on psychological functioning, disorders, treatment, and so much more. More specifically, psychological research on mental illness has provided society with information on the etiology (that is the source or origins of mental illness) through developing innovative ways of assisting individuals, families, and other groups. This research is conducted by faculty members in post-secondary education institutions as well as researchers in professional organizations, government agencies, and independent not-for-profit organizations such as the National Alliance on Mental Illness (NAMI) and the Psychiatric Research Association (PRA). These organizations also work to disseminate credible research about mental illness, treatment, and recovery to the public. However, just conducting research would not have made the change alone. It takes members of the general public, psychologists, and professional psychology organizations such as the American Psychological Association (APA) applying research to develop and support legislation, such as the Americans with Disabilities Act (ADA; APA, 2008). As education is one of the key ways to reducing the stigma of mental illness that far too often exacerbates distress and prevents help-seeking (Corrigan et al., 2014; Maranzan, 2016), psychological research has and continues to contribute to increased knowledge and understanding of mental illness, evidence-based interventions, and recovery (Corrigan et al., 2014).

BOX 1.1

ADA Definition

The Americans with Disabilities Act (ADA; APA, 2008) prohibits discrimination against people with disabilities, including mental or psychiatric disabilities.

Notwithstanding this progress, there is much more to do to understand and ideally prevent the pain that most often accompanies untreated and undertreated mental illness. Although people with mental illness are no longer summarily jailed, we still need more compassionate and well-trained human service providers, researchers, and informed policy makers to address the more than 50% of people in US jails and prisons with a diagnosed – and often untreated – mental illness (Roth, 2018).

PEOPLE IN PSYCHOLOGY WHO HAVE CHANGED THE WORLD

Speaking of how psychology has impacted the world, it is important to recognize that the field of psychology does not change the world – it's the people in the psychology field that change the world. As such, there are numerous psychologists and others using psychology whose work continues to make a difference in people's lives. You've likely heard of others, perhaps including Wilhelm Wundt, who established the first dedicated psychology laboratory and the scientific foundation of psychology (Benjamin, 1997). It's also important to know about others, including Mary Whiton Calkins, who was denied her doctoral degree in psychology from Harvard because she was a woman, yet made multiple contributions to the field, including election as the first woman president of the American Psychological Association in 1905 (Young, 2010). How about Kenneth Clark and Mamie Phipps Clark, the first African Americans to earn doctoral degrees in psychology from Columbia University in 1940 and 1943 and whose work and expert testimony demonstrating the effects of internalized racism contributed in many ways, including the 1954 U.S. Supreme Court decision that declared laws upholding racially segregated schools unconstitutional (Karera, 2010)? Or, Frank Parsons, social reformer, lawyer, and professor, who is considered the father of the vocational guidance movement. With increasing numbers of immigrants from both the countryside and overseas, Parsons established the "Breadwinner's College" at a settlement house in Boston at what was to become the Boston Vocational Bureau in order to assist individuals to find employment that suited the individual (Parsons, 1909; Pope & Sveinsdottir, 2005). We offer these examples – as well as those in Box 1.2 – to illustrate that psychology is a diverse, evolving field that increasingly welcomes and indeed needs people with diverse experiences and perspectives – including YOU – to participate.

BOX 1.2

Example Role Models

For additional inspiration and role models, check out these resources:

www.apa.org/pi/oema/resources/ethnicity-health/psychologists/
www.activeminds.org/blog/10-african-african-american-psychologists-you-should-know/
https://feministvoices.com/

Beyond the diversity of people who have and continue to contribute to psychology, psychology itself is a dynamic, scientifically informed profession. We'll explore these and other specialty areas as well as different ways to be involved in psychology in Chapter 2 and subsequent chapters. We'll also go into more depth about career options, as well as ways to make the most of those options, for people with or aspiring to conclude their formal education with bachelors through doctoral degrees in Part IV of this book.

Application: how might psychology help you change the world and/or achieve your goals?

Clearly, *psychological knowledge makes a difference in people's lives*. Psychology and psychological science promote well-being and help solve real-world issues. You can make a difference in small ways such as using your knowledge and access to inform your behavior, such as via educational and career success, and in larger ways!

Whether you're dabbling, reading this book on your own, reading it as a required or recommended text, or declaring (or further committing to) a major or advanced degree in psychology, psychology offers multiple ways to help you understand yourself and others. It also helps you to leverage your knowledge to change the world, perhaps beginning with making your own life and career decisions. Building on this, this book serves as a guide for making the most of college and post-college experiences focusing on 1) career/life planning and decision-making and 2) healthy professional and personal relationships.

Consistent with our celebration of the diversity of human experience and psychology, we recognize that you – our readers – also have a broad range of life, work, and career knowledge and experience, as well as degrees of decidedness about your next steps (Hammond, 2017) that we plan to address. We also know that life and career development are life-long processes and the world of work is changing rapidly, so there's almost always something new to learn, develop, and do! If you're reading this for fun (and we hope you are, even if it's assigned reading for a course), we encourage you to engage with the material, particularly material that's new or challenging for you. Take time to reflect and consider your options – you're worth the investment! At the same time, if you've already mastered some material, then we encourage you to appreciate the validation, consider additional ways to apply that knowledge and/or skills, and check out the *Next steps: Advanced move* section, found at the end of most chapters.

All the above leads us to encourage you to reflect on your unique array of interests, abilities, values, and goals, all of which can – and likely will – continue to develop throughout your lifetime. As such, it doesn't matter if you're a full-time or part-time student or are just beginning to think about higher education and your next steps. It doesn't matter if you're 16, 60, or 106 or how long it's been (or hasn't) since you've considered your career possibilities. It also doesn't matter whether you know exactly what you want to do or where you want to go career and life-wise, are still figuring it out, or even if you're just beginning to think about what you might want to "do with your life". In addition, although it helps to have resources (think money and connections), they're not required. With self-knowledge, appropriate choices, planning, focused work, and a little luck, most people can build a deeply satisfying life that includes meaningful work and positive relationships, even in today's challenging economy – which leads to our next question for self-reflection:

DOES UNDERSTANDING YOURSELF HELP YOU UNDERSTAND AND WORK BETTER WITH OTHERS?

And its corollary: Why do people seek to understand themselves better?

Don't they have anything better to do? Perhaps – yet the quest for self-understanding is one of the oldest cross-cultural human desires/goals.

BOX 1.3

Reflection – the Unexamined Life

Consider the quote below by Socrates, then consider the questions below the quote:

The unexamined life is not worth living.

– Socrates (Plato, 38a5–6)

Do you agree with Socrates' statement? Why or why not?
How might you apply this statement or revise it today?

We are who we are, right? Well, sort of. Although there are some aspects of ourselves that are more fixed than others (consider, for example, some of our physiology), there is much more that is adaptable and responsive, including intelligence, skills, personality, and many of the ways we think and act. As long as we're alive, there's potential for growth and change – and awareness is generally the first step in intentional action toward growth and change (Prochaska & Norcross, 2001; Sue et al., 1992).

Self-awareness and understanding are also an important component of self-compassion, and with that, empathy for the human condition, including the difficulties in making and sustaining even much desired change. So how does that connect with understanding others? Empathy is the key to understanding ourselves and others, which, in turn fosters positive relationships (Elliott et al., 2011). So – the answer to this question is an unequivocal "yes" – understanding yourself helps you understand and, therefore, better relate to or deal with others. Thus, self-understanding (that is, an examined life) is a worthwhile investment of your time and energy, particularly when that self-understanding inspires action!

More specific to this book and the *process* of life and career decision-making, preparation, and action – is that understanding or knowing yourself is fundamental to choosing, planning, and implementing a career and life path. Knowing yourself, your interests, your values, what's meaningful to you – as well as the challenges you're likely to encounter, ideally with a good plan for addressing them – is an excellent foundation for thoughtfully engaging in the ongoing process of making decisions about your life and work, including your career.

BOX 1.4

Definition of Career and Vocation

For the purposes of this text, we define career as a sequential, and ideally meaningful, work trajectory. Vocation may refer to a career, category of work, or work itself, whether that work generates financial compensation (as in pay) or not (as in caregiving; Richardson, 2012).

We'll explore and offer information as well as guided processes for deciding upon, preparing for, and implementing the next steps in your career journey throughout this book, so we invite you to keep reading.

Psychological knowledge also promotes mental health. For example, research and our experience indicate that many people who are undecided about their career path are relieved to learn that it's a normative (that is common) experience to be undecided, not only at the start of one's career, but often during it (Biemann et al., 2012). Many are also happy to know that there are research-informed ways, including the bibliotherapy that's offered in this book, to make informed career-related decisions – and that, for most people, career and life decision-making are ongoing, life-long processes.

We hope it's encouraging that you don't have to make a life-long commitment about your career today or even this year. Furthermore, it's likely that you'll either choose or have to adapt your career at various points, perhaps even make significant life and career shift. Nonetheless, it's still smart to invest the necessary time and energy to consider your life and career goals and then take action at your earliest opportunity. That doesn't mean you have to know exactly what you want to do, but if you have a general direction (for example, that you want to do something in psychology), that's a good beginning. No matter your current status, the key to career decision-making, planning, and preparation, is to make informed decisions, which we'll go into in more depth in Chapter 3, and to remain open and adaptable (Kegan, 1995; Kegan & Lahey, 2009; Lent & Brown, 2013) to new opportunities and experiences, which we'll also explore throughout this book.

BOX 1.5

Definition of Bibliotherapy

Bibliotherapy is the process of using one or more books or other written materials to help oneself psychologically, in this case, to make informed decisions about one's career in psychology (or not).

WHAT DOES THE PATHWAY FROM WHERE YOU ARE NOW TO YOUR CAREER IN PSYCHOLOGY LOOK LIKE?

To begin with the end in mind means to start with a clear understanding of your destination. It means to know where you're going so that you better understand where you are now and so that the steps you take are always in the right directions.

(Stephen R. Covey, 1989, p. 98)

To start the process, as suggested by Covey, let us explore options for people at different education levels in psychology. This won't give you an exact endpoint, but for most, it's a great starting point for your efforts to identify the direction for *your* career. You don't have to follow anyone else's path, but it's good to be aware of the trends and options. Knowing the trends helps you to begin to focus on those areas of psychology and its intersections with other fields that might be of greater interest to you. So, once you complete your formal education (at whatever level you decide to stop – at least temporarily), you may join or rejoin the workforce, or shift your employment. Are you curious about what might happen? Most of us are. So, let's take a look at the numbers in order to answer the question, where might you end up with your bachelor's degree in psychology. To start, it's important to realize 1) that not all individuals with a bachelor's in psychology go further in their education, and 2) of those that do, a good number obtain their graduate degrees in fields other than psychology. This tells us two things: 1) that a bachelor's in psychology is great preparation for the future, and 2) that you have many ways to put your knowledge of psychology to work. We encourage you to keep this in mind as you explore the remainder of the book.

Example educational paths in psychology

The Center for Workforce Studies at the American Psychological Association (2021) has compiled statistics to help us better understand the most popular careers for people with degrees in psychology (and we appreciate their permission to use the figures in this section). Let's take a look at their data for a minute. For the most recent year available (APA 2019b), 3.7 million individuals held a bachelor's degree in psychology. By the way, some of you reading this book may have a bachelor's degree in a field other than psychology – this does not mean that you cannot move into psychology – you will see later that many people do obtain degrees in psychology after completing a bachelor's degree in another field. So, of the 3.7 million people who had a bachelor's degree in psychology, approximately 2.1 million, or 57% stopped at a bachelor's degree (we'll look at where they went in a minute). Of the approximate 1.618 million individuals (43%) who continued their education and obtained a graduate degree. . .

- Approximately 27.7% completed either a master's, or a doctorate/professional, or both degrees in (a) field(s) outside psychology.
- Approximately 14% obtained either a master's or a doctorate as their highest degree in psychology.

Let's qualify this a bit. First, while some bachelor's degree recipients moved directly into a doctoral/professional degree program (28,899; 0.8%), a larger proportion earned a master's degree separate from their doctoral degree in psychology (110,741; 3.0%). Second, some individuals either earned a master's degree in psychology and then a doctorate/professional degree in another field (18,493; 0.5%) or did the reverse – earning a master's degree in a field other than psychology before earning a doctorate/professional degree in psychology (18,601; 0.5%). It is important to recognize that only 4% of the individuals graduating with a bachelor's degree go on to complete a doctorate in psychology (APA, 2018a, 2018b, 2020b) – in many instances because they've realized that they can do the work that they want to do with either a bachelor's or a master's degree. In addition, quite a few people combine their knowledge and experience in psychology with another field, creating their own niche in the world of work. So, additional experience can be a plus.

Interestingly, when people with a bachelor's degree in psychology move into other fields, the majority stick rather close to the core component of psychology, which is understanding and working with people. Here are examples of the most popular directions: Social Work (17%), Special Education (8%), P-12 teaching or School Counseling (each at 7%), other education or business administration (each at 4%). For those of you with diverse interests, you should note that at the other end of the spectrum, there are small groups of individuals who earn their masters in fields such as Forestry Sciences, Operations Research, Ecology, Mathematics, Computer Systems, and Criminology. As you can see, a major in psychology can lead to a wide variety of careers. Similarly, at the doctoral/professional level, individuals who earn these degrees after completing a bachelor's in psychology are most likely to complete degrees in Law (21%), Medicine (13%), or Educational Administration (5%). Smaller percentages of individuals complete doctoral/professional degrees in a wide variety of areas that are too numerous to list here. For more information and ideas, visit APA's Center for Workforce Studies (CWS) website and look for the links to "pathways" for bachelor's degree holders.

Overview of occupations for people with degrees in psychology

We've just discussed educational pathways for those with psychology bachelor's degrees, noting that individuals may also move into psychology after completing a bachelor's degree in another field. While that is an option, we are hoping that, by using the information and activities in this text, you will be able to find your path more quickly and make better use of the opportunities along the way. Let us turn now to an overview of the occupations chosen by those with various levels of education in psychology. This overview is important so that you can begin to consider the various directions that you can take a career grounded in psychological knowledge. We present this information not so that you mimic the survey respondents (unless this seems to be a good fit), rather so that you can see your options and move toward a career that allows you to have the impact on the world that you would like to have. For example, consider an individual who obtained their bachelor's degree in psychology and master's in ecology. Consider their ability to help create campaigns that raise awareness of the human impact on the earth or understand the ecology of communities (of people of color, of older individuals, etc.) and assist urban planning and renewal staff to create communities that support the people living there. We hope that, through the discussion here and the examples presented throughout the text and further discussed in Part IV, you will begin to see the particular niche for you.

The next three sections will be discussing the results of APA's (2018a, 2018b) survey of psychology graduates. The data on which the figures are based is drawn from the

Bureau of Labor Statistics and National Science Foundation data representing respondents with degrees in psychology at various levels. The respondents reported on the career or occupation that they entered after completing their degree. While you will notice that there are some similarities in career direction, there is also great diversity in the range of occupational categories (APA, 2018a, 2020b) included in these figures and the report. The similarities across education levels include careers in occupations that interact with people in different ways – administrative or management jobs, service or health care occupations (including social work), and occupations in the area of personnel, training, and labor relations. Of course, the specifics of the occupation differ. For example, individuals working in a mental health organization with a bachelor's degree will have different responsibilities than those with master's level training and, perhaps, licensure. Similarly, those with a doctoral degree are likely to engage in a different type of clinical work as well as be more likely to manage or run the organization. A similar situation arises with research careers, with individuals on a research team or as part of a research lab all assisting in the conduct of the research and reporting of the results, however, the exact tasks will depend on the degree of training and background.

Overview of occupations for people with bachelor's degrees in psychology

In Figure 1.1, individuals with bachelor's degrees in psychology chose careers in many different areas. Here are some popular examples: marketing and sales, teachers, accountants, auditors, and other financial specialties, counselors, personnel, training, and labor relations specialists, and a category labeled *writers, editors, PR specialists, artists,*

FIGURE 1.1 Most Frequently Reported Career Directions of Psychology Bachelor's Degree Holders
American Psychological Association. (2021). *Careers in psychology. [Interactive data tool].* www.apa.org/workforce/data-tools/careers-psychology.aspx. Used with permission.

entertainers, broadcasters. As you can see, these are large categories that can mask differences in career opportunities that may be of greater interest for you. Here are some examples to consider:

- Many students will use their skills in psychology to strengthen the ability to perform in other career fields, such as nursing, human resources, social work, dieticians, or criminal justice. Some will minor in psychology while majoring in their other field, while others will major in psychology while minoring in the other field of interest. It's best to speak with advisors in both areas to ensure that you are structuring the best route for you to your goal.
- Other students may be oriented toward business and use their major in psychology to become effective managers, work in marketing or public relations, or work in fields such as personnel administration, training, or labor relations. They may combine their degree in psychology with majors in various business majors.
- Another group may be more interested in public/government service, public policy, advocacy, or work with non-profit organizations. Again, combining majors and minors is likely to assist you in reaching your goals.

These examples provide some idea of the variation in directions one can take one's career at the bachelor's level. Throughout this book, we will provide a variety of examples in order to help you to see the amazingly large number of opportunities in and with psychology. Taking the time to explore these suggestions, as well as your interests, skills, values, and goals now can help you to maximize the effectiveness of your undergraduate education and open doors for have the impact you desire on the world. However, what if you are thinking about completing a master's degree? Do those who complete this next level of education follow the same paths as for those with bachelor's degrees? The answer to that is "sometimes". There is, of course, overlap across all three levels of education, however, there are also differences. We will discuss the most popular career directions for those completing master's degrees in psychology next.

Example occupational paths with master's degrees in psychology

The word-cloud in Figure 1.2 represents the most frequently chosen paths for those completing master's degrees in psychology. We discussed above the similarities to career options for those with a bachelor's degree and remind you that the most significant difference is degree of responsibility and complexity of the tasks you would be assigned. For example, a social worker with a bachelor's degree has different responsibilities than one with a master's degree. Similarly, individuals with interests in personnel, training, or labor relations with a master's degree are more likely to manage a group or unit than those with a bachelor's degree. Those who desire to teach may do so at either the P-12 level or may be qualified to teach at certain post-secondary institutions. Let's examine how research and practice (therapy) foci in psychology can take you in many directions.

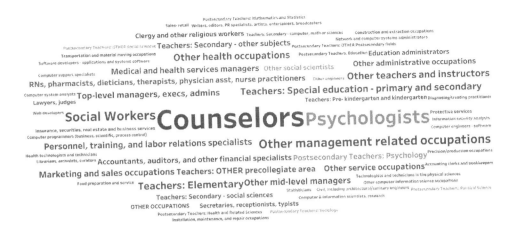

FIGURE 1.2 Most Frequently Reported Career Directions of Psychology Master's Degree Holders

American Psychological Association. (2021). *Careers in psychology. [Interactive data tool].* www.apa.org/workforce/data-tools/careers-psychology.aspx. Used with permission.

Research pathways

Right now, you may be asking "what if I want to do research?" or "what if I want to be a counselor or psychologist?" Those are options, too. Let's focus on them for a bit now. Let's start with research. Research can have three foci. First, research can be conducted to build our understanding of a topic. This is the type of research conducted by psychologists both as faculty members and as researchers for hospitals, government, and other organizations. This is how we tend to think of research. In fact, research is so important to psychology that most psychology departments provide a significant amount of training in research and statistics. However, this training is also useful in another way – conducting research that applies theory to real world settings – sometimes called "applied research". One example of this is called *program evaluation*. This field can be both a great use of your research skills and provide opportunities to advocate and address the social justice issues that are important to you.

As you can see, in the world of work, research is used in a wider variety of contexts, all of which require information gathering and synthesizing, critical analysis, and drawing conclusions. Thus, two major directions for those with an interest in research are 1) to build theory, knowledge, and understanding of a topic; and 2) to apply research skills and thinking to solving current issues and problems or otherwise advancing societal goals.

Practice pathways

With regards to becoming a counselor or psychologist, you may be aware that these individuals take on an added responsibility for people's lives and so are generally certified (particularly in the P-12 setting) or licensed to practice their career. They work in private practice settings, mental and health care settings, as well as in P-12 schools (as counselors, school counselors, school psychologists, and similar titles) and post-secondary educational institutions (in campus counseling centers, academic advising offices, career counseling centers, placement centers, and residence halls). This topic will be addressed further in Part IV.

Example occupational pathways with doctoral degrees in psychology

As you can see in Figure 1.3, there are other options for people with doctoral degrees as well as those that are similar to the options for those with a master's degree. Here are some examples: Lawyers or judges, web developers, actuaries, librarians/archivists/curators, and a category labeled *writers, editors, PR specialists, artists, entertainers, broadcasters.* As you can see, these are large categories that can mask differences in career opportunities that may be of greater interest for you. Here are several examples to consider:

- Within the *Lawyers or Judges* category (APA, 2020a; Novotney, 2017)
  - The psychologist who uses an additional degree in law to teach law and ethics in psychology as a faculty member and/or trainer
  - The psychologist who works for the American Psychological Association or other organization as a lobbyist to Congress is a professional advocate for a broad spectrum of mental health issues, including insurance coverage, reimbursement equity, equity in funding for training, and research funding

FIGURE 1.3 Most Frequently Reported Career Directions of Psychology Doctoral Degree Holders

American Psychological Association. (2021). *Careers in psychology. [Interactive data tool].* www.apa.org/workforce/data-tools/careers-psychology.aspx. Used with permission

- • The psychologist who conducts culturally sensitive forensic evaluations to ensure that contextual factors and psychological research on human behavior are incorporated into the proceedings (Melton et al., 2017)
- • Within the *Top-Level Managers, Execs, Admins* and the *Other Management related Occupations*
    - • The psychologist who manages the major assessment corporations (i.e., PAR, Inc.; The Myers Briggs Company)
    - • The psychologist who runs a non-profit school or organization
    - • The psychologists who run major consulting companies such as RHR International
    - • The psychologist who manages a mental health clinic, counseling center, or hospital-based psychological services department

These examples provide some idea of the variation in directions one can take one's career, even at the doctoral level, which often seems to students as the most restrictive degree. It's not that it's restrictive – it's just that a doctoral degree prepares you to more deeply understand and apply psychology to the world in specific ways. In addition, students often see the overlap between career opportunities with a master's and a doctoral degree. This is an important point to consider – do you need a doctoral degree in order to do what you want to do? For example, there is significant overlap in the work of master's level clinicians/therapists and doctoral-level clinicians/therapists. Recall that only 4% of the individuals graduating with a bachelor's degree go on to complete a doctorate in psychology (APA, 2018a, 2018b, 2020b). We encourage you to use all the resources we've mentioned (and any that you come up with that we haven't) to explore your options and define your goal/direction and begin to develop your plan for achieving those goals.

CHAPTER SUMMARY

Psychology is one of the most popular undergraduate majors in the U.S. (NCES, 2011). It's also a career with wide-ranging opportunities to change and or make a difference in the world around you. In this chapter we introduced you to psychology as both an educational and career choice, as well as suggesting ways in which psychology has an important role to play in changing the world around us. In looking at the data, we find that a little more than half of those with bachelor's degrees in psychology (APA, 2018a, 2019b) have not sought out graduate degrees and have satisfying careers that use their psychology knowledge. We found that these individuals have found employment in fields as diverse as accounting/auditing, software development, personal trainer, public relations, aerospace, health occupations, and protective services (APA, 2018a, 2020a). As with all data, it highlights larger groupings of data, thus, within these groupings you will find individuals engaging in very unique combinations of psychology and other occupations. The important takeaway for you, if you're among the many who conclude their formal education with a bachelor's degree is that with a little research and support, you can find a very satisfying direction for your post-degree career life. Finally, we introduced you to the first step in finding your unique way to contribute to the world through your knowledge in the field of psychology – becoming more aware of who you are and what you bring to the world.

EXERCISES

1   Start a journal to record your thoughts and reactions to the chapter.
2   Think about the courses you are taking this semester. Which ones are most interesting? Why? Talk with the instructor about the field behind the course.

Next steps: the advanced move

1   We encourage readers interested in knowing more about specific topics to look up and read the references for this and subsequent chapters.
2   The life/career visioning exercise (with credit to Marydee Spillett, one of our early career counselors, who introduced this helpful exercise). Sit quietly, closing your eyes if you're comfortable doing so, and in sequence (not necessarily all at the same time), imagine yourself at the oldest age you can, looking back on your life. What type of work would you have liked to have done? Where? With whom? What's your daily schedule? What values did you build upon? What were your accomplishments? – Write or draw your inspiration in your journal or other safe place so you can refer to it whenever it would be helpful.

REFERENCES

American Psychological Association. (2008). *Resolution on the Americans with disabilities act.* www.apa.org/about/policy/disabilities-act

American Psychological Association. (2014). *Psychology: Science in action.* www.apa.org/action/science/science-of-psychology.pdf

American Psychological Association. (2018a). *Careers in psychology. [Interactive data tool].* www.apa.org/workforce/data-tools/careers-psychology.aspx

American Psychological Association. (2018b). *Degrees in psychology. [Interactive data tool].* Retrieved January 15, 2021, from www.apa.org/workforce/data- tools/degrees-psychology

American Psychological Association. (2019a). *Advocacy.* www.apa.org/advocacy

American Psychological Association. (2019b). *Preparing for the future: The psychology workforce of the 21st century.* Retrieved January 31, 2021, from www.apa.org/workforce/presentations/future.pdf

American Psychological Association. (2020a). *Careers in psychology and law.* Retrieved December 28, 2020 from www.apadivisions.org/division-41/education/students/careers

American Psychological Association. (2020b). *Career pathways and the psychology major.* Retrieved January 31, 2021, from www.apa.org/workforce/presentations/career-pathways.pdf

American Psychological Association. (2021). *Degree pathways in psychology.* *[Interactive data tool].* www.apa.org/workforce/data-tools/degrees-pathways.aspx.

Association for Psychological Science. (n.d.). *Advocacy issues.* www.psychologicalscience.org/advocacy/issues

Benjamin, L. T. (Ed.). (1997). *A history of psychology, original sources and contemporary research* (2nd ed.). McGraw-Hill.

Biemann, T., Zacher, H., & Feldman, D. C. (2012). Career patterns: A twenty-year panel study. *Journal of Vocational Behavior, 81*(2), 159–170. doi:10.1016/j.jvb.2012.06.003

Corrigan, P. W., Druss, B. G., & Perlick, D. A. (2014). The impact of mental illness stigma on seeking and participating in mental health care. *Psychological Science in the Public Interest, 15*(2), 37–70. doi:10.1177/1529100614531398

Covey, S. R. (1989). *The 7 habits of highly effective people: Powerful lessons in personal change.* Fireside.

Elliott, R., Bohart, A. C., Watson, J. C., & Greenberg, L. S. (2011). Empathy. *Psychotherapy, 48,* 43–49. doi:10.1037/a0022187

Hammond, M. S. (2017). Differences in career development among first-year students: A proposed typology for intervention planning. *Journal of the First-Year Experience & Students in Transition, 29*(2), 45–63.

Jensen, M. P., & Turk, D. C. (2014). Contributions of psychology to the understanding and treatment of people with chronic pain: Why it matters to all psychologists. *The American Psychologist, 69*(2), 105–118. doi:10.1037/a0035641

Karera, A. (2010). Profile of Mamie Phipps Clark. In A. Rutherford (Ed.), *Psychology's feminist voices multimedia internet archive.* www.feministvoices.com/profiles/mamie-phipps-clark

Kegan, R. (1995). *In over our heads: The mental demands of modern life.* Harvard University Press.

Kegan, R. & Lahey, L.L. (2009). *Immunity to change: How to overcome it and unlock potential in yourself and your organization.* Harvard Business Press.

Lent, R. W., & Brown, S. D. (2013). Social cognitive model of career self-management: Toward a unifying view of adaptive career behavior across the life span. *Journal of Counseling Psychology, 60*(4), 557. doi:10.1037/a0033446

Maranzan, K. A. (2016). Interprofessional education in mental health: An opportunity to reduce mental illness stigma. *Journal of Interprofessional Care, 30*(3), 370–377. doi:10.3109/13561 820.2016.1146878

Melton, G. B., Petrila, J., Poythress, N. G., Slobogin, C., Otto, R. K., Mossman, D., & Condie. L. O. (2017). *Psychological evaluations for the courts: A handbook for mental health professionals and lawyers* (4th ed.). Guilford Press.

National Center for Education Statistics. (2011). *Digest of education statistics.* Table 290. Bachelor's, master's, and doctor's degrees conferred by degree-granting institutions, by sex of student and discipline division: 2009-10. http://nces.ed.gov/programs/digest/d11/tables/dt11_290.asp

Novotney, A. (2017). Helping courts and juries make educated decisions. *Monitor on Psychology, 48*(8), 70.

Parsons, F. (1909). *Choosing a vocation.* Houghton-Mifflin.

Plato. Apology 38a in *Plato in twelve volumes* (Vol. 1, Harold North Fowler, Trans.). Harvard University Press.

Pope, M., & Sveinsdottir, M. (2005). Frank, we hardly knew ye: The very personal side of Frank Parsons. *Journal of Counseling & Development, 83,* 105–115. doi:10.1002/j.1556-6678.2005. tb00585.x

Prochaska, J. O., & Norcross, J. C. (2001). Stages of change. *Psychotherapy, 38*(4), 443–448.

Richardson, M. S. (2012). Counseling for work and relationship. *Counseling Psychologist, 40*(2), 190–242. doi:10.1037/0033-3204.38.4.443

Roth, A. (2018). *Insane: America's criminal treatment of mental illness.* Basic Books.

Stamm, K., & Fowler, G. A. (2019). *Planning your career path in psychology.* American Psychological Association.

Sue, D. W., Arredondo, P., & McDavis, R. J. (1992). Multicultural counseling competencies and standards: A call to the profession. *Journal of Counseling & Development, 70*(4), 477–486. doi:10.1002/j.1556-6676.1992.tb01642.x

Wampold, B. E. (2011). *Qualities and actions of effective therapists.* American Psychological Association Continuing Education. www.apa.org/education/ce/effective-therapists.pdf

Whiston, S. C., & Blustein, D. L. (2013). *The impact of career interventions: Preparing our citizens for 21 st century jobs.* National Career Development Association. (www.ncda.org) and the Society for Vocational Psychology (www.div17.org/vocpsych/).

Young, J. (2010). Profile of Mary Whiton Calkins. In A. Rutherford (Ed.), *Psychology's feminist voices multimedia internet archive.* www.feministvoices.com/mary-whiton-calkins/

CHAPTER 2

Connecting your goals to the education needed

ORIENTING QUESTIONS

1. What are some ways people can be involved in psychology?
2. How can you learn (more) about specializations in psychology?
3. What are some other related occupations that build on psychological knowledge?
4. How do you want to contribute? What role(s) do you want to play?
5. What level *and type* of education will you need to reach your potential goal(s)?

DOI: 10.4324/9780429296413-3

WHAT ARE SOME OF THE WAYS YOU CAN BE INVOLVED IN PSYCHOLOGY?

Building on our discussion in Chapter 1, we know that psychological knowledge makes a difference in people's lives. Furthermore, psychology is an area of study that can help you understand yourself and others better – and potentially contribute to making the world a better place. This chapter will help you explore some specific ways to become involved with psychology at various educational levels. It will also help you develop skills to more fully consider your options for a meaningful career in psychology.

The world of work is complex, with many different types of careers (more than 20,000!), each requiring skills and ways of thinking that are similar to some other occupations, while also being different from other occupations. For example, individuals interested in research might conduct research (gathering, analyzing, and reporting information) for a wide range of organizations.

The examples in Table 2.1 are just a few of the ways in which research skills are used in the world of work. Although these examples don't fully represent the diversity of subfields or settings in psychology (more on that later), this list was purposefully constructed to demonstrate the differing levels of education needed to engage in research work. For example, many of these organizations hire individuals with bachelor's or master's degrees to engage in various research tasks. To illustrate, one of us worked as a research analyst for a state legislative body along with people with bachelor's, master's, and doctoral degrees in their roles as lobbyists, community activists, and experts from various organizations.

TABLE 2.1 Applying Research Skills in the World of Work

Organization	Type of research
Legislature	Gather and analyze topics related to proposed legislation
Lobbyists	Gather and analyze data related to contracting organization's agenda
Community Activist	Gather and analyze data related to the focus of the sponsoring organization's agenda
Marketing	Design experiment/gather data related to impact of various marketing techniques
Pharmaceutical Company	Collaborate with other researchers to design and test potential drugs to ameliorate psychological and other disorders
Testing Companies	Conduct research to update existing tests or create new ones
Educational Institution	Design and conduct research studies to evaluate effectiveness of the institution at providing education to students

(Continued)

TABLE 2.1 *(Continued)*

Organization	Type of research
Businesses and Governmental Agencies	Design methods for selecting/promoting employees; evaluate effectiveness of processes and procedures; design research to evaluate the effectiveness of teams and/or the organization's culture
Mental Health Agency or Hospital	Conduct research related to client/patient issues, as well as the types of research mentioned earlier for business/governmental organizations.
Research Libraries	Use research skills to develop sophisticated methods for finding information needed by patrons.
Research Centers or Universities	Participate in collaborative research projects by assisting in all aspects from literature searches and research methodology design through implementation, data analysis, and reporting.

Some of you may have an interest in helping people as a counselor or therapist. While you, too, would be using your research skills to better understand the client's or patient's concerns and goals, you might be interested in some of the other ways people with this type of interest apply their skills, a few examples of which are shown in Table 2.2.

TABLE 2.2 Applying Helping Skills in the World of Work

Organization	Type of Helping
Clinic or Community Mental Health Center and Private Practice Settings	Conduct intake interviews; conduct assessments; develop treatment plans; provide diagnoses, psychoeducation, counseling, and therapy to individuals, couples, and families
Educational Organizations	Conducting assessment, diagnosis, advocacy, psychoeducational intervention, and therapy to students, teachers, and parents or guardians; design and/or evaluate educational interventions and work with teachers to improve learning for all students
Hospitals, Medical Centers, and Corrections	Conduct intake interviews, counseling, psychoeducation, and therapy to patients & inmates
Business, Government, and Security Organizations	Conduct intake interviews, counseling, and psychoeducation to employees; design interventions to address diversity, skill, and other psychological topics affecting organizational and personal effectiveness.

Similar to research skills, helping skills can be used in a variety of organizations by a variety of professionals, trained at varying levels to conduct aspects of this work. Two differences that you will quickly observe is that 1) more of these positions require some sort of certification or licensure, and 2) that while some of these types of helping require a bachelor's degree, others require graduate level or other specialized training. In addition, you will likely find that individuals approach helping people from different perspectives aligned with their professional training and expertise. In addition to health service psychologists (i.e., clinical, counseling, and school psychologists), professionals in allied fields such as marriage and family therapists, clinical social workers, counselors, pastoral counselors, and psychiatrists are just a few of the types of individuals providing counseling and otherwise using helping skills and who bring a different philosophy and focus to helping people.

According to the US Bureau of Labor Statistics (BLS, 2020), the large majority (88.5%) of working psychologists in the U.S. are health service psychologists with doctoral degrees in clinical psychology, counseling psychology, or school psychology (BLS, 2020). Of these, clinical psychologists are the most numerous, followed by counseling psychologists, and then doctoral level school psychologists (NCES, 2011, 2017). The BLS (2020) also reports that 1% of active psychologists hold doctorates in Industrial Organizational (I-O) psychology and 10.4% earned doctorates with majors in many other psychological specializations, some of which we'll review later in this chapter.

Overall, although a doctoral degree is the entry level credential for most psychologists, there are multiple ways – at all levels of education – to build your career in psychology, which we'll review in this chapter and explore more fully and specifically in Part IV of this book. As you read, reflect, and think about how you might be involved with psychology, it's important to consider the levels and, within those levels, types of advanced (i.e., graduate) education necessary to pursue and attain your potential (or actual) goals. For example, if you want to be a licensed therapist, the primary options are to earn a doctoral degree in health service psychology or a licensure-qualifying master's degree in an allied profession. Similarly, if you're considering broader or different ways to be involved with psychology that require graduate training, it's important to consider those possibilities in your decision-making and planning. At the same time, although decision-making and planning is important, it's also important to remain adaptable and open to future possibilities. One thing we know – the world is changing and so are you!

APPLYING YOUR EDUCATION: MAJOR CATEGORIES OF WORK IN PSYCHOLOGY AND RELATED FIELDS

At this point, whether you've just begun to think about, are in the process, or are clear about the differences between psychology and allied professions, let's move on to considering five major ways you can engage in psychology. Keep in mind that these are simply five major ways; there are – and likely will be – many more, so if you're considering an area that doesn't fit within our categories, we encourage you to include that among your possibilities to investigate. In addition, if you want to think about this some more, read on and see the *Next steps: the advanced move* section of this chapter. So, psychologists and others apply their knowledge of psychology and desire to help others in five general ways. They do so by: 1) providing mental health or other psychological services; 2) conducting research; 3) teaching; 4) administrative or organizational service; and 5) advocacy and policy work. Let's take a look at each in turn.

Mental health or other psychological services

Most people have seen a psychologist portrayed on TV or in a video and so have some familiarity with psychotherapy, therapy, and counseling. As noted earlier, the majority of psychologists provide direct service to individuals, couples, families, and other groups, as therapists in independent practice, hospitals, agencies, and similar settings (BLS, 2020). Licensed psychologists use their knowledge of people and psychology to help individuals and groups develop and heal, understand themselves and others better, learn more effective ways of functioning and interacting with others, change unhealthy habits, develop skills to understand the world to inform their decision-making, and more. Psychologists are also qualified to administer, score, and interpret the results of a wide array of psychological assessments. Similarly, psychologists with specialty training may conduct forensic and other legal assessments as well as serve as expert witnesses. Psychologists also contribute to people's mental health indirectly. For example, psychologists with specialized training in one or more of the vast array of psychological specialties, such as I-O, cognitive, and social psychology, provide psychological services and therefore provide indirect mental health services through research and dissemination, teaching, consultation, and evaluation services.

There are many advantages to working as a counselor or therapist. It is a fulfilling career that directly helps people – because, as we noted earlier, psychotherapy works! You don't have to be perfect or perfectly evolved to be a counselor or therapist – but it is important that you know yourself, your biases, and your challenges – because in working with others, it's likely your own "stuff" will emerge. Thus, becoming a therapist, while rewarding, is also challenging, and requires a life-long commitment to becoming more fully aware, knowledgeable, multiculturally competent, and more skilled. In summary, master's level practitioners are generally expected to use and apply psychological knowledge and skills in their work, while doctoral level practitioners often do that and contribute to the knowledge base. Furthermore, practice and research, which we'll explore next, are recursive, in that each informs the other.

Research

Many psychologists conduct research to understand the basic science that underlies psychological functioning (e.g., brain function) and applied research (e.g., how therapy works) to help people solve their mental health problems, help individuals understand themselves better, engage with others more effectively, and achieve their goals in life. They may also do translational research that applies psychological theory to real world problems. Students at all levels can learn about research in classes – and often gain first-hand experience working with a faculty member and/or member of a research team.

Research psychologists and some academic psychologists, including faculty at many colleges and universities, often dedicate a significant proportion of their professional time to conducting research that builds on prior knowledge, answering as yet unaddressed questions, building theory, and testing hypotheses. They may test their hypotheses directly through carefully designed experimental and quasi-experimental studies, communicating the results in context (that is, what was already known, what wasn't, what this study was designed to investigate, the method by which the study was conducted, the results, and a discussion of those results, often including implications for practice and recommendations for future research). Overall, psychologists and others contributing to psychological knowledge through research and scholarship disseminate the results of their research at peer-reviewed professional conferences and in peer-reviewed journals, and therefore generally contribute to the growing knowledge base in psychology.

Some undergraduate (bachelor's degree) and more master's programs offer opportunities to learn more about and gain front-line experience conducting research by working with faculty and, often advanced students, on specific studies, projects, or even an entire line of research. There may also be opportunities to present the work you contributed to at a professional conference (a wonderful opportunity to learn and develop your network) and/or to contribute to a professional journal article or other written report. If you're serious about the possibility of pursuing a doctoral degree, research experience, particularly at the level that results in conference presentations or publications is a plus!

While some of you are likely to desire to conduct research (or, to develop that interest in the future), others may be more interested in applying research in your practice or work. We cannot stress strongly enough how important understanding the strengths and limitations of research is to effective work, including practice, in psychology. The field is a relatively new field, so it's important to stay current because knowledge can advance rapidly, which is likely to have an impact on your work.

Teaching

Psychologists – and people with training in psychology – also use their knowledge of psychology to teach. In addition to the content (that is subject matter knowledge), psychological research informs educational theory and practice, so teaching, regardless of setting or level, is, in large part, applied psychology.

Psychologists and others with psychological knowledge, including the applied psychological knowledge in education, teach at the preschool through 12th grade (P-12) level. Most public P-12 schools require teachers to hold a state-issued teaching certificate, which is generally awarded upon completion of a specific course of study at the bachelor's degree level that often includes a major in education, which is based in psychology. Some jurisdictions offer options for alternate routes including earning a certificate of advanced standing (a post-baccalaureate certificate), master's degree in teaching, and emergency certification. Furthermore, some alternate programs, such as Teach for America, provide their own training in how to teach within the parameters of their programs. Independent, parochial, and other non-public schools may also welcome teachers with other qualifications including education and training in psychology and psychology-related fields.

At the post-secondary level (colleges and universities), a minimum of a master's degree is required to teach undergraduate courses, while a doctorate is often required to teach at the graduate level. Most psychologists with full-time faculty appointments at four-year colleges and universities have earned a doctoral degree in psychology, with a specialization in one of the subfields in psychology. Many of these individuals will hold the rank of *Assistant Professor, Associate Professor,* or *Professor.* Depending upon the institution, either a master's or a doctoral degree may be required for *Instructor* or *Lecturer* positions. At some two-year community colleges, a master's degree, with a minimum of 18 graduate credits in psychology, is sufficient to qualify as a full or part-time faculty member. A final type of position at the post-secondary level is that of *adjunct faculty* – that is, employment on a course by course or similar basis that may not require the same level of education or training as full-time faculty positions. However, although adjunct teaching can be a good way to gain experience, share your knowledge and experience, or supplement your income, it's important to know that adjunct teaching, even full-time, rarely pays a living wage (June & Newman, 2013), which is a value and consideration for most people in career decision-making and planning.

Across levels and courses academic psychologists teach courses ranging from introduction to psychology through specialty or specialization areas such as social or experimental psychology. Most full-time faculty and some adjunct faculty (i.e., part-time faculty) advise students, conduct research, serve on committees to improve the program and/or institution, as well as writing grants and presenting at conferences. In addition, psychologists who teach in clinical training programs, provide clinical supervision to advanced students providing therapy and other client services in university-sponsored field work.

Administrative or organizational service

Psychological knowledge is an asset in work and life that extends to managing and leading groups of people. This particular way of implementing a career in psychology crosses all *industries.* By the way, *Industries* are groupings of similar types of workplaces used by the federal government (U.S. Bureau of Labor Statistics, 2021) to better understand the pattern of employment and productivity across society. While the U.S. Bureau of Labor Statistics (US BLS) lists over 100 industries, the BLS groups them into ten meta-categories, one might say. These ten major categories include: Construction; Education & Health Services; Financial Activities; Information; Leisure & Hospitality; Manufacturing; Natural Resources & Mining, Other Services (except public administration); Professional & Business Services; and, finally, Trade, Transportation, & Utilities. One would expect to see individuals with training in psychology in two of these categories (Education & Health Services, as well as Professional & Business Services). Would you expect to see them at administrative levels in the Leisure & Hospitality or the Information industries? The latter is particularly interesting as it contains the following business sectors: publishing, motion pictures, data processing and related, and telecommunications.

Depending on one's interests, skills, abilities, and training, psychologists and others using psychological knowledge may assume leadership roles such as director of an agency, research, or clinical services. They may also serve as a communications coordinator or provide therapeutic or administrative support. Psychologists and others using psychological knowledge also contribute administratively and organizationally in other venues such as business, education, professional organizations, and public service that we'll explore with greater depth later in this chapter.

Thus, individuals, such as yourself, may decide to use your knowledge of people to provide a service to people, to manage people, or to lead an organization. Psychologists (and others) apply psychological knowledge to contribute to the development, maintenance, and improvement of effective organizations both generally and as related to psychological services. They may also offer professional consultation, program evaluation, and accreditation support. Furthermore, in some settings, psychologists contribute through collaborating with others to design more effective processes and procedures, develop strategies to help the organization become more successful, design systems for managing crises, and ensure ethical behavior and research.

BOX 2.1

Example Role Model

Rosie Phillips Davis (formerly Bingham), Ph.D., ABPP, is a Professor of Counseling Psychology at the University of Memphis. She served as 2019–2020 President of the American Psychological Association, and prior to her presidency, served as Vice President for Student Affairs at the University of Memphis. www.apa.org/about/governance/president/rosie-phillips-davis

Advocacy and policy work

Psychological knowledge makes a difference in people's lives. As just one example, discussed in Chapter 1, the dissemination and application of the growing body of psychological knowledge contributed to better treatment of people with mental illness, and reduced stigma, which is likely to encourage more people to seek help – and promotes, in a virtuous cycle, more research and education.

Psychological knowledge and advocacy also helps people – by influencing policy, legislation, judicial rulings (e.g., the Clarks' contribution to ending legal school segregation), and thus positively influencing people's lives. Psychologists and others using psychological knowledge contribute to the development of legislative, governmental, and other policy initiatives designed to promote human welfare. They may serve as expert witnesses in a variety of areas including vocational psychology. People with advanced degrees in psychology and the law, including psychologists with juris doctorate (JD) degrees, advise, represent, and, when necessary, defend psychologists and others. Last, but not least, psychologists and others using psychological knowledge also work to educate legislators and other policy-makers and otherwise engage in advocacy to promote the broader work of the profession.

BOX 2.2

Reflection

Are you interested in any of these ways of being involved related to psychology? If so, in what ways? How might your interests relate to your choice of major and making the most of your educational opportunities?

PSYCHOLOGICAL SPECIALTIES, SUBFIELDS, AND RELATED OCCUPATIONS

The decision to choose to further investigate or pursue a career in psychology is an important first step. However, it's only the first step. The next, as we briefly introduced earlier, is to consider if any (or any combination) of the major ways people use their education in psychology and/or are employed in psychology careers. It might help to go back and re-read that section, noting your response to the descriptions and, for those areas you're particularly interested in, noting the level of involvement (e.g., researcher or research assistant), which loosely corresponds with the highest level of education you might pursue, to inform your decisions. A third step is to consider (and decide) if you'll pursue an educational specialty in psychology, which could include specific areas to investigate or research (e.g., anxiety), populations to work with (e.g., children), a specialized subfield in psychology (e.g., I-O psychology), allied field (e.g., social work), or related occupation. As we've shared before, if you know, or even have a pretty good idea of, where you're going, it's smart to plan – and take action – to reach those goals. For now, continue to develop your ideas, as we will discuss specialties in greater detail in later chapters.

At the same time, if you're sure or pretty sure about a potential career in psychology but are not sure about potential specializations, we want to assure you that's a good option too. Some people decide to pursue advanced study, including master's degrees in *general psychology* (sometimes with different names such as *psychological science* or *psychological studies*), to immerse themselves in the broad field while they figure out their next steps. Others pursue a general (or more focused) master's degree to gain additional knowledge and skills to strengthen their applications for doctoral study (more on that later). Still others choose to pursue a career in general psychology because they particularly appreciate the overarching principles and practices of the profession and aspire to (or do) work from a generalist (i.e., integrative) perspective and perhaps contribute to the field as a whole. In this way, general psychology is a specialization – and it is so important that APA established the Society of General Psychology as its first division – and it remains Division 1!

In the next section, we'll provide additional information, first about psychological specialties and subfields, then about related occupations, to further help you make informed life and career decisions. Keep in mind this is just an overview and there are other ways, some of which we'll explore in more depth throughout this book, to learn more about specialties, subfields, and related occupations. Keep reading. . .

Psychological specialties and subfields

Specialties, also known as specializations, are subfields of education and work in a career or profession that share the larger goals of a profession or occupational field – then extend that knowledge. For example, the subfields of cognitive psychology, developmental psychology, and social psychology all focus on understanding the mental processes and functioning of individuals from different perspectives. Similarly, there are a number of specializations in psychology that are focused around the application of our understanding of psychology to directly helping people using their training in therapy, assessment, and similar skills in the HSP subfields which include counseling psychology, clinical psychology, and school psychology. These specializations share the same principles, including ethical standards, of the larger profession. Here are examples:

- Most Counseling Psychology doctoral programs prepare people to be scientific practitioners, focusing equally on science (e.g., research) and practice (e.g., direct service, including counseling and psychotherapy). Counseling psychology emphasizes human strengths, understanding people in context (i.e., person–environment interaction), multicultural competence, social justice – and respect for vocational/career development (Brady-Amoon & Keefe-Cooperman, 2017; Goodyear et al., 2016). Most U.S. counseling psychologists have training in vocational psychology (Scheel et al., 2018) and some, like the authors, further specialize in Vocational Psychology (SVP, 2017).
- Clinical Psychology, the largest of the health service psychology specialties (NCES, 2011, 2017), is often the first field people consider when they consider an advanced degree in psychology and the possibility of clinical practice (e.g., providing psychotherapy). Clinical psychology is an excellent choice if your goal is to specialize in assessment, treatment, and/or research of mental illness and other psychological disorders. Similar to other health service psychology specializations (i.e., Counseling Psychology), a master's degree is good preparation for assistant level work – and a doctoral degree, generally Ph.D. or Psy.D. – is required for licensure and direct client service.

- School Psychology is another unique specialty area within health service psychology and the third largest specialty area in psychology (NCES, 2011, 2017). As the title suggests, most school psychologists work in school settings. They generally provide testing, assessment, and support for students with identified disabilities or identify disabilities. School psychologists, who minimally have earned a master's degree in school psychology and qualified for a certificate to work in public schools in a specific jurisdiction, are one of only a few exceptions to the general rule that a doctorate is required to call oneself a psychologist (another is psychologists in the military). At the same time, people who hold a doctorate in school psychology, currently comprising about 11% of school psychologists (NASP, 2019), are also eligible for licensure and thus, practice outside school settings, including independent practice.
- Industrial/Organizational Psychology (I-O) is another, smaller, specialty relevant to career decision-making and planning. I-O is an applied, integrative field that focuses on workplace issues at the individual through systems level. I-O psychologists and professionals with master's degrees in I-O primarily work in higher education, industry, and government as researchers and consultants (SIOP, 2016).

A good resource for learning more about these as well as other specialties in psychology that fall under the "all other" category, including Developmental, Educational, and Forensic Psychology, is the *Occupational Outlook Handbook* (BLS, 2020), its online equivalent O*Net online (www.onetonline.gov), people with education and experience in those fields (perhaps your professor?), and the websites of these professions and related professional organizations. Be careful, however, some websites that purport to provide unbiased information are carefully disguised advertisements or other propaganda, so it's a good idea to check the validity of a site with someone knowledgeable about the specialty, vocational or career counseling, or information such as a reference librarian.

Professional organizations such as the APA www.apa.org/about/index and Association for Psychological Science (APS; www.psychologicalscience.org/about) are also good resources for learning more about psychology and psychological specialties. As a start, we encourage you to consider how each of these professional organizations approaches and contributes to psychology. We also encourage you to explore APA divisional listings (www.apa.org/about/division/) – and follow up to learn more about any that particularly interest you. As an aside, it's OK – and in fact, fairly common – for members, including student affiliates to join more than one!

Related occupations that build on psychological knowledge

Psychology is a popular area of study – and general interest. However, other fields (or, professions) utilize or build on psychological knowledge. Since Chapter 12 will discuss these fields in greater depth, we'll only speak briefly about them here. As you journal, note any of the related fields briefly outlined here that you'd like to learn more about either as a career goal or interim step on your potential life/career journey.

The first area is allied professions that we introduced earlier. If you want to be a master's level therapist, some areas to consider are professional counseling also referred to as mental health counseling, marriage and family therapy (MFT), and clinical social work. As an aside, professional counselors also have training in career counseling, which we think is a plus. Moving from therapy to counseling and indirect student services, another related profession to consider is school counseling. School counseling, the current preferred professional term for what used to be called Guidance counseling (because guidance is only part of what school counselors do today) is a profession to consider if you want to promote the personal, social, academic, and career development of all children in P-12 school settings.

Much of what we know as business, including human resources, management, market research and analysis, sales, and training and development are founded on or informed by psychological research and principles. Moreover, many psychologists and people with psychological training in diversity, career development, and more, work as business consultants. Similar yet distinct in some ways from business, psychological knowledge informs the many ways people offer and deliver executive, job, and life coaching.

Health care is another broad area that's informed by psychology. As just a few examples, nurses and other front line health care providers work with the public, often under stressful circumstances. A kind word, a good connection, can facilitate healing. Similarly, psychological knowledge helps people who work as advocates for people with disabilities as well as those who provide direct care and support to others.

In addition, the broad field of education, as discussed earlier (under teaching) and education, as previously discussed, is, in many ways, applied psychology. In fact, psychology informs just about everything – so this and other psychology courses are a good investment regardless of your life/career path.

HOW DO YOU WANT TO CONTRIBUTE?
WHAT ROLE(S) DO YOU WANT TO PLAY?

Now we come to the crux of this book – asking how you want to contribute; how you want to be involved in psychology. We hope this chapter has inspired you to think (further) about your potential involvement in psychology and role(s) that interest you. This is a good time to reflect on those thoughts as well as your values, interests, and goals – and, if you haven't already done so, treat yourself to a journal. An old-fashioned notebook will do, but if you prefer a digital format, go for it. Ideally, you'll use this journal as a private, uncensored outlet to write (prose, poetry, however you choose), draw, paint, sing, or otherwise collect your ideas. Most people find the process of collecting their ideas helps their thinking. In addition, having them mostly in one place (not your head) facilitates reflection and further consideration, which is essential in life/career decision-making and planning.

BOX 2.3

Why I Write

"I write entirely to find out what I'm thinking, what I'm looking at, what I see and what it means. What I want and what I fear" (Joan Didion, 1976, p. 270, para. 8).

As you journal, we encourage you to reflect on your values – and how you prioritize them. For example, most people say that they want a career that pays well – yet it's important to consider how compensation (which includes salary) ranks in your life and career priority listing. For example, would you accept a position that paid well yet was otherwise unsatisfying? What would make a position unsatisfying or, conversely, satisfying to you? Your thoughtful considered responses will give you some insight into your life and career values – and therefore what matters most to you. Values are fundamental to life and career decision-making and planning. Along these same lines, some people consider their vocation or work a calling, both in the religious/spiritual and secular sense (Dik & Duffy, 2009). This is a lot to think about, consider, and journal, but don't fear, we will go into more depth and detail about ways to assess or identify your career values in Chapter 3.

Similarly, consistent with our integrative approach to career/life planning and decision-making, including healthy relationships, we understand that work and careers are just part of life, important parts to be sure, but just parts. There are a number of excellent life/career planning and decision-making guides that address this. One of our favorites is the popular *What color is your parachute?* by Richard N. Bolles (2019), which has been updated every year since its initial publication in 1970 (yes, that's a long time)! Bolles' approach is loosely based on Holland's and Strong's theories and their widely used interest inventories (i.e., the Self-Directed Search and the Strong Interest Inventory) that inform this book, and that we'll return to in more depth in subsequent chapters.

As we discussed earlier, our work is also informed by psychological theory and research, including Sunny Hansen's *Integrative career planning for adults* (2002) that addresses the importance of starting where you are – respecting all parts and aspects of one's life – as you move forward. Similarly, putting to rest the belief that there's an inherent conflict between work and family life, this book is also informed by Greenhaus and Powell's (2006) position that work and family life have the potential to enrich each other – and do, often giving returning students and career changers and enhancers (Brady-Amoon & Hammond, 2014) an advantage (Motulsky, 2010). In this same vein, Donald Super's (1980) Life-Plan/Life Space theory and his life rainbow are perhaps the best-known description and illustration of the interaction among the various aspects (or, roles) of a person's life, some of which are more common in specific age ranges than others.

As you consider your current commitments and future goals, it's important to keep in mind that no one can make more time. We all have the same 24 hours, 7 days per week.

However, we can work to allocate it going forward consistent with our priorities. For example, if you want to make a good life-career decision and plan, it will be important to allocate sufficient time to read this book, reflect, do the exercises, journal, and more.

HOW MUCH TIME SHOULD YOU INVEST IN CAREER PLANNING?

Envisioning your life and career goals, including the role(s) you might take, is also essential to making informed decisions about the level and type of education you will need to reach those goals. At the same time, it's important to be prepared for the opportunities you will seek as well as happenstance opportunities (Krumboltz, 2009). The best place and time to start is NOW. So, if you're currently in school, regardless of status (part- or full-time) or level, we encourage you to make the most of your training opportunities.

If you have a good idea that you want to pursue a career in psychology and have not yet completed your bachelor's degree, then it's smart to major in psychology. If you've already committed to another major, you can still pursue a career in psychology, but it will likely take some additional work beyond your bachelor's degree, possibly at the graduate level (i.e., master's or doctoral degree). If you're an advanced undergraduate (i.e., bachelor's degree) candidate who declared a major other than psychology and are considering changing your major to psychology or adding it as a second major or minor, we strongly recommend exploring your options with an advisor who is knowledgeable about the curriculum at your college or university to make informed decisions. There is no reason to delay one's planned graduation – because, similar to people who've committed to another major, you can still pursue a career in psychology. As an aside, neither author of this book majored in psychology as an undergraduate – yet we both earned doctorates in psychology, are licensed as psychologists, and more!

OVERVIEW OF EDUCATION IN PSYCHOLOGY

Most psychologists have earned a Ph.D., a doctor of philosophy degree, with a major in psychology or their specialty area within psychology. The Ph.D. is a theoretically informed research degree that requires, among other things, an independent research dissertation. Increasing numbers of psychologists have earned the more recently established Psy.D., doctor of psychology degree, which follows a scholar-practitioner model of training. Still others have earned an Ed.D., a doctor of education degree with a major in their specialty area within psychology. Notwithstanding these differences, the overall goals of doctoral training in psychology are the attainment of advanced knowledge as well as professional development and socialization.

If your goals include earning a doctoral degree in psychology, it's important to make the most of your undergraduate education, including mentoring and research opportunities, to increase your likelihood of admission to these extremely selective programs. Similarly, it's important to research potential programs and mentors to identify potential programs and mentors that would be a good fit for you. Furthermore, as higher education represents a significant investment of time and money (including lost or deferred wages), it's important to investigate opportunities for funding, which may include graduate assistantships. We'll cover the application process for both master's and doctoral programs in future chapters. For now, it's important to consider the costs and benefits of doctoral study – to set the stage for life/career decision-making.

There's more variety in master's and post-master's (sub-doctoral) training in psychology, including degrees and specializations. Some master's programs are academic, others research focused, and still others are career focused, including master's programs in I-O and school psychology. Similarly, as we noted earlier, master's degree programs in several allied professions may be another good option for people who want to pursue that option. Given the diversity in master's programs, it's important to do your research to identify the programs that will best meet your goals.

What level and type of education will you need to reach your potential goal(s)?

When you know – or at least have a better idea about – your goals, then the level and type of education you need will become clearer. In this chapter, we explored five major ways people can be involved with psychology at multiple levels. We also provided brief descriptions of related occupations that build on psychological knowledge. Overall, we emphasized that *psychological knowledge makes a difference in people's lives.*

One of the ways you can leverage psychology is to engage with the material in this book to reflect on your values, interests, and abilities, to begin to lay the foundation for life and career decision-making. When you have ideas about where you'd like to go (even as possibilities), then you can start preparing to choose the appropriate level and type of education to reach your goals. With that in mind, you can then systematically investigate, make informed decisions about your next steps to maximize success. Some questions to ask yourself at this stage include: How directly to I want to be involved with psychology? As a contributor to the knowledge base, someone who applies psychological knowledge in my work in psychology? In an allied field? In a related occupation? Some people choose a career path or destination first and then determine the best educational route for them. Others consider their career and educational options concurrently. What matters most is you make an informed decision consistent with your values and life goals. Moreover, no matter where you are on your higher education journey, it's important to recognize that the appropriate education, training, and degree is necessary but not sufficient for life and career success. There's so much more to make the investment that a good education should be – a worthwhile one that will pay dividends in the currency (values) that matter to you.

While we're encouraging you to explore – and consider possibilities, we urge you NOT to unnecessarily limit yourself – you're not too young, too old, or too whatever you might think. Far too many people, particularly women, people of color, first generation students, nontraditional (i.e., older students) students underestimate themselves, comparing themselves with people with much more experience, training, and resources – therefore diminishing their own potential.

CHAPTER SUMMARY

This chapter introduced you more deeply to psychology as a field. Following an introduction to the two major directions that careers in psychology can take (research and applied), a more in-depth description of five major categories of work in psychology was provided. The second part of the chapter focused on helping you to begin to understand specialties and subfields in psychology and related fields. The chapter wraps up with an overview and introduction to education in psychology.

EXERCISES

1   Go to the website of the American Psychological Association. Find the "Divisions" web page and review the list of Divisions (groups of psychologists with similar interests). Find two–five that most interest you and go to their website. After you review the information there, consider whether you might enjoy working with people with these interests and ways of working together. Think about how this helps you to see where you might go with your career in psychology.

2   Outline your day – current and future. What does your life look like now? In a typical day, how many hours do you dedicate to work and/or school? Loved ones? Self-care, including sleep? What would a typical day look like in the future? What will you do to get there?

3   Draw a picture, make a collage, and/or write a list of what you want your life to look/be like in ten years. If ten years is too long a horizon for you, make it five, or whatever is comfortable. (The goal here is to see it, to plan it, to reach it).

Next steps: the advanced move

1   Think about your experiences in life. Which ones are most interesting? Why? Which experiences were the least interesting? Why? Then, consider the differences between the two. What might they tell you about your future in psychology?

2   The best sources for information about allied professions are people in your network who are happily engaged in those professions and the professional societies for those professions. Do you know someone with a career that interests you? Can you arrange conversation? Check out the BLS and O*net websites to find professional organizations that interest you.

3   The "how many hours are you going to work/invest in planning/preparation" exercise.
a.   Step 1: Reflect on your life. How long do you intend/think you need to work? To earn an income? Keep in mind that most people need to work (or be able to work) to support themselves until they're at least 65, maybe longer given longer lifespans.
b.   Step 2: Subtract your current age from the age you estimated in Step 1. This is the number of years you expect to work, pursue your career(s).

   c.   Step 3: Multiply the number of years you calculated in Step 2 by 48 weeks (allowing a generous four weeks' vacation and holidays). This is the number of weeks you're estimating you'll work.

   d.   Step 4: Multiply the number of weeks you estimated in Step 3 by 35 (keeping in mind that many positions require much more than 35 hours per week) to arrive at the number of hours you expect to work.

   e.   Step 5: Reflect on the number of hours you estimate you'll work. Do you want to do something you like? That you're good at? How much time are you willing to dedicate to make good decisions about your career path?

REFERENCES

Bolles, R. N. (2019). What color is your parachute? In *A practical manual for job-hunters and career-changers*. Ten Speed Press. www.jobhuntersbible.com/

Brady-Amoon, P., & Hammond, M. S. (2014, July). Women's midlife career transitions: Barriers, risks, and opportunities. In V. E. Sojo (Convener), *Risk factors for working women's wellbeing, functioning and growth: What we know and what we can do*. Presentation to the 28th International Congress of Applied Psychology, Paris, France.

Brady-Amoon, P., & Keefe-Cooperman, K. (2017). Psychology, counseling psychology, and professional counseling: Shared roots, challenges, and opportunities. *The European Journal of Counselling Psychology, 6*(1), 41–62. https://doi.org/http://dx.doi.org/10.5964/ejcop.v5i2.105

Didion, J. (1976, December 5). Why I write. *New York Times*, p. 270, para. 8. www.nytimes.com/1976/12/05/archives/why-i-write-why-i-write.html

Dik, B. J., & Duffy, R. D. (2009). Calling and vocation at work: Definitions and prospects for research and practice. *The Counseling Psychologist, 37*, 424–250. https://doi.org/10.1177/0011000008316430

Greenhaus, J. H., & Powell, G. N. (2006). When work and family are allies: A theory of work-family enrichment. *Academy of Management Review, 31*(1), 72–92.

Goodyear, R. K., Lichtenberg, J. W., Hutman, H., Overland, E., Bedi, R., Christiani, K., . . . Young, C. (2016). A global portrait of counselling psychologists' characteristics, perspectives, and professional behaviors. *Counselling Psychology Quarterly, 29*(2), 115–138. https://doi.org/10.1080/09515070.2015.1128396

Hansen, L. S. (2002). Integrative life planning (ILP): A holistic theory for career counseling with adults. In S. G. Niles (Ed.), *Adult career development: Concepts, issues and practices* (3rd ed., pp. 57–75). National Career Development Association.

June, A. W., & Newman, J. (2013, January 4). Adjunct project shows wide range in pay and working conditions. *The Chronicle of Higher Education*. www.chronicle.com/article/Adjunct-Project-Shows-Wide/136439

Krumboltz, J. D. (2009). The happenstance learning theory. *Journal of Career Assessment, 17*, 135–154. https://doi.org/10.1177/1069072708328861

Motulsky, S. L. (2010). Relational processes in career transition: Extending theory, research, and practice. *The Counseling Psychologist, 38*(8), 1078–1114. https://doi.org/10.1177/0011000010376415

National Association of School Psychologists. (2019). *School psychology credentialing fact sheet [handout]*. Author.

National Center for Education Statistics. (2011). *Digest of education statistics*. Table 290. Bachelor's, master's, and doctor's degrees conferred by degree-granting institutions, by sex of student and discipline division: 2009–10. http://nces.ed.gov/programs/digest/d11/tables/dt11_290.asp

National Center for Education Statistics. (2017). *Digest of education statistics*. Table 318.30. Bachelor's, master's, and doctor's degrees conferred by postsecondary institutions, by sex of student and discipline division: 2014–15. https://nces.ed.gov/programs/digest/d16/tables/dt16_318.30.asp

Scheel, M. J., Stabb, S. D., Cohn, T. J., Duan, C., & Sauer, E. M. (2018). Counseling psychology model training program. *Counseling Psychologist*, *46*(1), 6–49. https://doi.org/10.1177/0011000018755512

Society for Industrial and Organizational Psychology, Inc. (2016). *Guidelines for education and training in industrial-organizational psychology*. www.siop.org/Portals/84/docs/SIOP_ET_Guidelines_2017.pdf?ver=2019-05-02-093416-833

Society for Vocational Psychology. (2017). *Society for vocational psychology, a section of the society of counseling psychology of the American psychological association*. www.div17svp.org/

Super, D. E. (1980). A life-span, life-space approach to career development. *Journal of Vocational Behavior*, *16*(3), 282–298. https://doi.org/10.1016/0001-8791(80)90056-1

U.S. Bureau of Labor Statistics (BLS). (2020, August 18). Occupational employment and wages, May 2020: 19-3031. Clinical, Counseling, and School Psychologists. https://www.bls.gov/oes/current/oes193031.htm.

U.S. Bureau of Labor Statistics (BLS). (2021, September 15). Industries at a Glance. https://www.bls.gov/iag/tgs/iag_index_alpha.htm.

CHAPTER 3

Career decision-making and management for psychology

ORIENTING QUESTIONS

1. What is career decision-making?
2. What is career management?
3. What information will help you make good decisions about your career in psychology – both as a student and as a professional?
4. What steps will help you to make an effective decision about your career direction?
5. How do you identify information you need to make a decision?
6. Who or what resources can help you in this process and how do you access them?

DOI: 10.4324/9780429296413-4

INTRODUCTION

"You can't make decisions based on fear and the possibility of what might happen."

(Michelle Obama, 2007)

This chapter will present information related to the process of making decisions about and planning one's career. Why should we do this? Because we are two to four times more likely to accomplish our goals if we write them down (Morisano et al., 2010). Developing a plan to reach a goal not only increases the likelihood of reaching it, it also frees up our mind to focus on other things since, by having a plan, we no longer need to worry about what to do to reach the goal we set (Masicampo & Baumeister, 2011)! We will start with an overview of decision-making, which is central to the process of making a plan – move on to discussing the information needed to make effective decisions and describe a method for developing a plan for completing your undergraduate degree with an eye toward your post-graduation goals. Finally, we will introduce resources for making career decisions, which we'll explore more fully later in the book, particularly in Chapter 6. By the way, many things and people influence our thinking about our career. Taking a minute to think about these influences and what they've taught us is a good start to this process. You can use the suggestions in Box 3.1, "Discussion", to support your reflection and discussion.

BOX 3.1

Discussion

Our thinking about work is shaped by the people, activities, and events to which we are exposed. Make a list of people, activities, and/or events that have affected your thinking about your career. When finished, discuss with one or two peers or advisors. What did you learn from this discussion about influences on your and others' thinking about careers?

DECISION-MAKING

We make decisions, plan projects or activities, and carry them out in many realms of our life. Some of these decisions are *bigger* in that they are likely to have a larger impact on our life, while other decisions are smaller – yet can still have an influence. Thus, we can think about decision-making on two levels. The first, or *micro* level, is a decision between options, such as when you've been reading about different specializations in psychology and related areas and decide that one option either does or does not seem to meet your interests. Another micro-level decision might be to learn more about *informational interviewing* or *job shadowing* (both are ways to learn about occupations). The second, or "macro" level is the entire process of making a decision about your career direction. At this level *career decision-making* alerts us to the stages involved in decision-making – the process of identifying alternatives and deciding on a small number that seem to better match our criteria; the process of exploring those options in-depth through research, experiences, and conversations with relevant others; and the process of evaluating those options to determine which might be a better fit for you (Gati & Tal, 2008). In order for you to master the process well, we are providing detail about the process in the next section.

Decision-making comes more easily to some people than others. Why? Primarily, because some individuals have more experience with decision-making and planning and recognize the applicability or transferability (in psychological terms) of these skills to career decision-making while others learned these skills in workshops or classes that have taught this decision-making and/or planning skills. Most students who have made a decision about their college major fall into one of these three categories – whether they realize it or not. This section is about helping you to fill in the gaps in your understanding about the mechanics and processes of making career decisions and managing your career in psychology. Given the importance of this process, we've provided an overview of the steps, or process, of career decision-making and planning, which is central to career management. Regardless of your experience of decision-making and planning in general or career decision-making and planning in particular, we encourage you to read this section with an eye to refining your skills. Whether you're refining skills, learning them for the first time, or something in between, we'll take it step-by-step in order to ensure that you have the skills and knowledge you need to make good decisions and plans.

CAREER DECISION-MAKING PROCESS

Making decisions related to your career path requires 1) knowledge of the decision-making process, 2) knowledge of ourselves – values, interests, personality/interpersonal style, skills, and goals, 3) knowledge of the world of work and methods to prepare to both enter and succeed in that world, and 4) knowledge of the skills needed to make those decisions. This chapter will provide you with an overview of this process. Please note that, if we look only at the decision-making process, we might notice that there are similarities to other types of decision-making. Think about the decisions you might have already made today – to get up in the morning, dress yourself, eat, go to class or work, to study, or to drive carefully between activities. These may not seem like decisions, however, think about times when you didn't do these things and you are likely to see that in actuality, you did make a decision. Let's look at the steps in making a decision in Table 3.1.

TABLE 3.1 Steps in Making a Decision

1	Recognize that you need to make a decision.
2	Define the decision you need to make – what is part of this decision and what is not? Sometimes, we need to break decisions down into smaller pieces in order to improve our ability to make decisions.
3	Learn about the decision – how is it different from or similar to other decisions that you've made in the past? What's important to attend to about this decision?
4	Brainstorm possible decision options – rarely is there only one option or outcome. If there seems to be only one, explore that option and ask yourself "what assumptions am I making about the decision and/or outcomes?" Clearly understanding the different aspects of your decision often helps to generate options about which you can decide.
5	Evaluate the decision options. Some options may require information or other resources you can access, others to which you currently have no access, or may require more time to access than you currently have available. Other options may have limited applicability to the decision as you are experiencing it. Therefore, reviewing the options to eliminate those that are least likely to work is often helpful.
6	Make a decision – or decide when you're going to make a decision, based on the best information you have at that time.
7	Lay out the steps for implementing the decision.
8	Implement your decision and monitor what happens.
9	Review the outcomes from your decision – are they as you intended, or do you need to make adjustments?
10	If the outcome was not as expected, go back to step 2, re-define the decision, and work through the process again.

Hopefully, you can see where you've used a similar process to make decisions in your life. So, when we speak about career decision-making, we are actually applying the above general decision-making process specifically to making some type of decision about one's career. You most likely have already applied this process when you first decided to study psychology or make psychology your major. For those of you who started your post-secondary education with another career goal in mind, you've most likely used this process more than once. When we apply this process to making decisions about your career, the process looks like this:

1   Realize that you need to make a decision related to your career. Here are some examples of decisions you might need or choose to make about your career while you are an undergraduate student:

   a.   which major to declare (such as to major in Psychology)

   b.   what work and life goals you plan to achieve post-graduation

   c.   what subfield, if any, you might pursue to be qualified to engage in the work you want to do

   d.   what extra-curricular activities to engage in to best prepare you for the next steps you will need to take

   e.   which graduate program to apply to, or which job to take after graduation

2   Define the decision. As it relates to making career decisions, this means that you are clear about the decision you need to make, since the manner in which you define the problem affects the solutions you will come up with, as well as affect other people's ability to assist you in solving the problem. For example, if you believe that you need to make a choice of major and do not have enough information about the careers related to that major, perhaps the actual decision that needs to be made is related to which information sources you believe are reliable and how to obtain the information about the major(s) to which you are attracted.

3   Learn about the decision. This is the most important step. The more you know about and understand the boundaries and implications of the decision you are about to make, the more effective will be that decision. Use all of your resources – information sources (print and internet), people, etc.

4   Once you've learned all you can about the decision, think about the decision options – even not making a decision is an option (and a decision!).

5   Evaluate your options. Which options have a higher probability of moving you toward your goal? Which ones might be more challenging to implement? Are you up for that challenge?

6   Make the decision! Even if you don't have "all" the information – few people do – make your decision. In most instances, there are points at which you can change that decision (particularly if it's a big one like choosing a major). However, give it a go and lean into your decision.

7   Now that you've made a decision, lay out your plan for implementing it. We'll discuss this more in the Chapter 6, so we won't discuss it here.

8   Implement your decision plan.

9   Review the outcomes to see if the decision is working for you.

10 If the decision is not working out as planned, return to step 2 and apply your new understanding to re-define the decision – work through the process from there.

BOX 3.2

Vignette – The Case of Zoe

Zoe is a first-year student at RMU and is undecided about her major. She likes people and finds that people come to her for help with their everyday problems. She feels good about being able to help people and finds that her solutions tend to work for the people she talks with. In high school, Zoe did well in her art classes, earning a full scholarship to RMU based on her skills. In addition, she sang in the choir and acted in the high school and community theaters. Zoe is unsure that a career in art or music is the best path for her, as she is really enjoying the required psychology courses. What could Zoe do to test out her suspicion that psychology might be a better major for her?

CAREER MANAGEMENT: THE NEXT STEP

Simply put, career management is the process of adapting one's initial career plan as one learns more about the details of achieving one's career goal. Managing one's career begins as soon as one has made a choice. Why? Because, at this stage, one is beginning to identify activities to reach that goal – to create a plan that can guide you toward your goal. For example, once you've decided to study psychology, you might begin to see that there are many different subfields in psychology – such as cognitive, developmental, industrial/organizational psychology, or social psychology – or that there are different ways people implement a career in psychology, such as researcher, instructor, clinician, or consultant. In addition, occupations change over time. You may want to "try out" these areas by talking to a psychologist who knows about that area, taking a course, or joining a research team that conducts related research. You also might interview someone who works in the area in which you are interested or obtain an internship to gain experience in that particular setting. All those ideas and more will help you gain information to assist you in deciding whether this might be a good direction for you, as well as to help you gain experience in the types of activities and skills that are useful in most subfields in psychology. Career management uses the same skills as career decision-making – because we continue to make decisions – however, the decisions are related to carrying out tasks or activities that will help us learn more about our career direction and to move toward the career goal we set.

Let's think about an example. Many students believe that if they go to classes and get a good grade, then they will get into graduate school. In addition, they believe that graduate school is just like their undergraduate program. These two beliefs prevent students from seeing and preparing for the reality of graduate school work (or, employment) – often until they are applying for graduate school (or, a job). First, we want to dispel these two crippling myths. Post-secondary education has both classroom-based and non-classroom-based learning opportunities to help you prepare for your career. In addition, the practice of psychology (whether research or practice-focused) requires the development of both one's mind and one's skills. Thus, when your advisor or instructor encourages you to join the psychology club or a research team, they are not just trying to make you do busy-work. Building your network and being on a research team are ways to develop a number of important skills. For example, let's look at the skills you can build by participating on a research team. Consider which of these might also help you in other ways:

1   Research skills, such as gathering data (from people or other sources), entering and editing data, identifying a research topic and question, conducting a literature review to learn what we know about a topic, formulating that information into a meaningful "review" to communicate with others about this topic, developing research questions, analyzing the data, preparing conference presentations, presenting your findings at conferences, and publishing your findings in a professional journal.
2   Critical thinking skills, such as deciding what evidence (often from the research literature) is needed to improve the discussion of your main research topic. Another example is reviewing a draft manuscript to give helpful feedback.
3   Collaboration skills, such as working with another research team member to generate research terms for a literature search, assisting other research team members in data gathering, and engaging in conversations about the next direction for the research project.
4   Other (strongly correlated with) employability skills, such as recognizing and acting on one's responsibility to carry out your part of a project, showing up for meetings on time, staying at the meeting the entire time, completing the tasks you commit to as agreed, asking for assistance and guidance when you are not sure about how to do something, responding to feedback from your mentors and supervisors, treating your fellow research team members with the respect that you want them to treat you, and other skills.

The above skills are just a few of the things that you learn (or, hone) by being on a research team. Don't forget that you will likely need recommendations and the more faculty members know you, your skill-set, and work, the more effectively they can support you with suggestions for additional opportunities for development and letters of reference for applications to various types of experiences, graduate school, and beyond. By the way, if you'd like to learn more about career readiness or employability skills, you can learn more by visiting your campus or local career placement office for information from the National Association of Colleges and Employers (NACE, www.naceweb.org/career-readiness/competencies/career-readiness-defined/) or the American Psychological Association's Center for Workforce Studies (APA CWS; www.apa.org/workforce/data-tools/qualifications-job-advertisements)

Thus, in career management, you are using the skills and knowledge you gained in making a career decision to implement and refine, or adjust, your plan. The goal of ongoing career management is to allow you to control what you can and take advantage of new information or opportunities that may help move you toward your career goal. This may seem overwhelming, however, remember, this, like much in life, is a one step at a time process. You will find that, as you explore psychology via coursework and extra-curricular activities, your understanding of psychology as a field with options and paths will grow. This will lead you to revise or update your career plan.

BOX 3.3

Vignette – The Case of Carlos

Carlos is a sophomore at MSU. He is interested in helping people. He had a friend whose aunt had been diagnosed with schizophrenia and chose psychology as his major in order to help people struggling with psychological issues such as this. Last semester he took a course in neuropsychology – the study of the brain – and realized that he was really interested in the physical aspects of the brain's and the body's functioning. Now he's wondering if he should change over to Biology and get his PhD so that he can conduct research on how the brain works differently in people with schizophrenia. What are the pros and cons to switching or remaining in psychology versus changing to biology as a major? What would you do?

CAREER DECISION-MAKING INFORMATION: VALUES, INTERESTS, PERSONALITY, AND SKILLS

We've laid out the process of making a career decision first so that you can begin to recognize how much experience you have in making decisions. You can use your prior decision-making experience to help you make more effective career decisions. The next step is to understand the types of information needed to make a good career decision – whether it is a decision to major in psychology, to minor in a related subject (such as biology, business, criminal justice, sociology, or statistics), to join a research team, apply for a job or graduate school, or even when to retire from the workplace! There are four major types of information that are needed to make most career decisions. They all boil down to how well you know yourself, your specific situation, and the educational and occupational worlds (Parsons, 1909).

BOX 3.4

Frank Parsons

Frank Parsons (1854–1908) started the Vocational Bureau in Boston, Massachusetts to help immigrants and young people make effective choices as to work so as to lead a successful life. He is considered to be the "father of Vocational Guidance", now called "career guidance" or "career counseling".

Parsons (1909) suggested that people need to understand their own "aptitudes, abilities, interests, ambitions, resources, limitations, and their causes" (p. 5). In addition, he suggested that one must have knowledge of the available occupations (or, *world of work*), how to be successful in those occupations, and the likelihood that the occupation will continue to exist. This includes information about the tasks and activities, preparation needed, availability of positions, advantages and disadvantages, and the potential for growth. Finally, Parsons suggested that one uses *true reasoning* to evaluate the options in light of the individual's characteristics, which we now refer to as "decision-making". In the next few sections, we'll discuss these types of information and how to access them, if you haven't already. By the way, as a result of the research and work of both vocational psychologists (who study career development and decision-making) and career counselors, we now know that there are more skills, knowledge, and abilities needed to make good career decisions and plans; however, as a simple heuristic, Parson's model is a good short-cut.

Values

Values can be defined as "organized sets of general beliefs, opinions, and attitudes about what is preferable, right, or simply good in life" (Šverko & Vizek-Vidović, 1995, p. 5). We make many of our decisions based upon values related to the options among which we are deciding. Values include such things as the importance of spirituality or religion in our lives, how important it is to have money or friends or the latest technology. There are so many values that psychology has had a hard time creating an overarching theory of values. Thus, subfields in psychology, such as vocational psychology, have created mini-theories.

BOX 3.5

Definition of Mini-theories

Mini-theories are focused theories that organize knowledge and information around a portion of a larger topic. A mini-theory does not presume to explain the entire topic – only that portion relevant to the particular aspect of the topic to which it applies.

Applied to career development, values might be defined as "what we want from a career". It might be money, or status, or to solve a problem we see as "important". And that's the key – a value is something that is "important" to us. As a result, values underlie our decision-making. For example, if we asked you to choose between spending a Saturday evening going out with a group of people you know or staying home, you would likely have a preference. However, the preference you have this week might be different than the preference that you might have next week due to a variety of factors, such as: you might be tired, you just spent two days travelling, or you haven't seen this group of people for several years. In addition to that preference, you might also value keeping connected to people you know more than spending time by yourself or vice versa. To begin to understand the values that you have, think about decisions you make about where you spend your time. On a specific day, you decide to study versus spend time with friends or exercising or something else. When you do so, in essence, you are preferring one thing over another. A preference on any one day is likely to be influenced by factors on that day, while the more frequently you prefer that one thing over others the more likely that the preference is an indication of a value. Table 3.2 is a list of values that people often associate with their career or work. Are any of these of interest to you?

Finally, values have a strong influence on our choices and motivation (Chase et al., 2013). Incorporating values into the goals you set has been shown to increase student achievement and help you persist to reach your goal. Thus, understanding what it takes to reach your goals and understanding how an action supports you achieving your values can help you to reach that goal.

TABLE 3.2 Example Work Values

Advancement	High income	Prestige
Adventure	Independence	Public contact
Artistic creativity	Influence others	Recognition
Challenging	Interest in career field	Security
Competition	Leadership	Specific geographic location
Creativity	Leisure time	Stability
Entry w/o additional training	Mentally stimulating	Supervision
Fast paced	Moral fulfillment	Time freedom
Flexibility	Physically challenging	Variety
Helping others	Power	Working alone

BOX 3.6

Values Reflection

Turn to the person next to you (or find another willing partner for this exercise) and take turns describing two–five values that are important to you. They can be things, people, outcomes, etc. They must just be important to you. Have the other person take notes. Once you've both shared your values with each other, discuss how you think they might impact your career path.

Interests

Interests are one of the oldest ideas linked to career choice. They are the subject of a 15th-century book in Spain (see Chabassus & Zytowski, 1987) and were discussed as part of a set of treatises written in Arabic by a group of authors located in the area now known as southern Iraq (see Chabassus & Zytowski, 1987). Continuing into the present, most major theories of career development incorporate interests as a core variable (Super et al., 1963, 1996; Lent & Brown, 2013). Thus, those things to which we attend with the greatest interest are likely to provide clues to an effective choice of major and to an effective choice of specialization within a major – such as choosing to focus on cognitive, developmental, clinical, or counseling psychology. By extension, we are more likely to be comfortable with and have more interesting interactions with people who have similar interests to ourselves. Two of the most frequently used measures of career interests include Holland's *Self-Directed Search* (SDS; Holland & Messer, n.d.) and the *Strong Interest Inventory* (Gruter & Hammer, n.d.). In addition to the SDS, Holland also developed a method for organizing interests and work personalities into groups that can be linked to careers – typically called the Holland Hexagon (also known as the RIASEC theory; Holland, 1997). The latter was first developed by E.K. Strong, Jr. during World War I to assist the military more effectively match soldiers to the occupations in the military. Both the SDS (first published in 1979) and the Strong Interest Inventory have been continuously updated and revised and can be completed and interpreted with the assistance of a career counselor on your campus career office, from a local career counselor, or online. Make sure that, if you do the online version and have questions, you speak with someone with the training to answer your questions. Examples would be your academic advisor, a career counselor, or counselor in the campus or community counseling center.

BOX 3.7

Interests Reflection

Take a moment to write down a few sentences about two things that you find most interesting. Decide on a few words that best represent the topic of your interests. Then, go to your library's website and put the word "psychology" and the keywords from one of your interests into the "topic" search boxes. Review the articles that come up. If there are a large number, think of a second term related to your interest and refine your search. Talk with your neighbor or other willing partner about the results.

Personality

Personality influences our career choice in several ways. Personality is often talked about in two ways – personality characteristics and interpersonal style. While personality characteristics are linked to career interests (Holland, 1997; Su et al., 2015), interpersonal style, as reflected in the frequency and way we prefer to interact with others is related to different ways of playing out a career. For example, a psychologist who is more extraverted may be drawn to tasks and careers that involve more direct contact with people such as the ways many child psychologists, consultants, and advocates work. Similarly, a psychologist who is more introverted yet interested in some of these areas might be drawn toward conducting research on the effectiveness of interventions with children, gathering and synthesizing information on trauma-informed education prior to working with a school system, or preparing materials for a local group to advocate for at-risk youth. If you look carefully at our examples, you may notice that we intentionally used examples from similar situations (just changing the specific activity). This was intentional, since, while we have preferences in the way we do things (as evidenced by the slightly different tasks highlighted), it doesn't mean that we can't do things outside our comfort zone. It just means that it may take a bit more effort.

Getting back to personality, it may surprise you to know that interests and personality are more highly correlated than you would think. One of Holland's early measures (Vocational Preference Inventory; Holland, 1985) used occupational labels to identify both personality style and vocational interests. Like the measures of interests, these measures of personality and the interpretation materials to help you apply this information to your career choice process, can be completed with the assistance of your campus career counselor or a career counselor in the community.

BOX 3.8

Personality Reflection

Ask someone who knows you well to list ten words that best describe you. Then, ask them to give you feedback on how these descriptors might relate to the type of work you might do, the setting you might work in, or the way you might work (for example, as part of a team or alone). Write a reflection on what you heard.

Skills

Many of us have found that some things come easier to us than to other people – and the reverse. Skills that are more "natural" are indicators of strengths that could lead to and/or support a career in a particular direction. Think about yourself and your friends – what are you good at (or, what comes more easily for you) that your friends are not? Do you find yourself helping others with math? Sharing tips with a teammate about how to improve their swing, throw, dunk, etc.? Organizing their rooms or lockers or work, or even an event? You may already know that you are good at certain tasks or activities (read that you have these "skills"), however, sometimes we are not aware of, or exposed to, skills that we might be good at. Paying attention to and thinking about what we are good at is one way of beginning to think about those parts of psychology that might be a better fit for us. We encourage you to think and journal about your skills because although some may be very valuable for career-decision making and management, there may also be some skills that you would like to spend a lot of time doing, but not have to depend on them for your salary.

Skills are one of the most visible and, thus, accessible aspects of careers. They are also the most frequently developed (rather than inherited) aspects of careers. For example, how many of you were born knowing how to use a computer, microscope, or phone? You've developed these skills through learning and/or experience. In addition to skills that are directly related to your career, you will develop skills that help you function in the workplace, and skills that you choose not to use in the workplace. For example, you may have hobbies. Some people are more skilled at their hobbies than at their work, yet they do not want to work for pay at those hobbies. There are a variety of reasons for this. You might find it worthwhile to speak with someone with a hobby to which they are committed to learn how they thought about and decided which (work or hobby) would take on which role in their life.

Skills can be one of the easiest or most difficult type of information to gather when one is researching careers. Why? For two reasons. First, many careers are heavily oriented toward taking action – such as athletes, airline pilots, and landscapers, while others are focused more on abstract thought (Holland, 1973). Careers that utilize more mental activity than action are hard to notice. So, for example, while we *see* teachers using their teaching skills in the classroom, we don't see them reading textbooks, taking classes, and planning these classroom activities. Another example would be a researcher, such as a social psychologist. They read the research literature on their research topic, identify questions that haven't been answered, talk with others about their ideas, and think up research studies to answer those questions. It can look like they are not *doing* anything – it's just that the *doing* is mostly in their heads. Second, many careers are invisible to most of us because the work is behind the scenes – for example, the psychologist who consults on a psychological thriller movie, consults with a business to update their hiring processes and procedures so as to not disadvantage individuals from under-represented groups, or who conducts psychological evaluations on astronauts to ensure that they can tolerate the stresses of space flight. These are unlike occupations that are visible to us in our daily lives – teachers, doctors, postal carriers, store clerks. Sometimes invisible (and less visible) occupations become more visible, such as the way the work of three African American mathematicians was highlighted in the movie *Hidden Figures* (Melfi, 2016) or via the NBC show entitled the *Profiler* (Campbell et al., 1996–2000). Until *Profiler* appeared, psychological profiling as an occupation had remained invisible, meanwhile, after it appeared there was a tremendous increase in interest in psychological profiling as a career.

BOX 3.9

Skills Reflection

Think about what you are good at – regardless of whether or not you like doing it. List up to ten things that you are good at, then sort and organize into groups of related things. Consider whether or not you would be happy spending 40 or more hours per week doing that thing (or, group of things) to support yourself and/or others. Which skill or group of skills would you be willing to use (and ideally develop) on a regular basis for at least ten years?

BRINGING IT ALL TOGETHER: GOAL SETTING AND CAREER PLANNING

We've now discussed the major components of career decision-making and management. In this section, we will talk about what you can do with these components. We've discussed decision-making and seen how skills in decision-making directly apply to career decision-making. We've also seen that when you make an initial career decision (such as to major in Psychology), you often find there are new decisions to make – such as the particular subfield within psychology that most attracts your focus and might be the direction in which you want to take your career. There will be other decisions, such as about electives, a minor to complement your major in psychology, joining professional organizations, participating on a research team, and/or engaging in activities related to the professional organization or research team. Some of you will already have seen where we're going – hurrah for you! Even so, let's go through what one does at this point to make sure that we're all on track to move toward creating a career plan.

Step 1 – Define the decision to be made: Do you have enough information to make an informed decision about your career/major? To complete this step, bring together all your notes about your values, interests, personality, and skills, as well as any additional information, such as favorite hobbies and feedback from others about your strengths and growing edges. At this point we will not take into consideration financial or monetary issues as this topic will be addressed in a later chapter.

BOX 3.10

Definition of Growing Edges

In this text, *growing edges* will refer to things that one does not do as well as one would like or as well as one needs to do them. This term is used to emphasize the mutable nature of abilities and skills – one can develop and/or change many things about oneself in order to support moving toward a goal, whether that goal is to achieve something, to engage with the world in a certain way, etc.

Step 2 – Review and summarize the information. You might use "post-it notes" with one piece of information on each. Then, put them on a flat space (e.g., a wall) where you can re-arrange them until they form one or more groups with common themes. These themes might be indicative of the types of activities you want to engage in, the issue of greatest concern to you, the type of people you want to work with as colleagues or clients, etc.

BOX 3.11

Kuder Career Guidance Software

The Kuder company developed software to assist individuals identify career options. It is named after an early pioneer in the vocational guidance field named Frederic Kuder (1904–2000). They have versions of the program for individuals in the education system (K-12), career and technical education, as well as for

(Continued)

BOX 3.11 *(Continued)*

those in post-secondary education and/or the workforce. If you are affiliated with an education institution, contact that institution's student services office, career counseling, or career placement office to obtain access to the system. If you are not affiliated with an education system, you are able to obtain access directly from the Kuder Company (www.kuder.com)

Step 3 – Evaluate the information. Do you feel that you have enough information to make a decision? Do you see patterns that make sense? If the answer is *yes*, then move on to the next step. If you are not sure that you have all the information you need (and this is often the case), then the answer is *no*. If the answer is *no*, the next step is to figure out what's missing. Look at each of the types of information, reflect on, and write down what you know about yourself and your situation. There will be some areas where you can write what seems like *reams* of information – then there are those where you may have trouble getting started. That's your clue that indicates that you need more information. If this is the case – and in many instances it is, then it's time to use your resources (advisor, instructor, advanced students in psychology, this book, the Kuder Journey program, career counselor, etc.) to fill in the gaps in your knowledge. Each time you fill in the gaps in your knowledge, you move closer to making that decision. In the next section, we'll talk about identifying resources to help fill in the gaps.

Step 4 – Making the decision. However, this isn't the end of the process – it's just the beginning! You will want to consider what else you do and learn in order to make the most of your opportunities. We will speak more about this planning process in Part II.

How do you figure out where to go or what to do?

Once you realize that you need more information to make you comfortable with deciding or with moving on to the next decision, you need to figure out what information you need and where to find that information. Let's look at identifying what information you need. So, you know that you need information and you are unsure where to obtain it or who might have that information. Let's flip this around – who seems to already have that information? Your psychology instructors? Fellow students? Who else might already have been in exactly your shoes and so might have figured out where to find that information? Make a list and start to contact the people on your list. You might start by talking to your classmates, instructor, or advisor. Once you are comfortable talking with people you know, you might want to try talking to professionals or people who you don't know well. Examples of these types of individuals includes your campus career counseling or career placement office staff and individuals who work in jobs related to your interests. To help you with that, we'd like to introduce the concept of informational interviewing.

BOX 3.12

Informational Interviewing

Informational interviewing is the process of gathering information through personal contact (Bolles, 2021). To conduct an informational interview, one must find someone who is doing a job that one is interested in, contact that person for a focused (about 20 minute) interview. This time should be used learning as much information as one can about the work and type of people who do the work. More information is provided later in the text, or see *What Color Is Your Parachute?* (Bolles, 2021) for more on information.

Richard N. Bolles, in his book *What Color is Your Parachute?* (2021), describes the results of a survey of successful job hunters. This survey revealed that those who were the most successful had spent time talking to people in various businesses and organizations before they began actively seeking job interviews. These individuals had tapped into a valuable source of career information – other individuals in the workforce. Through talking to others, they gained a better understanding of the relationship between their skills/experience and specific career fields. They also learned first-hand what type of work environment different jobs offered and were able to use this information to decide exactly what they wanted to do, target their job search, and market their skills effectively to employers. You can use this same method to learn more about psychology and its subfields. Besides being a highly effective means of gathering information, informational interviewing also helps most people develop confidence in approaching others – a skill that's valuable in many other career and life domains. A set of guidelines to help you start informational interviewing, as well as example questions can be found at the end of this chapter in Next steps: the advanced move.

As you can see, there are many resources to tap into to find out more about psychology. Start with someone you know or who is easy to talk to. At the end of your conversation, always ask if there is someone else or another resource that you should consider. This will help you to build your list of resources for information. Eventually, you will find that you have enough information to make your decision and move on to the next step in your planning and moving toward your career in psychology.

CHAPTER SUMMARY

In this chapter, we reviewed and discussed the concepts of career decision-making and career management. In so doing, we drew your attention to the decision-making processes that you are likely to already use and compared them to the career decision-making process so as to make the transfer of skills from one area to another easier for you. In addition, the major types of information needed to make the choice of a major (such as choosing to major in psychology) were described. Furthermore, we discussed an approach to figuring out the "next" information you need to improve your thinking about and planning to build your career in psychology.

EXERCISES

1   Often, our career direction is shaped by our family. We develop our sense of work from seeing and hearing about the work that others do, as well as learning how to deal with work-related issues from hearing how those around us work. One way of understanding how our thinking about work and career is shaped is by creating a *career/work genogram*. Please draw a basic family tree (defining "family" your way), starting with yourself, your parents/guardians, and then including other important people (e.g., siblings, aunts/uncles). Then note on the tree each person's occupation or primary employment (broadly defined). Then, reflect on any patterns that emerge – and how family attitudes about work influenced you.

2   Review the links on the American Psychological Association's Undergraduate Psychology webpage (www.apa.org/ed/precollege/undergrad/index). While some of the links are for your instructors, links under "Careers in Psychology" have helpful information.

Next steps: the advanced move

1   Visit your campus career center or the Kuder website. Complete the surveys of values, skills, and interests and review the results. Take note of which types of career options are suggested by the questionnaire results. Note the non-psychology career results. Why? Because they can give you clues to areas of specialization within psychology. For example, if Marketing is listed, you might explore how psychology is applied to understanding people's purchasing choices. Whereas, if Biology is listed, you might explore Neuropsychology or the psychology of the human–animal bond (yes – there are really a group of psychologists studying this topic!). Talk over the results with your campus career center personnel, your advisor, or a local career counselor.

2   Conduct an informational interview with a psychologist. Below are listed guidelines for arranging for and carrying out an informational interview, as well as example questions you might use:

a.   Guidelines for informational interviewing

   i.   The purpose of informational interviewing is to help you decide what you want to do and where you want to do it. It is not a way to get a job interview.

   ii.   Be sure you have located and reviewed the available information (online and in print) about the particular career field, company, organization, or business before you begin interviewing others for information. Libraries, public relation officers, personnel directors, Chambers of Commerce, and occupational organizations and associations are sources that provide information.

   iii. Start with people you know. Ask them if they know someone who is working in psychology, counseling, mental health, or research (depending upon your interest).

   iv. Contact the individual (or, organization) and ask for an appointment. Always ask for an appointment ahead of time. State specifically that you are interested in learning more about a particular career field, industry, or business. Ask for 20 or 30 minutes of the person's time and be sure to keep the meeting within that time frame.

   v. If the person you speak with recommends someone else as a source of further information, always ask if you may tell the new contact that they referred you to him or her when contacting the recommended individual.

   vi. Write down the information you received, the name of the person with whom you spoke, and date of your conversation for your records. Later, you can compare information received from different sources.

   vii. Send a thank you note after the informational interview.

  b. Example Questions for an Informational Interview

   i. Describe a typical day.

   ii. What do you like least about your job? What do you like most about your job?

   iii. What types of changes are occurring in your field?

   iv. How did you get into this type of work? What is your background?

   v. What type of training/education is needed for this job?

   vi. What type of advancement opportunities does this company offer? How do salaries in this field compare with other fields?

   vii. What suggestions do you have for anyone interested in obtaining this type of position? Who do you suggest I talk to for further information?

REFERENCES

Bolles, R. N. (2021). *What color is your parachute? 2020: A practical manual for job-hunters and career-changers*. Ten Speed Press.

Campbell, Clifton, Kronish, Stephen, Moses, Kim, & Sander, Ian (Executive Producers). (1996–2000). *Profiler* [TV series]. Three Putt Productions; NBC Studios

Chabassus, H., & Zytowski, D. G. (1987). Occupational outlook in the 15th century: Sanchez de Arevalo's mirror of human life. *Journal of Counseling & Development, 66*(4), 168–170. https://doi.org/10.1002/j.1556-6676.1987.tb00838.x

Chase, J. A., Houmanfar, R., Hayes, S. C., Ward, T. A., Plumb Vilardaga, J., & Follette, V. (2013). Values are not just goals: Online ACT-based values training adds to goal setting in improving undergraduate college student performance. *Journal of Contextual Behavioral Science, 2*(3–4), 79–84. https://doi.org/10.1016/j.jcbs.2013.08.002

Gati, I., & Tal, S. (2008). Decision-making models and career guidance. In J. Athanasou & R. Van Esbroeck (Eds.), *International handbook of career guidance* (pp. 157–185). Springer. https://doi.org/ 10.1007/978-1-4020-6230-8_8

Gruter, J., & Hammer, A. L. (n.d.). *Strong interest inventory*. The Myers-Briggs Company. Search Results | The Myers-Briggs Company (themyersbriggs.com)

Holland, J. L. (1985). *Vocational preference inventory (VPI) manual*. Psychological Assessment Resources.

Holland, J. L. (1997). *Making vocational choices: A theory of vocational personalities and work environments* (3rd ed.). PAR.

Holland, J. L. (1973). *Making vocational choices: A theory of vocational personalities and work environments*. PAR.

Holland, J. L., & Messer, M. A. (n.d.). *The self-directed search*. PAR. https://www.parinc.com/Products/Pkey/396

Lent, R. W., & Brown, S. D. (2013). Social cognitive model of career self-management: toward a unifying view of adaptive career behavior across the life span. *Journal of Counseling Psychology, 60*(4), 557. https://doi.org/10.1002/j.2161-0045.2013.00031.x

Masicampo, E. J., & Baumeister, R. F. (2011). Consider it done! Plan making can eliminate the cognitive effects of unfulfilled goals. *Journal of Personality and Social Psychology, 101*(4), 667–683. http://dx.doi.org/10.1037/a0024192

Melfi, T. (2016). *Hidden figures* [Movie]. Twentieth Century Fox.

Morisano, D., Hirsh, J. B., Peterson, J. B., Pihl, R. O., & Shore, B. M. (2010). Setting, elaborating, and reflecting on personal goals improves academic performance. *Journal of Applied Psychology, 95*(2), 255–264.

Obama, M. (2007, February). CBS 60 Minutes. *S49 Obama 2007: Launching his candidacy*. https://www.cbs.com/shows/60_minutes/video/OThu8YhEgiQJjeRhA_Jou78lPwX8epI3/obama-2007-launching-his-candidacy/

Parsons, F. (1909*). Choosing a vocation*. Houghton Mifflin Company.

Su, R., Murdock, C., & Rounds, J. (2015). Person-environment fit. In P. J. Hartung, M. L. Savickas, & W. B. Walsh (Eds.), *APA handbook of career intervention: Vol. 1: Foundations* (pp. 81–98). American Psychological Association. http://dx.doi.org/10.1037/14438-000

Super, D. E., Savickas, M. L., & Super, C. M. (1996). The life span, life space approach to careers. In D. Brown & L. Brooks (Eds.), *Career choice and development* (3rd ed., pp. 121–178). Jossey-Bass.

Super, D. E., Starishevsky, R., Matlin, N., & Jordaan, J. P. (1963). *Career development: Self-concept theory*. College Entrance Examination Board.

Šverko, B., & Vizek-Vidović, V. (1995). Studies of the meaning of work: Approaches, models, and some of the findings. In D. E. Super & B. Šverko (Eds.), *Life roles, values, and careers: International findings of the work importance study*. Jossey-Bass.

PART II

Practical guidance, unwritten rules, and planning to reach your goals

CHAPTER 4

Practical guidance for building your foundation for career success

DOI: 10.4324/9780429296413-6

INTRODUCTION

Good plans – and actions – start with a good foundation. As we continue to build on the content and processes introduced in previous chapters and set the stage for the sections that follow, we turn our attention now to more practical guidance for making the most of your educational and other career-preparation experiences and opportunities.

For many people, including people interested in careers in psychology (that's you!), college is an early career stage (Lent et al., 1994). By earning a bachelor's degree at any age or career/life stage, people demonstrate their ability to meet multiple evaluators' expectations, develop advanced writing and communication skills, work in teams and individually, and more – all skills that are essential for professional work and other aspects of life. So, whether or not your college education is (or was) specifically career focused, that education, particularly when augmented as suggested here (and by multiple mentors), is good preparation for career and life success. Let's review some of the basics.

ACADEMIC SKILLS AND PROFESSIONAL DEVELOPMENT

Making the most of the time you're investing

As a psychology student (and emerging professional), it's your responsibility (and a privilege) to invest the necessary time and energy to make the most of your educational and professional opportunities. The complexity of psychology, particularly at the graduate and professional levels, requires *more* than that minimum – in terms of time, effort, and results. This is reflected in most college/university grading systems in which an A is reserved for outstanding or exceptional performance. (We know that's disappointing to some, but isn't it better to know?) In general, you'll earn a passing grade for performance that meets minimal standards – but back to expectations (above), psychology is a highly competitive, evolving field so we encourage you to do your best – and get assistance before you think you need it (more on that later too). Furthermore, keep in mind that you'll need (and perhaps want) letters of recommendation, referrals, and more – so when you have the opportunity to engage in formal (or informal) learning and/or professional development, it's wise to invest the necessary time and energy to do your best and, in so doing, make the most of your opportunities.

Learning

How do people learn? How do we remember what's important to us? What about motivation and beliefs we have about our abilities? Does any of that change as we move from high school to college? To graduate school? To professional levels? You bet it does – and significantly too!

Learning in psychology and related fields is a lifelong process. It doesn't stop when you earn a particular degree or degrees. Learning is also an active, culturally informed, and often collaborative process that builds on prior knowledge. The deeper level of learning required to prepare for most careers in psychology requires active engagement and deliberate practice over time (Ericsson et al., 1993). We learn how to learn by working with others, developing, practicing, and refining those skills and our understanding of each other and the topic or subject at hand. Furthermore, many psychology students are surprised at the amount of reading (or the audio equivalent) required for classes, the complexity of much of that reading, and therefore the time it often takes to understand and apply the presented material.

Learning requires development and application of progressively more complex skills, ranging from memorizing facts and terms, to reading for understanding, to the ability to synthesize and evaluate published literature on a particular topic. As such, memory is necessary but not sufficient for learning. Knowing essential terminology and facts (often starting with memorization) is foundational to understanding as well as application, synthesis, and other advanced educational and professional outcomes (see, for example, Bloom's Taxonomy; Bloom et al., 1956). Yet there are degrees of knowing at all these levels. For example, it's easier to recognize you know something than to recall or apply that information. That's why simply highlighting or reading your notes and saying to yourself, "yes I know that", is generally not sufficient in psychology (and many other fields). So, give yourself the gift of time to really learn the terms and concepts you need to know. That will set the stage for understanding, applying, communicating, and, at more advanced levels, contributing to professional knowledge.

What you currently know is separate from your capacity to learn (Farrington et al., 2012). Moreover, developing skills and attitudes that support learning increases your capacity to learn. Learning is a complex process and making the most of it requires going beyond the basics, such as showing up and engaging with the professor and others to *make meaning* of or integrate the information for later application. This will also set the stage for re-learning, which when necessary, is much quicker than learning something the first time.

Critical thinking

Critical thinking is another essential skill for careers in psychology (APA, 2013) – and life. Critical thinking is not, as some mistakenly believe, negative or pessimistic. It's actually the opposite. Critical thinking, at its best, is curious, explorative, and investigative. It's a way of systematically evaluating the available evidence (e.g., is it from a reliable, knowledgeable, source? Is it biased?), synthesizing, and analyzing that evidence, arriving at tentative conclusions while remaining open to new information including feedback. Furthermore, critical thinking, like the scientific method, another time-honored investigative approach, also informs recommendations and future research.

As a set of skills, the practice of critical thinking in psychology includes basing one's arguments, assignments, and work on generally accepted (e.g., peer-reviewed journal articles and books) psychological principles, theory, and empirical evidence, which may include your own as well as others' experiences and observations. This requires thinking as well as attending to feelings, intuition, or inspirations, which are important sources of information – and may be your inclination or preference (Belenky et al., 1986; Myers, 2015). However, regardless of your preferences for taking in and sharing information, critical thinkers reflect on and take action to minimize their own biases and response to evidence. They seek information that both confirms and challenges their thinking so they don't fall prey to *confirmation bias*, the tendency to accept information that supports or confirms our current thinking (APA, 2013; Ross, 2018). They also recognize the limitations of generalizability, for example, that while their experiences and observations are valid for them, others may (and often do) have different experiences and perceptions. Moreover, critical thinking encompasses "willingness to accept critical feedback and to adjust based on such feedback; openness to possible failures from time to time; and the ability and desire to cope with frustrating and ambiguous learning tasks" (Conley, 2007, p. 8). Overall, critical thinking, including adaptability, persistence, and flexibility, is an important skill for educational and career success in psychology – and life.

Academic writing and presentation skills

Communication is another essential skill for careers and life. However, many people find writing, particularly academic and professional writing, challenging, requiring a higher level of thinking, writing skills, and attention to style than needed in face to face, email, text and other forms of communication. Some people (often students) add to the challenge by trying too hard to sound "smart", for example, by using passive voice and referring to themselves in the third person. If you're in the latter group, we remind you that active voice and first person are preferred (APA, 2020) – and have been for some time. More on that shortly.

If you aren't yet a good writer, this is the time to practice, share your work, get feedback, revise, and use all the resources available to you (e.g., college/university writing center) to improve your writing and presentation skills. Writing, both for assignments and for your own edification, is a time-honored way of advancing thinking and making new connections, which is key to advancing learning (Lang, 2013). Many people have had the experience of trying to explain something, particularly in writing, and realizing that they know more about the topic than they thought they did, or worse, don't know enough or don't have their thoughts and/or information sufficiently organized to make their point or otherwise complete their task. If you, like us, can relate to this at any level, then you have more evidence that writing is a way to consolidate and reinforce learning as well as communicate – and have a better understanding why writing is so important for careers in psychology.

This is also a good time to reference (pun intended) APA style, the most frequently used style and style guide for student papers through publications in psychology. Similar to other respected writing styles and formats (e.g., MLA, Chicago), the *Publication Manual of the American Psychological Association* (7th ed., 2020) offers a wealth of guidance on writing well including citation and reference formats, guidance on academic honesty, authorship, and more. Furthermore, the *APA Publication Manual* is the go-to source for current guidelines for academic and professional writing in psychology. As a quick adden-dum, it's also smart to follow any additional guidelines provided by your instructor, col-lege, department, program, or publisher. Keep in mind that many published works (i.e., articles and books) are formatted in the publisher's own style (for example, with extra spaces between paragraphs and reference entries) for ease of reading, so are not good format models for student assignments (and other work). In response to student questions about the importance of style and formatting (and why they matter for grades), one of us often shares advice from an editor at a conference years ago that presenting your paper in the best possible light, with proper grammar and style/format, is similar to dressing up for an important interview to present yourself well. So, our advice is to present your work in the best possible light by attending to content *and* formatting it correctly.

The library and literature searches

Information literacy is related to critical thinking and the important tasks of communica-tion (i.e., writing, presentation skills, and reading) in psychology. There's no shortage of information. In fact, it often feels like there's too much information coming at us from multiple sources – perhaps because there is! How do you, as someone interested in a career in psychology, decide what's valid? Useful in a particular context or not? Sure, sometimes the distinction is obvious, however, when you don't know whether the infor-mation you're seeing (and increasingly hearing) is valid for your education and career in psychology, what are some ways to decide?

As we discussed earlier, critical thinking and scientific methods are excellent guides for determining the validity of evidence – and information (APA, 2013). Building on that, it's important to consider the *basis* of the evidence or information (verified facts, a body of research, or, less compellingly, someone's opinion) and the *source* of that information. In psychology and, indeed, most other disciplines, credentials, including degrees, and relevant experience matter.

Your local library, and for academic/educational research, your college/university library, are excellent sources of valid information. Most libraries house extensive hard copy collections, including books and a vast array of electronic resources including peer-reviewed, also known as refereed, journal articles. Peer-reviewed journal articles, books published by respected academic presses such as this one, and other resources in curated collections (i.e., selected by academic librarians in consultation with faculty) are more likely to be good resources than those generated in a random internet search. This is par-ticularly important when you're starting with a low knowledge base because, at that point, you may not have sufficient information to make an informed decision about the validity of the information you find. For example, let's say you want to know more about career interest inventories. Sure, you could type career interest inventories in your preferred web browser, which would generate good sources – and even more sort-of-good and not-so-good sources. However, using your college/university library (or career center in this case), would increase the likelihood that your results would fall into the *good sources* category. Furthermore, don't underestimate the assistance a good librarian, particularly a reference librarian, can provide. Some librarians also have expertise in information literacy and can help/teach you how to use the vast array of library resources, including inter-library loan, more efficiently and effectively.

Expectations

Psychology is a field with multiple opportunities, in which there always seems to be something to do, to achieve, and at the same time, is often highly competitive. As such, it's easy to fall into the trap of comparing ourselves with *our perceptions* of others (or their social media projections), rather than comparing ourselves with earlier versions of ourselves. This includes taking regular stock of your progress relative to your goals, actively seeking opportunities to learn and grow, celebrating your successes – and building a good foundation for your career.

GETTING AND STAYING IN THE MOST HELPFUL AND PRODUCTIVE HEADSPACE

Self-regulation

Self-regulation is an empirically supported psychological construct that informs and supports learning and, as such educational, career, and life success (APA, 2013). At a fundamental level, people who appropriately manage their own thoughts, feelings, and behaviors, not suppressing them, but directing them, in the service of their own, as well as others' goals are more successful than those who allow themselves to be moved by transient feelings. In terms of career self-management, self-regulation is demonstrated and strengthened by "goal setting, study, and time management" (Lent & Brown, 2013, p. 560).

One way to promote self-regulation is by making pacts or commitments with other people (for example, sharing your goals and timelines with a trusted peer or mentor). It's also enhanced through interaction with others such as peers, professors, coaches, and identifying and using resources, including online resources. Self-regulation is associated with intrinsic and extrinsic motivation – and success (Deci et al., 2017; Ryan & Deci, 2019).

Motivation

Some of us are intrinsically (internally) motivated to learn and know more, while others are more extrinsically motivated, which means they are motivated by external goals and rewards, such as others' approval of parents, teachers, and/or their peers' approval. Furthermore, many students are motivated to achieve to reach their long-term career and life goals. Others find it easier to focus on shorter term goals, such as earning a particular degree, passing a course or assignment, which brings us to grades.

Grades, particularly the cumulative grade point average, are educational outcome measures (Bandura, 1997; Brady-Amoon & Fuertes, 2011). As such, grades are an indicator of college success, which for many, sets the stage for career success. Most, but not all, college students want to earn high grades. Some are dedicated to earning an A, which although varying from institution to institution and by level (e.g., undergraduate and graduate), is generally considered an indicator of outstanding work. A high grade point average (GPA) is often necessary for admission to competitive graduate programs in psychology and related fields including some careers in education, and may be a relevant entry-level consideration for other careers. However, some students are content with a final passing grade (which varies by level). Regardless of your approach to grades, formal education remains a unique opportunity to develop knowledge and important work and life skills. These skills include effective respectful communication, accountability (APA, 2013), and persistence (Browning et al., 2018), all of which are associated with career and life success.

It may seem counterintuitive to explore the role of self-efficacy and other beliefs we have about our abilities in a chapter on practical guidance – yet our beliefs, attitudes, and mindsets are strongly associated with academic and career performance (APA, 2013, 2017; ASCA, 2019). Furthermore, these thoughts, both specific and general, and associated feelings, influence and are influenced by our behavior, including the actions we take (or don't) toward educational and career/life success.

In some ways, people's attitudes, beliefs, and mindsets relevant to academic and career performance are aligned with their personal and professional values. For example, honesty, including academic honesty, which is foundational to professional integrity, can be both a personal and professional value (Lang, 2013). As such, many psychology programs promote the development of students' knowledge as well as personal and professional values as illustrated by professional ethical guidelines, codes, and standards (APA, 2013, 2017). Although some values, such as honesty and integrity remain constant, ethical guidelines in psychology and related fields are updated regularly to reflect evolving understanding and the current context, much like our own values and related behavior.

Notwithstanding all this, you may be aware of inconsistencies between your personal values and attitudes, beliefs, and mindset for success. For example, you might believe that all people deserve the opportunity to succeed – but not you. If, on reflection or, as is more common, through interaction with others, you discover you hold one or more incongruous beliefs, then those beliefs are important to reconcile. Moreover, some attitudes, beliefs, and mindsets are so ingrained, natural to us, and automatic, that we may not be aware (or fully aware) of them.

This is a good time to consider if your current attitudes, beliefs, and strategies are effective. Do they work as well as they could? Many times, what was effective at one point in time is no longer effective (and may be limiting us now or in the future). Read on for psychological and other research-informed ways to make the most of both your academic and career preparation.

Self-efficacy

Bandura's concept of *self-efficacy* (1977, 1997), as extended by Hackett and Betz (1981) and Lent et al. (1994) introduced earlier, is important here. Self-efficacy, the belief people have about their ability to achieve a goal, is foundational to the sustained action necessary to achieve that goal. Beliefs, including those we have about ourselves and our abilities, are not sufficient for success however, research demonstrates they undergird and support sustained, productive action to reach those goals, including overcoming (or going around) barriers and other challenges (Bandura, 1997). Most of this research has been in specific areas, particularly perceived achievement in career decision making and performance in science, technology, engineering, and mathematics (STEM) and related areas (Brady-Amoon, 2008; Brady-Amoon & Fuertes, 2011).

Self-efficacy is also associated with overall college student performance. To illustrate, one of our recent studies with an intentionally diverse sample of undergraduate students with majors in the liberal arts including psychology, found that self-efficacy, self-rated abilities, and adjustment accounted for 15% of the variance in academic performance, operationalized as GPA. This 15% was significantly higher than the 2.41% accounted for (or predicted by) prior academic performance operationalized as high school grades. Moreover, with this diverse sample, SAT scores accounted for *no* variance; they didn't make any difference (Brady-Amoon, 2008; Brady-Amoon & Fuertes, 2011). The bottom line here is that, for most people, the beliefs we have about our own abilities greatly influence behavior, which in turn, influences performance.

However, much like other self-beliefs (e.g., self-rated abilities, self-confidence, and self-esteem), more isn't better (Brady-Amoon & Fuertes, 2011). A good goal is to work toward a realistic assessment of your current (self-rated) abilities and future abilities (self-efficacy) and areas for improvement – to guide your academic, career, and life development. This is another area in which a trusted advisor or mentor can help.

Growth mindset

Growth mindset, the knowledge that skills and competencies are not fixed or static; they can be cultivated and developed (Rattan et al., 2015) is important here too. Together with a growth mindset, we can develop expertise through hours of dedicated deliberate practice (Ericsson et al., 1993). Moreover, we don't have to do this by ourselves. We can improve our mindsets and reach our goals faster when we work with teachers, mentors, coaches, and other experienced guides (Michael, 2019; Vygotsky, 1978). This is exciting – because it means that those of us who haven't yet accomplished what we would like to can likely do so. It also means that those of us who have accomplished what we would like to have additional untapped potential.

Grit

Grit, perhaps the most popular of the psychological constructs associated with career and life success, is, by the author's own admission, likely a combination of multiple constructs

(Duckworth, 2016). As such, it's helpful to consider how our beliefs about ourselves, hard work, and persistence contribute to success. Do you have the stick-to-itiveness to see things through? Are you someone who gives up easily? What's that all about? Is that helping or hindering you? Keep in mind that grit, like all the other mindsets and skills we've explored, is not something you either have or don't, it's a way of thinking and acting that you can develop, in many of the same ways we develop and attain mastery of other mindsets, skills, and practices. Beliefs without action are insufficient. Yet the beliefs described here – and more – inform essential skills that are foundational to academic, career, and life success.

When we focus ourselves on getting and staying in the most helpful and productive head space, adopt a growth mindset (Dweck, 2016; Rattan et al., 2015), and take a compassionate learning stance toward ourselves, we can consider suggestions for improvement (even lower grades than we'd like) as opportunities to learn. And true (*mastery*) learning, even when challenging, is fundamental to career/life success, including the pursuit of academic degrees in psychology!

MORE PRACTICAL GUIDANCE

BOX 4.1

Insides versus Outsides

"Don't compare your insides with other people's outsides."

Stress, anxiety, and other barriers – and how to overcome them

Many people, perhaps most, experience stress, anxiety, and other barriers to life and career success, some much more than others. While a little stress or anxiety can be helpful, for example, giving us extra motivation to meet a deadline, too much is counterproductive and can be debilitating (Bandelow & Michaelis, 2015; Carter et al., 2017; Sapolsky, 2004; van der Kolk, 2014). Interestingly, although stress and anxiety are frequent conversational and popular press topics, Harris' (2020) review of the scientific literature found no consensus definition of stress. Furthermore, although we often share some stressful experiences with others, individuals typically appraise and respond to stress in uniquely personal ways (Frankl, 2006; Harris, 2020; Taylor, 2006). In contrast, the clinical (applied scientific) definition of anxiety is "fear or apprehension that is out of proportion to the situation" (Black & Grant, 2014, p. 123). Although reasonable people may disagree about what's out of proportion for a particular situation, research shows that anxiety disorders, which are diagnosed when anxiety interferes with a person's functioning, are the most frequently diagnosed mental health concern (Bandelow & Michaelis, 2015; Remes et al., 2016; van der Kolk, 2014).

Fortunately, there are research-informed ways to address stress, anxiety, and many other barriers. Whenever possible, it's best to prevent them by using good strategies, like those we suggest in this book. Moreover, we can research and use a variety of approaches including connecting with our support system (Taylor, 2006), spirituality (Sapolsky, 2004), meaning making (Frankl, 2006), and cognitive reframing as coping (Lazarus & Folkman, 2012). Building on this, it's also good practice to monitor your own emotional and physiological response (e.g., where you feel stress in your body), engage in appropriate self-care, including giving and receiving social support to put stressors, including those that are unavoidable, into context. In this way, you're building your own resiliency narrative. At the same time, if you or someone you care about is experiencing high levels of stress, anxiety, or other concerns, it's important to seek help. You might start with joining or starting your own support group. If you're a student, your college/university health or counseling services offices is another good resource. Please don't ignore serious problems – and when appropriate, contact the relevant hotline for more immediate help and referrals.

Beyond this, it's also likely you've already encountered barriers along the way – and will meet more en route to achieving your life and career goals. Sometimes these barriers are relatively minor (e.g., a poor grade – for you). One way to handle barriers like this is to consider if there's something you can learn from the disappointment – and, if so, resolve to put that new insight to work to increase your opportunity for improved outcomes moving forward. At other times, barriers are more significant – or harder to address. For example, let's say your application to a competitive program or position was not successful. After an initial cooling off period (24 hours is a good guideline), in addition to reflecting on your application process and materials, this could also be a good time to attend to your deeper feelings and thoughts about the opportunity. Are you OK with the rejection? Maybe you didn't really want it, maybe it's not right for you, and something else would be better. Do you still want it? More than ever? How then can you channel your disappointment into going around, over, or under that barrier, which in this example, likely means strengthening your application for the next time or similar position?

Professors, advisors, and mentors

It's often game-changing for students to talk with faculty. Professors and other teaching faculty generally pursue that specific career path to help students develop knowledge, skills, and/or competencies in a particular area and often, the broader discipline. The overwhelming majority of faculty members want you to meet course and program requirements as outlined in the syllabus and other applicable guidelines. In addition to making the most of course preparation and classes, we encourage you to take the time to meet with your professors during office hours and any optional meetings they offer. Given the importance of professors, advisors, and mentors in career development and success, we'll explore this further in upcoming chapters, particularly Chapter 7 that focuses on relationships in professional life.

Considering the resources to stay engaged in your education and development

Resources such as financial assistance, career development and placement assistance, and access to needed information, experiences, training, and/or mentoring can help you make the most of your learning and career development opportunities. The first place to start, if you're a student (or potential student) is your current or prospective college/university. Most offer an extensive array of services to support student enrollment (e.g., student financial assistance) and success (e.g., career development and placement assistance). Many also offer additional services to support student success such as writing centers, tutors, counseling and, often, supplemental support services for students from groups historically underrepresented in higher education and the professions. So check them out – and read on for further information about student financial assistance and career planning and placement services.

Student financial assistance

If you're a student or potential student, it's helpful to learn what you can about student financial assistance available through your institution or potential institutions. The best way to start is by reading all the published (including online) information and meeting with administrators and staff in your or your potential school's financial aid office (even if it's called something else). These knowledgeable people can help you sort through the often-confusing information and terms, identify, apply for, and confirm your eligibility for different types (e.g., grants, loans, and work) and sources of financial assistance. They can also help you make informed decisions about accepting or declining specific offers such as a loan or work study opportunities.

BOX 4.2

Explore Options

"Don't pay for what you can get for free."
Old bumper sticker published by a financial aid professional association.

While we recommend against paying for services you can (and should get) for free such as those available through your college/university financial aid office, it can be helpful to explore your options with knowledgeable people, including advisors, mentors, family and friends, and reference librarians at your local public library, which often have extensive college and career resources. Overall, in making these decisions, it's important to consider the costs, both short-term such as projected payments and campus-based work obligations, and longer-term such as student loans, as well as the costs (not limited to financial) of declining a specific aid offer, deferring, or deciding not to pursue a particular program of study or degree.

The career planning and placement center

We'd also like to encourage you again to check out – and use – the services of your college/university career center. Many offer career decision-making and planning workshops, administer, score, and interpret vocational assessments such as the Strong Interest Inventory and Self-Directed Search described earlier, and more. Some of these and others offer individual and/or group career/vocational counseling and placement services. Some centers also make their services available to alumni, sometimes for a modest fee.

In some ways, things are easier now than they've ever been. In other ways, it's harder – and it's definitely more complex. For example, it's easier now than ever before in recorded history to be admitted to a college or university. However, it's just as hard to graduate today as it was 50 years ago as that approximately 50% graduation rate has remained steady (and it's worse for people from marginalized groups). So – when you make the decision to pursue a degree, give it all you've got, seek out and use all the services offered, and make the most of it!

CHAPTER SUMMARY

This chapter offers practical suggestions for making the most of your educational and therefore career preparation opportunities. It includes sections on learning, critical thinking, academic and professional writing and presentation skills, and using the library and other resources. This chapter also provides practical guidance for cultivating and maintaining a positive productive mindset for career and life success, an ongoing challenge and opportunity for most of us in light of increasing expectations and the changing world. The chapter concludes with brief sections on managing stress, anxiety, and other barriers, and a brief note on identifying and using resources – all of which we'll expand on in upcoming chapters.

EXERCISES

1   Listen to Carol Dweck's Ted Talk on Growth Mindset, take the online Grit, and/or Mindset questionnaires. Choose one or two areas to further develop.

2   Find out about the services your library offers. Meet with one or more reference librarians to learn more about how they can help you. If there's a special psychology reference librarian, meet that person.

3   Learn more about the services offered by your college/university counseling center. If they offer stress management seminars or workshops, take one.

Next steps: the advanced move

Learn more about college success as it relates to career preparation. One good book (tried and true) is *Thriving in College and Beyond: Research-Based Strategies for Academic Success and Personal Development* (2013) by J. B. Cuseo, A. Thompson, M. Campagna, and V. S. Fecas, published by Kendall-Hunt.

REFERENCES

American Psychological Association. (2013). *APA guidelines for the undergraduate psychology major: Version 2.0.* www.apa.org/ed/precollege/undergrad/index.aspx

American Psychological Association. (2017). *Ethical principles of psychologists and code of conduct.* www.apa.org/ethics/code/index

American Psychological Association. (2020). *Publication manual of the American psychological association* (7th ed.). https://doi.org/10.1037/0000165-000

American School Counselor Association (2019). *ASCA school counselor professional standards & competencies.*

Bandelow, B., & Michaelis, S. (2015). Epidemiology of anxiety disorders in the 21st century. *Dialogues in Clinical Neuroscience, 17*(3), 327–335. https://pubmed.ncbi.nlm.nih.gov/26487813

Bandura, A. (1977). Self-efficacy: Toward a unifying theory of behavioral change. *Psychological Review, 84,* 191–215.

Bandura, A. (1997). *Self-efficacy: The exercise of control.* W. H. Freeman.

Belenky, M. F., Clinchy, B., Goldberger, N. R., & Tarule, J. M. (1986). *Women's ways of knowing: The development of self, voice, and mind.* Basic Books.

Black, D. W., & Grant, J. E. (2014). *DSM-5 guidebook: The essential companion to the diagnostic and statistical manual of mental disorders* (5th ed.). American Psychiatric Association.

Bloom, B. S., Englehart, M. B., Furst, E. J., Hill, W. H., & Krathwohl, D. R. (1956). Taxonomy of educational objectives: The classification of educational goals. In *Handbook 1: Cognitive domain.* McKay.

Brady-Amoon, M. (2008). *The association between self-efficacy and self-rated abilities and college students' adjustment and academic performance* (Doctoral dissertation). Fordham University.

Brady-Amoon, P., & Fuertes, J. (2011). Self-efficacy, self-rated abilities, adjustment, and academic performance. *Journal of Counseling and Development, 89*(4), 431–438.

Browning, B. R., McDermott, R. C., Scaffa, M. E., Booth, N. R., & Carr, N. T. (2018). Character strengths and first-year college students' academic persistence attitudes: An integrative model. *Counseling Psychologist, 46*(5), 608–631. https://doi.org/10.1177/0011000018786950

Carter, R. T., Lau, M. Y., Johnson, V., & Kirkinis, K. (2017). Racial discrimination and health outcomes among racial/ethnic minorities: A meta-analytic review. *Journal of Multicultural Counseling & Development, 45*(4), 232–259. https://doi.org/10.1002/jmcd.12076

Conley, D. (2007). *Toward a more comprehensive conception of college readiness.* Educational Policy Improvement Center.

Cuseo, J. B., Thompson, A., Campagna, M., & Feca, V. S. (2013). *Thriving in college and beyond: Research-based strategies for academic success and personal development.* Kendall-Hunt.

Deci, E. L., Olafsen, A. H., & Ryan, R. M. (2017). Self-Determination theory in work organizations: The state of a science. *Annual Review of Organizational Psychology and Organizational Behavior, 4*(1), 19–43. https://doi.org/10.1146/annurev-orgpsych-032516-113108

Duckworth, A. (2016). *Grit: The power and passion of perseverance.* Scribner.

Dweck, C. S. (2016). *Mindset: The new psychology of success* (Updated). Random House.

Ericsson, K. A., Krampe, R. T., & Tesch-Romer, C. (1993). The role of deliberate practice in the acquisition of expert performance. *Psychological Review, 100*(3), 363–406.

Farrington, C. A., Roderick, M., Allensworth, E., Nagaoka, J., Keyes, T. S., Johnson, D. W., & Beechum, N. O. (2012). *Teaching adolescents to become learners. The role of noncognitive factors in shaping school performance: A critical literature review.* University of Chicago Consortium on Chicago School Research.

Frankl, V. E. (2006). *Man's search for meaning* (60th anniv). Washington Square Press and Pocket Books.

Hackett, G., & Betz, N. E. (1981). A self-efficacy approach to the career development of women. *Journal of Vocational Behavior, 18*, 326–339.

Harris, B. N. (2020). Stress hypothesis overload: 131 hypotheses exploring the role of stress in tradeoffs, transitions, and health. *General and Comparative Endocrinology, 288*(113355), 1–55. https://doi.org/10.1016/j.ygcen.2019.113355

Lang, J. M. (2013). *Cheating lessons.* Harvard University Press.

Lazarus, R. S., & Folkman, S. (2012). Cognitive theories of stress and the issue of circularity. In *Dynamics of stress: Physiological, psychological and social perspectives.* Springer. https://doi.org/10.1007/978-1-4684-5122-1_4

Lent, R. W., & Brown, S. D. (2013). Social cognitive model of career self-management: Toward a unifying view of adaptive career behavior across the life span. *Journal of Counseling Psychology, 60*(4), 557–568. https://doi.org/10.1037/a0033446

Lent, R. W., Brown, S. D., & Hackett, G. (1994). Toward a unifying social cognitive theory of career and academic interest, choice, and performance. *Journal of Vocational Behavior, 45*, 79–122. https://doi.org/10.1006/jvbe.1994.1027

Michael, R. (2019). Self-efficacy and future career expectations of at-risk adolescents: The contribution of a tutoring program. *Journal of Community Psychology, 47*(4), 913–923. https://doi.org/10.1002/jcop.22163

Myers, K. B. (2015). *Introduction to type* (7th ed.). Consulting Psychologists Press.

Rattan, A., Savani, K., Chugh, D., & Dweck, C. S. (2015). Leveraging mindsets to promote academic achievement. *Perspectives on Psychological Science, 10*(6), 721–726. https://doi.org/10.1177/1745691615599383

Remes, O., Brayne, C., van der Linde, R., & Lafortune, L. (2016). A systematic review of reviews on the prevalence of anxiety disorders in adult populations. *Brain and Behavior, 6*(7), e00497. https://doi.org/10.1002/brb3.497

Ross, L. (2018). From the fundamental attribution error to the truly fundamental attribution error and beyond: My research journey. *Perspectives on Psychological Science, 13*(6), 750–769. https://doi.org/10.1177/1745691618769855

Ryan, R. M., & Deci, E. L. (2019). Research on intrinsic and extrinsic motivation is alive, well, and reshaping 21st-century management approaches: Brief reply to locke and schattke (2019). *Motivation Science, 5*(4), 291–294.

Sapolsky, R. M. (2004). *Why zebras dont get ulcers* (3rd ed.). Owlbook and Freeman.

Taylor, S. E. (2006). Tend and befriend: Biobehavioral bases of affiliation under stress. *Current Directions in Psychological Science, 15*(6), 273–277.

van der Kolk, B. (2014). *The body keeps the score: Brain, mind, and body in the healing of trauma.* Viking.

Vygotsky, L. S. (1978). *Mind in society: Development of higher psychological processes.* Harvard University Press.

5

The unwritten rules of success

It doesn't just happen by accident

ORIENTING QUESTIONS

1. What are you glad you know about succeeding in the psychology major and related careers?
2. How do you fit in yet stay true to your values – and yourself?
3. What are some ways to foster creativity?
4. What are some ways to see a project through to completion?
5. How do you prefer to work? Alone and/or with others? What are some ways to make the most of both ways of working?
6. What are your priorities? How can you be your best self?

DOI: 10.4324/9780429296413-7

INTRODUCTION

Many people who pursue a career in psychology want work – and a life – that's fulfilling in the ways that matter to us. Most of us also know this will take commitment, perseverance, hard work, positive mindsets, and a host of practical guidance, the highlights of which are discussed in Chapter 4 – yet, as you might expect, there's more. That's why this chapter builds on earlier chapters by focusing on unwritten "rules" of success. These aren't rules, per se, but guidance, tips, and hints for success that some, often more privileged people, know and act upon (sometimes unconsciously), yet many people with successful careers in psychology (and other fields), including us, wish we had known earlier in our careers. That knowledge might have saved us – and can potentially save you – from some easily avoidable mistakes and missed opportunities.

Good thing (see Chapter 4) we're self-efficacious (Bandura, 1997), have a growth mindset (Dweck, 2016), are resilient, gritty (Duckworth, 2016), and have good senses of humor! Once again, if you know some, most, or even all of this (wow!), then consider this a refresher – and cultivate a sense of gratitude for the people who taught you these unwritten rules, even if they and you might not have known these were important things to know. However, since there's a lot in this chapter and you can't possibly know what you don't know, we encourage you to read on with an open mind to maximize your opportunities!

SUCCEEDING IN THE PSYCHOLOGY MAJOR AND RELATED CAREERS

BOX 5.1

Inspiration to Get Started

If you didn't already start, start now!

We begin this exploration of unwritten rules for success at the bachelor's degree level because, as we discussed earlier, a bachelor's degree is foundational to most, if not all, careers in psychology. If you haven't yet started your degree, great – you'll have a head start with this additional information. If you're currently pursuing your bachelor's degree, that's also great; you have time to adjust if necessary, and finish strong. If you've already earned your bachelor's degree, congratulations – and keep reading. Furthermore, although we expect the majority of our readers will earn undergraduate degrees with majors in psychology, this book (and chapter) also applies to people with other undergraduate majors (like both of us) interested in pursuing a career in psychology – and career development itself.

Responsibility

One of the most important unwritten rules for college, careers, and life is to meet your responsibilities, to meet them well, and on time. (If you already know that, great – keep practicing and read on. If this is new, keep reading and start practicing.) Responsibility and its cousin, reliability, are key components of conscientiousness, arguably one of the most significant individual factors in academic and career success (Schmidt, 2014) that, like many other factors associated with success, can be developed (Javaras et al., 2019).

What does conscientiousness look like from an unwritten rules' perspective? As just a few examples, if you're unclear about an assignment (when is it due? what does X mean?), do your best to figure it out (e.g., check your syllabus, consult with a classmate or colleague), then if you still have questions, ask your professor or supervisor (politely, of course). Similarly, it's wise to consider your current obligations and commitments before taking on new commitments so if you say you'll do something you can – and will. If, despite your best efforts, you have to be late or absent for a class, meeting, or other important obligation, take responsibility and advise your professor or supervisor at your earliest opportunity. Similarly, if you need or want an extension to submit an assignment, ask as early as possible. In summary, an unwritten yet essential rule of success is meeting (and when appropriate and possible exceeding) your responsibilities!

Another, often unwritten rule is that it's better to be proactive than reactive. Whenever possible, talk with your professor, advisor, or supervisor *before* things hit a crisis point. Don't make decisions (such as dropping a class) with insufficient information. And don't go to other professors with the same question if you don't like the answer from the first professor. That wastes everyone's time . . . and we talk with each other.

Recognizing, responding, and following up on opportunities

Some people miss opportunities because they don't know about them, which is more easily remedied, or recognize them. As the sayings go, opportunities may be disguised as hard work, problems, and/or seemingly impossible situations. Others recognize an opportunity (at least to a degree), yet fail to respond or follow up appropriately. There are many potential reasons for this such as insufficient planning, time, and fear of rejection or success (yes that's real). Regardless of the reasons, if we intend to respond (e.g., by submitting a good application) or follow up (contacting someone who offered to help), but either don't follow up or don't follow up well (e.g., with a hastily written application), we have, in reality, rejected that opportunity. In many cases, not making a decision is a decision *not* to apply or follow up – and results in you disqualifying yourself.

Another critically important unwritten rule is that opportunities don't always announce themselves. Many times, you have to do your own research and networking to identify potential opportunities – or create them yourself. Moreover, there are degrees of good opportunities. In addition to determining how good an opportunity is, it's important to consider the timing. Some good opportunities come along so rarely, like the proverbial once in a lifetime opportunity, they are definitely worth your serious consideration. Some of those – and others – are time-sensitive (e.g., reserved for first year students and/or with a firm deadline) while others (e.g., those that open up every semester) are more easily postponed. How do you know any/all of this? Here's another shout out for professional networks, professors, advisors, and mentors – and encouragement to talk with peers, particularly more advanced peers. What opportunities did they pursue? What are they glad they knew? Wish they'd known? The student peer-to-peer network is generally a good resource, however, it's almost always helpful to use your critical thinking skills and verify important information with a trusted and knowledgeable advisor. At the risk of being obvious, our final recommendation for this section is to thank the people who tell you about opportunities, help you, and support you. It may seem old fashioned, but thank you notes (email is OK for some) make a positive difference. Practice gratitude, and be generous expressing it. It will set you apart – and may open up even more opportunities – so you can take another step toward your goals and your best life!

Professional skills and building a professional identity

What are some unwritten rules for developing professional skills and building a professional identity in psychology? In addition to dedicating the necessary time and effort (including consultation with others) to develop your knowledge, skills, and ability to communicate effectively, we can learn a lot from observing others and learning from their experiences (Park & Schallert, 2019). As such, finding opportunities to interact with faculty and fellow students in your program can help you further develop your skills, your understanding of the profession, and build those important professional interaction skills. More formally, we strongly recommend you take full advantage of opportunities to engage with others as part of coursework, research teams, and professional organizations, and related activities. Whether it's studying together, working on a group project, or actively participating in discussions and chats, you can expand your behavioral repertoire and professional identity by observing and interacting with others (Park & Schallert, 2019).

Learning how those in your field and subfield communicate, interact, and expectations for various career paths can facilitate your career trajectory. As a result, it's helpful to become engaged with your department, any specialty organizations that might be of interest to you, as well as national, regional, and/or state professional organizations. Please note there are local, smaller versions of most national organizations such as the Southeastern Psychological Association and the Illinois Psychological Association. These offer opportunities to become involved that are closer to "home" and, are often, less costly. Engagement in regional and/or state-level organizations is also a pathway to engagement at the national level, should you feel more comfortable going this route to achieve your career goals.

Respecting yourself – and others

As you interact with other people, we encourage you to respect – and be kind to yourself. This is not cheesy self-help, it's a fundamental truth – and unwritten rule for success! Each of us comes to this process with different experiences, interests, talents, and more.

Sometimes we try to engage with others and find that they ignore, misunderstand, or rebuff us. It's often confusing and may even feel hurtful – particularly if you feel that you've done something to be supportive or helpful to the other person. There are many reasons for this. Sometimes it's obvious – they're stressed out or otherwise out of sorts. Other times, they may "hear" our statement differently than we intended and take offense or otherwise misinterpret what we've said. Many of you have the skills to cope with these types of challenging interactions. At the same time, if you notice this happening more than occasionally, it's a good idea to consult with a trusted friend, family member, advisor, or mentor to put things in perspective and, if applicable, help you identify one or more growth opportunities. If that's the case, you might also find it helpful to read books or take a course to improve your interpersonal skills, which are critically important for life and career success.

However, you may also encounter a person who is truly rude, very self-centered, biased, or a bully. If this happens, it's important to remember that respect starts with you! You can decide if, and if so, how you're going to respond. You might take a deep breath and walk away. You might decide to set other boundaries. However, harassment, intimidation, discrimination, bullying, and similarly demeaning behaviors are *never* acceptable. If these occur around you (to you or someone else), it's smart to seek out your support network to help you to process the experience and, depending on the severity and context, help you take appropriate action, which might include reporting the behavior. Moreover, if you or someone else is in immediate danger, seek safety first, then get help.

Coping with bias and discrimination

Although discrimination on the basis of race, ethnicity, gender, and many other identities is illegal in the U.S. and many other countries, bias, discrimination, and other injustices persist at multiple levels, often in hidden, unconscious ways. For example, systemic barriers to educational access and success (Armstrong & Hamilton, 2013; Brady-Amoon & Fuertes, 2011) and employment (Colella et al., 2017; Jackson, 2013) persist, lending further support to the theoretical proposition and observation that apparently neutral environments are, in fact, biased in favor of dominant groups (Betz, 1989, 2002; Freeman, 1979). As another example, good people who believe in equal opportunity and would never intentionally discriminate against another person on the basis of race, sex, or other legally protected (or other) identity, may unconsciously default to limiting, stereotypical, biased and discriminatory assumptions about other people. Such automatic thoughts, attitudes, and associated behaviors limit the people having and doing them, those on the receiving end, and society as a whole.

In addition to the well-documented negative effects of racism (Carter et al., 2017) and other systemic injustices, *implicit bias* manifests itself in many ways including the presumption of incompetence (Gutiérrez y Muhs et al., 2012; Niemann et al., 2020) and daily, often unintentional, slights referred to as microaggressions (Sue et al., 2019). Furthermore, decades of research shows that a simple reminder of common stereotypes of lower status identity groups before a related task is associated with increased performance anxiety and decreased performance compared with their performance without that harmful reminder (Steele, 2010). Overall, others' beliefs have the potential to negatively and positively affect people's self-perceptions, beliefs, and, therefore, educational and career success. It takes a great deal of strength to effectively cope with prejudice, bias, discrimination, and its sequela – but fortunately, none of us has to do it alone.

BOX 5.2

Reflection on Stereotypes and Coping

Reflection: The title of Dr. Claude Steele's (2010) well-written book, *Whistling Vivaldi*, is an illustration of one of the ways he and other Black men take action to disarm stereotypes about Black men so they're more likely to be treated respectfully, as all humans deserve to be treated. What are some of your coping strategies?

When faced with discrimination or similar poor treatment, it's important to take a step back to protect yourself, and honestly assess the situation. In so doing, it's generally helpful to consult with one or more trusted people who can help you put the situation into context, provide support, and, much like you might do when faced with harassment, intimidation, or bullying, help you decide how to move forward. For most of us, particularly people from groups historically underrepresented in higher education and the profession, social support, communities, and mentors make a significant positive difference (Gutiérrez y Muhs et al., 2012; Niemann et al., 2020; Sedlacek, 2004; Yosso, 2005). Moreover, multiple identities can be, and often are, an asset (Bentley et al., 2019; Brown, 2018).

As we discussed earlier, support networks can be helpful for processing experiences, generating alternative explanations and responses, as well as facilitating perspective-taking. Moreover, support networks can open up opportunities you might not have otherwise had – or even considered. As such, we encourage you to connect, or re-connect, with *your* community. This might include your extended family (however you define that), faith and other service organizations, and, of course one or more of the professional groups we discussed earlier. If you haven't yet found a network to join, start one!

This is another good reason for finding a faculty member/advisor who's knowledgeable about your academic program and potential career goals. While it can be helpful to have role models and mentors who share one or more of your important salient identities, those people aren't always available (fact – there are very few faculty of color) and, when they are, may not be the best advisor for you. We encourage you to keep in mind that faculty, advisors, and mentors who are or who appear to be different than you (e.g., in terms of race/ethnicity, and/or gender) are often excellent advisors/mentors (Albana, 2021). So, keep an open mind. Given the importance of advisement and mentoring, we'll explore these topics more fully in Chapter 7, which focuses on relationships in professional life.

CREATIVITY

Humans (that includes you) have the potential to be imaginative, insightful, and integrate knowledge and information in unique and innovative ways (Kahneman, 2011; Kounios & Beeman, 2015; Sprugnoli et al., 2017). As such, creativity is fundamental to psychology. So another, often unwritten, rule for educational and career success in psychology is to tap into and develop your creativity, openness to inspiration, and imagination to complement and extend your thinking.

One of the most important unwritten rules for developing creativity is to respect your own experiences, ways of knowing, intuition, and insights – yet remain open to learning and new information. Yes, we're encouraging you to *trust* yourself and, moreover, *be* yourself. What? You may be saying, "I want to give my professor, my supervisor, my boss exactly what they want". However, while it's important to meet (and when appropriate, exceed) expectations and base your work on evidence (see earlier chapters), psychology, at its core, is a creative field.

When you trust yourself and your creative processes, you're less likely to fall into the far too common trap of limiting yourself on an open-ended assignment or interview by trying to give your professor or prospective employer exactly what you *think* they want – instead of embracing your unique self and response. Although on one level that seems easier than taking creative risks, it takes a tremendous amount of psychic energy to attempt to "read" and give others what you think they want – and it often backfires. Students and professionals who limit their responses to what they think the other person wants miss opportunities to creatively explore ideas and, when applicable, get feedback. Prospective employees who limit themselves to what they think the interviewer wants forgo the opportunity to explore whether the potential job and employer is a good match for them in an interview (which means two-way) situation. Even when they earn a passing grade on the assignment or get the job, they – and the people they're with – miss out.

We have both had the experience where we've approached an assignment or project differently than other people, thought we'd failed or missed the mark on the project – and then learned we hadn't and that different can and often is another way of being right. Don't fall into the trap of thinking there's only one way to do something or that all the good ideas have been taken; because neither is correct! We encourage you to trust yourself and take appropriate creative/intellectual risks. That's one of the ways individuals and the field as a whole develops.

Another way to maximize creativity is to allow sufficient time for ideas to incubate and integrate with each other and your prior knowledge. If you've ever been up against a deadline, made that deadline (or worse missed it) and then thought "I should have included X", you know the benefit of dedicating sufficient time for tasks. You may have also had the experience of having an "eureka" or "aha!" moment in which, apparently out of nowhere, you have a solution, a new insight, or other brilliant (at least to you) idea (Kounios & Beeman, 2015; Sprugnoli et al., 2017). You may have also had the experience of working on something for a time, then, while doing something completely different (like taking a shower or taking a walk), getting new ideas (Kounios & Beeman, 2015; Sprugnoli et al., 2017). How do you set the stage for creativity? Research suggests preparation (e.g., cognition, attention, and time on task) promotes creativity. (Sprugnoli et al., 2017). For example, you can nurture creativity by reading widely and engaging in focused work sessions. It also helps to shift to related tasks toward the end of a work session to promote the incubation (and thus generation) of new ideas (Madjar et al., 2019) – that, like other ideas, are good to write down or record, so you don't lose them.

PERSISTENCE

No matter how lofty your goal or how worthy the goal seeker (that's you), you can be sure there will be challenges, difficulties, and other barriers along the way. It's helpful to remind yourself that challenges, difficulties, and barriers are opportunities to learn something new (perhaps about yourself), expand your skills, and remind yourself how much you wanted that goal. Sometimes that reminder is just what you need to stay with the task at hand – or the overall goal. When you really want, desire, aspire to something like a degree or career goal and encounter the inevitable difficulties, it's time to marshal your persistence and resources. This may include consultation and support to promote a positive mindset and/or adapt your approach, strategies, and, when appropriate, even one or more of your short- or long-term goals. That way you can keep going or start again and then keep going.

Persistence means staying with a task or project until it's done and done well. It also means regularly re-committing yourself to doing the necessary work to reach your goals. Most long-term goals, like earning a degree, require seeing multiple, sometimes simultaneous, tasks and projects through to completion – and that's not always easy. Some tasks and projects require you to step outside your comfort zone, develop new skills, and ways of interacting. Stepping outside your comfort zone can be scary, exciting, a sign you're on the verge of a growth spurt (Mohr, 2014) – or something different. We encourage you to pay attention to your feelings when faced with new challenges, including roadblocks, because, as we've said before, knowledge, including knowledge and awareness of your feelings, is power.

When unacknowledged and unaddressed, fear (and associated feelings like imposter syndrome; Clance & Imes, 1978; Orbe-Austin & Orbe Austin, 2020) can lead to self-sabotaging behavior, including premature abandonment of the tasks necessary to reach an important goal, and the goal itself. Two of the most common self-sabotaging behaviors are negative procrastination and maladaptive perfectionism (Korstange et al., 2019; Kurtovic et al., 2019). Negative procrastination is associated with depression, anxiety, and low self-esteem, all of which are counterproductive to reaching your educational and career goals – and maximum potential. However, although procrastination deserves its negative reputation, *adaptive procrastination* such as switching tasks to allowing time for thoughts and ideas to incubate then coming back to the first task can be a positive way of sustaining momentum (Chu & Choi, 2005). Similarly, maladaptive perfectionism that blocks or otherwise hinders progress is distinct from adaptive perfectionism, which is striving to do excellent work (Kurtovic et al., 2019).

BOX 5.4

Inspirational Quotes

Strive for excellence, not perfection.
"There is no try, there is only do." – Yoda
When the going gets tough, the tough get going.

In addition to your feelings, it's helpful to pay attention to your progress and lack thereof, so when you get off track, you can assess what's going on and get back on track as soon as possible. If that doesn't work, it might be yet another time to reach out to mentors, advisors, or your support system – but be careful about the latter. We've known students and professionals who, in a moment of distress, for example, thinking they failed an exam or missed an important deadline, made uninformed decisions (like dropping out in the middle of the semester or sending an angry email) they later regretted. Gather all the relevant information and take your time for big decisions. Consult wisely, then use your head and heart to make your best decision. And if you get conflicting advice (which happens), consider the sources. Does the person giving the advice know and support your goals? Does the person giving the advice have *current* knowledge about the implications of your decision? (This is where a faculty advisor and/or your professor can be an excellent resource.) Of course, you want all the above – to make good decisions that work for you and the people that matter to you.

INDIVIDUAL (ALONE-NESS) AND GROUP WORK

Much of the work required for educational and career success in psychology (and other fields) is individual work, that is work we do (by necessity or choice) alone, by ourselves. Whether you're preparing for class, writing a paper, or preparing for a presentation, you're in charge of getting started, persisting, and completing one or more tasks. Some of us prefer and thrive on individual work, so much so that, influenced by the dominant *individualistic* culture of the U.S., most schools and work places reward individual achievement.

Others prefer to work with others. We may learn and do better work in collaboration with others than by ourselves. We may also be lonely and feel isolated with too much (for us) individual (alone) work. We may be more *collectivist* in our orientation toward our family, identity, or other group. Regardless of our broader orientation, which like most broad categories, is better understood as a spectrum of preferences (Duffy et al., 2016), education and careers in psychology also require collaboration, often in the form of group or team work. Furthermore, some of these differences are associated with our personality or type preferences, such as the degree to which we draw energy from introspection and interior reflection and/or as many introverts do – and/or, as many extraverts do, through interaction with other people.

Whether you're participating in group discussions or contributing to group projects, you're responsible for doing your part – and helping the group stay on task – to accomplish your individual and the group's goals. Groups vary in size (two people are a group), structure (formal or informal), and how they function (including leadership). When you start a new group, you have the opportunity to set the tone for a collaborative group. When you join or are assigned to an established group, it's helpful to ask if the group has established norms or rules, and observe for other unwritten norms and related group dynamics, to maximize your belongingness and productivity in the group.

RESEARCH TEAMS AND LABS: THEIR ROLE IN YOUR PROFESSIONAL GROWTH

As we shared in Chapter 3, research teams and labs are comprised of groups of people who are working together to achieve a goal. As such, they are great places to learn and practice working both individually and collaboratively – and develop a host of academic and professional skills. Furthermore, from an unwritten rules perspective, it's important to know that many faculty lead research teams and labs both to help complete their research projects and help students develop both research and interpersonal skills to be successful in the field. For example, as part of a research team/lab, you would likely have the opportunity to observe and develop skills related to professional interpersonal functioning. How, you ask? Well, while there are tasks that you will do on your own (once you've been trained), there are group meetings, individual and group supervision, presentation practice, and traveling to present together, and other opportunities to interact with members of the team/lab. Each of these opportunities to interact with others allows you to observe others and practice your professional interpersonal skills. They also get to know you! Finally, you may also have an opportunity, at some point, to write up results from the work on the research team and/or present those results in a professional setting. Not only are the skills you develop doing this useful in your future career, the fact that you've presented or published research is a demonstration of your research skills, which is another asset on many employment and graduate school applications.

YOUR PRIORITIES – BEING YOUR BEST SELF

This book presents an empowerment process to help you to make informed career and life decisions – which is part and parcel with making the most of your opportunities to become a better version of your self. To be your best self, it's important to create time for reflection. It's also helpful to seek out and welcome support and feedback from others who can help you recognize your strengths as well as your growing edges as you move toward career and life success. Regardless of your career goals in psychology, your abilities and developing skills, including planning, critical thinking, resilience, interpersonal skills, creativity, and gratitude will go a long way toward helping you to develop and grow in this field (Arnout & Almoied, 2020; Häfner et al., 2013; Hartley, 2011; McBurney, 1996; Sharp et al., 2008).

One of the biggest challenges many people drawn to psychology and other helping fields face is that we "want to help". There are so many aphorisms that encourage us to focus on helping others before we attend to ourselves that we will not list them here (although, you could seek them out). Oftentimes we put others' needs in front of our needs. In moderation, this helps us to grow as professionals and as humans. In excess, it distracts us from acquiring the skills and knowledge to truly help others and provide for ourselves and our families in the way we desire (Rupert & Dorociak, 2019; Stevanovic & Rupert, 2004; Wise et al., 2012). Let's take an example. A mother and infant are in an airplane and the air masks drop from the ceiling (we can conclude that something challenging is happening in the cockpit!). The mother is concerned that the lack of oxygen will harm her baby's growing brain. What should she do? Although it might seem counterintuitive, the well-established guidance is for her (and all of us) to put the oxygen mask on ourselves *before* helping others, so we are able to help them. If we apply this to our lives as professionals, we might think about the long-term effects of trying to please everyone else before we take care of ourselves. It's important to apply what we know about stress management to ourselves – and regularly remind ourselves of that.

Another common challenge is trying to do too much. As we discussed earlier, many, if not most of us, have multiple responsibilities and opportunities, which makes prioritization critical. From an unwritten rules' perspective, it's helpful to know that it's OK to shift your priorities for a time, a season, or long-term. They key is being aware – and intentionally deciding upon or accepting a necessary shift and considering the impact of that shift on others. This is not an either-or decision, it's a matter of degree. Deciding to prioritize one or more aspects of your life (such as education and career) does not mean ignoring or neglecting other important aspects of your life (such as family or social support). At its best, prioritization allows you the freedom to pursue your highest goals for the time period you've designated. In higher education, that often means semester by semester. When your formal education is complete, you might, as many people do, decide to re-assess your priorities (and how you're spending your time and energy) annually on a date that matters to you. (We both use our birthdays for one of our reflection points.)

Keep in mind higher education and some professional careers are a privilege and a choice. You don't have to do this. Sometimes hard work pays off; and sometimes it doesn't – but you have a choice (to a point) about where you invest your creative energies. It's also important to note in all this and more that not making a choice *is* a choice – usually for the default position, which might not be consistent with your priorities. Another important unwritten rule is that higher education and, even more so, pursuing your life/ career goals, is a marathon, not a sprint. Marathoners know that although you can sprint part of a marathon, if you want to finish – and finish well, it's important to train well, take care of your health, and pace yourself.

Don't forget your health and important relationships

Self-care is more than a meme. It's also much more than whatever you see on your favorite (or not so favorite) social media feed or the equivalent. Self-care is a disciplined approach to taking care of yourself so you're able to attend to the other things that matter to you – and achieve your career and life goals. For most us, self-care includes proactively attending to the foundations of health such as nutrition, sleep, exercise, balance, and social support. Ideally, your self-care includes regular preventative health care and, when appropriate, early intervention with one or more trusted health care providers. Good health in all areas (or the best you can do because clearly, it's not all in our control) is associated with a host of benefits including stress management and educational, career, and life success. Adding to the unwritten rules, it's important to remember that *you* are responsible for doing your part to maintain your health and important relationships.

How do you do that? Well, this gets back to your values, priorities, and your current situation. For example, during a particularly busy time, some people prioritize exercise over sleep; others make the opposite decision. What matters most is that you make decisions that work best for you, when applicable, in consultation with the people who matter most to you.

CHAPTER SUMMARY

As the title indicates, this chapter focuses on unwritten rules, or, more accurately, guidance, tips, and hints for success that many people with successful careers in psychology wish they had known earlier in their careers, some of which they learned the hard way. It includes hints, tips, and recommendations for succeeding in the psychology major while developing professional skills and building a professional identity. It also includes sections on respecting yourself and others, creativity, persistence, research teams and labs, and wraps up with a reminder to clarify and work with your values and priorities.

EXERCISES

1   If your department student organization has a social media presence, "follow" them. Read interesting posts that relate to being successful.
2   Attend a meeting of the Psychology Club or other psychology student activity and introduce yourself to at least one student, ideally someone further along than you. Once you get to know them a bit, ask them about things to do to be successful in your program.
3   Speak with your academic advisor about being successful. You can ask something like "I'm trying to learn as much as I can through coursework, research team engagement, and other experiences. I'm interested in _____. Do you have any suggestions for getting started on this path?"
4   Meet with your academic advisor, professor, or other professional you admire. Ask that person "What is one thing about the field you know now that you wish you knew when you were where I am now?" Really listen to their response – and be sure to consider and, when applicable, act on their advice and send a thank you note!

Next steps: the advanced move

1   Review the descriptions of the faculty research teams at your institution and find a team that looks interesting. Prepare a few questions to help you learn more about that research team, then make an appointment to speak with the faculty member leading the research team. Ask the questions you prepared and any new ones that you think of as you converse with the professor.
2   Choose a professional organization in psychology and find the organization's website. Review the website, then answer the following questions:
    a)   What is the purpose of the organization?
    b)   Can I see myself as part of this organization?
    c)   How might I benefit from being a member of this organization?
    d)   How might I further explore this organization to see if I might want to join?

REFERENCES

Albana, H. F. (2021). *Faculty perceptions of dyadic advising relationships, power, and cultural consciousness on college student learning outcomes* (Unpublished doctoral dissertation). Seton Hall University.

Armstrong, E. A., & Hamilton, L. T. (2013). *Paying for the party: How college maintains inequality.* Harvard University Press.

Arnout, B. A., & Almoied, A. A. (2020). A structural model relating gratitude, resilience, psychological well-being and creativity among psychological counsellors. *Counselling & Psychotherapy Research.* https://doi.org/10.1002/capr.12316

Bandura, A. (1997). *Self-efficacy: The exercise of control.* W. H. Freeman.

Bentley, S. V., Peters, K., Haslam, S. A., & Greenaway, K. H. (2019). Construction at work: Multiple identities scaffold professional identity development in academia. *Frontiers in Psychology, 10.* https://doi.org/10.3389/fpsyg.2019.00628

Betz, N. E. (1989). Implications of the null environment hypothesis for women's career development and for counseling psychology. *The Counseling Psychologist, 17,* 136–144. https://doi.org/10.1177/0011000089171008

Betz, N. E. (2002). The 2001 Leona Tyler award address. Women's career development: Weaving personal themes and theoretical constructs. *The Counseling Psychologist, 30,* 467–481.

Brady-Amoon, P., & Fuertes, J. (2011). Self-efficacy, self-rated abilities, adjustment, and academic performance. *Journal of Counseling and Development, 89*(4), 431–438.

Brown, L. S. (2018). *Feminist therapy* (2nd ed.). American Psychological Association. https://doi.org/10.1037/0000092-000

Carter, R. T., Lau, M. Y., Johnson, V., & Kirkinis, K. (2017). Racial discrimination and health outcomes among racial/ethnic minorities: A meta-analytic review. *Journal of Multicultural Counseling & Development, 45*(4), 232–259. https://doi.org/10.1002/jmcd.12076

Chu, A. H. C., & Choi, J. N. (2005). Rethinking procrastination: Positive effects of "active" procrastination behavior on attitudes and performance. *Journal of Social Psychology, 145*(3), 245–264.

Clance, P. R., & Imes, S. A. (1978). The imposter phenomenon in high-achieving women: Dynamics and therapeutic interventions. *Psychotherapy: Theory, Research, and Practice, 15*(3), 241–247.

Colella, A., Hebl, M., & King, E. (2017). One hundred years of discrimination research in the Journal of applied psychology: A sobering synopsis. *Journal of Applied Psychology, 102*(3), 500–513. https://doi.org/10.1037/apl0000084

Duckworth, A. (2016). *Grit: The power of passion and perseverance.* Scribner.

Duffy, R. D., Blustein, D. L., Diemer, M. A., & Autin, K. L. (2016). The psychology of working theory. *Journal of Counseling Psychology, 63*(2), 127–148. https://doi.org/10.1037/cou0000140

Dweck, C. S. (2016). *Mindset: The new psychology of success* (Updated). Random House.

Freeman, J. (1979). How to discriminate against women without really trying. In J. Freeman (Ed.). *Women: A feminist perspective* (2nd ed., pp. 194–208). Mayfield.

Gutiérrez y Muhs, G., Niemann, Y. F., González, C. G., & Harris, A. P. (2012). *Presumed incompetent: The intersections of race and class for women in academia.* Utah State University Press.

Häfner, A., Stock, A., Pinneker, L., & Ströhle, S. (2013). Stress prevention through a time management training intervention: An experimental study. *Educational Psychology, 34*(3), 403–416. https://doi.org/10.1080/01443410.2013.785065

Hartley, M. (2011). Examining the relationships between resilience, mental health, and academic persistence in undergraduate college students. *Journal of American College Health, 59*(7), 596–604.

Jackson, M. A. (2013). Counseling older workers confronting ageist stereotypes and discrimination. In P. Brownell & J. J. Kelly (Eds.), *Ageism and mistreatment of older workers: Current reality, future solutions.* (pp. 135–144). Springer Science + Business Media. https://doi.org/10.1007/978-94-007-5521-5_8

Javaras, K. N., Williams, M., & Baskin-Sommers, A. R. (2019). Psychological interventions potentially useful for increasing conscientiousness. *Personality Disorders: Theory, Research, and Treatment, 10*(1), 13–24. https://doi.org/10.1037/per0000267

Kahneman, D. (2011). *Thinking, fast and slow.* Farrar, Straus and Giroux.

Korstange, R., Craig, M., & Duncan, M. D. (2019). Understanding and addressing student procrastination in college. *Learning Assistance Review, 24*(1), 57–70.

Kounios, J., & Beeman, M. (2015). *The eureka factor: Aha moments, creative insight, and the brain.* Random House.

Kurtovic, A., Vrdoljak, G., & Idzanovic, A. (2019). Predicting procrastination: The role of academic achievement, self-efficacy and perfectionism. *International Journal of Educational Psychology, 8*(1), 1–26. https://doi.org/10.17583/ijep.2019.2993

Madjar, N., Shalley, C. E., & Herndon, B. (2019). Taking time to incubate: The moderating role of "what you do" and "when you do it" on creative performance. *Journal of Creative Behavior, 53*(3), 377–388. https://doi.org/10.1002/jocb.362

McBurney, D. H. (1996). *How to think like a psychologist: Critical thinking in psychology.* Prentice-Hall.

Mohr, T. S. (2014). *Playing big: Find your voice, your mission, your message.* Gotham books.

Niemann, Y. F., Muhs, G. G. Y., & González, C. G. (2020). *Presumed incompetent II: Race, class, power, and resistance of women in academia.* Utah State University Press.

Orbe-Austin, L., & Orbe-Austin, R. (2020). *Own your greatness. Overcome imposter syndrome, beat self-doubt, and succeed in life.* Ulysses.

Park, J. J., & Schallert, D. L. (2019). Talking, reading, and writing like an educational psychologist: The role of discourse practices in graduate students' professional identity development. *Learning, Culture and Social Interaction, 22.*

Rupert, P. A., & Dorociak, K. E. (2019). Self-care, stress, and well-being among practicing psychologists. *Professional Psychology: Research and Practice, 50*(5), 343–350. https://doi.org/10.1037/pro0000251

Schmidt, F. L. (2014). A general theoretical integrative model of individual differences in interests, abilities, personality traits, and academic and occupational achievement: A commentary on four recent articles. *Perspectives on Psychological Science, 9*(2), 211–218. https://doi.org/10.1177/1745691613518074

Sedlacek, W. E. (2004). *Beyond the big test: Noncognitive assessment in higher education.* Jossey-Bass.

Sharp, L. R., Herbert, J. D., & Redding, R. E. (2008). The role of critical thinking skills in practicing clinical psychologists' choice of intervention techniques. *Scientific Review of Mental Health Practice, 6*(1), 21–30.

Sprugnoli, G., Rossi, S., Emmendorfer, A., Rossi, A., Liew, S.-L., Tatti, E., di Lorenzo, G., Pascual-Leone, A., & Santarnecchi, E. (2017). Neural correlates of Eureka moment. *Intelligence, 62,* 99–118. https://doi.org/10.0.3.248/j.intell.2017.03.004

Steele, C. M. (2010). *Whistling Vivaldi: How stereotypes affect us and what we can do.* W. W. Norton & Co.

Stevanovic, P., & Rupert, P. A. (2004). Career-sustaining behaviors, satisfactions, and stresses of professional psychologists. *Psychotherapy: Theory, Research, Practice, Training, 41*(3), 301–309. https://doi.org/10.1037/0033-3204.41.3.301

Sue, D. W., Alsaidi, S., Awad, M. N., Glaeser, E., Calle, C. Z., & Mendez, N. (2019). Disarming racial microaggressions: Microintervention strategies for targets, White allies, and bystanders. *The American Psychologist, 74*(1), 128–142. https://doi.org/10.1037/amp0000296

Wise, E. H., Hersh, M. A., & Gibson, C. M. (2012). Ethics, self-care and well-being for psychologists: Reenvisioning the stress-distress continuum. *Professional Psychology: Research and Practice, 43*(5), 487–494. https://doi.org/10.1037/a0029446

Yosso, T. J. (2005). Whose culture has capital? A critical race theory discussion of community cultural wealth. *Race, Ethnicity and Education, 8*(1), 69–91.

CHAPTER 6

Developing an action plan

ORIENTING QUESTIONS

1. What is an *action plan* and why do we need it?
2. How is an action plan different than a program of study?
3. What information do you need to make an action plan to complete your degree or other long-term goal? To complete the semester, quarter, or professional equivalent? The week?
4. How do you develop an action plan?
5. What if something happens and you can't complete your initial plan – or decide to do something different?

DOI: 10.4324/9780429296413-8

INTRODUCTION

Have you ever wanted to do something – to achieve a goal or complete a task – that had a deadline and found, to your dismay, that you ran out of time? It happens to all of us at one time or another – particularly when we've made more commitments than we have time to deal with. This is not uncommon in educational and professional (i.e., career) settings, as illustrated by research suggesting that lack of planning (or, time management) skills, is a major stressor for college students (Korstange et al., 2019). Students and professionals often benefit from learning (and re-learning) and practicing time-management skills such as those popularized by Stephen Covey and colleagues (Covey, 2013; Covey et al., 1994) as discussed in earlier chapters. When you make plans to achieve your goals, you're much more likely to achieve them than if you simply were to think about them (Locke & Latham, 2019; Schippers et al., 2020). In fact, planning one's time is so important to college and future success that not only faculty (van der Meer et al., 2010), but upper-level students identify time management as one of the most important learning outcomes from their college experience (Walker, 2008). Managing one's time effectively has been shown to be particularly helpful for non-traditional and part-time students (MacCann et al., 2012; Trueman & Hartley, 1996). Moreover, a large body of research shows that the benefits of investing the necessary time to make a plan include maximizing the likelihood of reaching that goal, increased academic and professional success, lower levels of stress, anxiety, and procrastination, and greater satisfaction with leisure time (Gortner & Zulauf, 2000; Krumrei-Mancuso et al., 2013; Locke & Latham, 2019; Macan et al., 1990; Misra & McKean, 2000; Mpofu et al., 1996).

In addition, keep in mind the best plans are highly individualized – and adaptable. Your plans will be *your* plans - reflecting your priorities; no one else's will be exactly the same. If you're concerned that creating an action plan (and checking it regularly) will take time – it will; however, we encourage you to consider the time it takes an investment in your future success. Moreover, if you're concerned an action plan will lock you in or set you up for failure, keep in mind that good plans are flexible and adaptable, so you can and should adapt them as your circumstances or plans change and when things don't work out the way you'd like. It's also important to leave room for spontaneity and to recognize that shifting schedules and falling behind are quite common and may be learning opportunities (what can you do differently next time?).

So, what is an action plan?

An action plan is an outline of the actions to help you reach or achieve a goal. The outline is more than a list – it designates timelines and time frames for completion. Planning can be targeted to a variety of time frames – a decade, a year, a semester or the equivalent, a week, or a day. The focus of the plan changes with each level. For example, a goal that can take about a decade to complete for full-time students is completing your post-secondary education, bachelor's through doctoral degrees. At this level, the focus of the plan is on achieving large goals such as successfully completing the coursework designated by your program for the year or completing your capstone project/thesis/dissertation. When focusing on your plan for the year, you can be more specific, listing specific course or tasks to complete. For example, students might list specific courses, joining Dr. So-and-so's research team, and applying for membership in Psi Chi, the international honor society in psychology. Meanwhile, planning at the weekly level is even more detailed. For example, if you're a student, your weekly plan might focus on tasks such as preparing for class by reading the material and completing assigned homework, attending a research team meeting, participating in recreational and/or spiritual endeavors, and doing the laundry.

Planning and SMART goals

Plans are affected by the clarity of the goal, so rather than stating a goal of "successfully completing the course", research shows it's more effective to state it in *S*pecific, *M*easurable, *A*chievable, *R*ealistic, and *T*ime-bound (SMART; Doran, 1981; Fielding, 1999; Wade, 2009) ways. Here is a definition for each: 1) *Specific* signifies that you are targeting a specific skill, task, or area for improvement, 2) *Measurable* represents the idea that you want to quantify or clearly state an indicator of progress, 3) *Achievable* goals are realistic, in other words, goals that stretch you a bit and yet are not completely out of reach (such as winning the Nobel Prize before you earn your BA/BS), 4) *Realistic* goals are those you have some degree of control over, and 5) *Time-bound* is that the goal has an endpoint and evaluation criteria to determine if you've achieved the goal or need to modify it. We've listed some examples in Box 6.1.

BOX 6.1

Example Goals – Typical versus SMART

Typical Goal	Smart Goal
Read the chapter	Spend 15 min. skimming the abstract, headings, tables, graphics, and chapter summary; 30–45 minutes reading each section, highlighting and taking notes; 60 minutes completing chapter exercises or relevant activities
Study for test	Spend 1 hr/wk reviewing notes, definitions, and chapter highlights
Do literature search for PSYC 1010 paper	Spend 2 hrs this week learning to use library search engines, asking Psychology Reference Librarian about advanced search techniques, and identifying articles to read

For example, let's say you want to exercise more. That's a good goal, but it's not SMART. To make it SMART, you'd identify what you're committing to do (e.g., walk for a half hour), how often (e.g., three times per week), and for how long (e.g., one month), and then track your achievement. That way your goal of exercising more would be specific, measurable, achievable, realistic, and time-bound. As a further illustration, using SMART, you could change a broad goal like "successfully completing the course" to "By the end of the semester, I will complete PSYC 2345 with a 'B' by attending at least 80% of the lectures, spending at least eight hours per week reading and studying the material, spending one hour per week reviewing the material studied during the previous week, and spending two hours per week working on the final paper for the class". Although this might on first glance appear overwhelming, this goal identifies what you're going to do to achieve that grade, the tasks you're going to do to achieve it, and is time-bound. This will allow you to create both a semester plan and the weekly plan that helps you to lay out the activities needed for each week in order to achieve this goal. Where it might be weak is whether or not it's realistic. It may not be realistic if you've overcommitted yourself by enrolling in an overload, have a job, a family, and a sick relative for whose care you are responsible (or, some combination thereof). The practice of proactively planning can assist you in preventing over-commitment and, if that happens anyway (and it does because life happens), seeing when you are becoming over-committed so that you can make a decision about how to deal with the over-commitment.

As career development in psychology begins with formal education, the plans and illustrations that follow focus on career preparation through completing your bachelor's or other advanced degree in conjunction with career and life development. However, these skills are not limited to college success – they are essential career/life management skills. If you've already mastered one or more steps or have earned your bachelor's degree, feel free to adapt the plan to meet your needs and reach your goals.

The remainder of this chapter will walk through the steps of creating three types of plans – a long-term plan to complete your degree, a semester plan to guide you through to a successful semester or equivalent, and a weekly plan to keep you focused each week on your important goals and tasks. Since you already have a program of study to organize your academic work, the action plans introduced in this book primarily focus on your career development activities. In order to assist you in your planning efforts, the forms that we will be using are available in the appendices and can be downloaded from the book's website as MS Word documents. The plans are set up as tables to allow you to add rows to accommodate other parts of your life. We want to be explicit in stating that the process introduced here is one that you can adapt to meet other long-term goals, as well as professional and educational goals. For example, a person does not just go out and run a 25K marathon. Those who do so successfully set up a training schedule and gradually build up their body (and mind) to accomplish this goal through achieving multiple small milestones. We hope that you find this process useful in all areas of your life.

CREATING A LONG-TERM PLAN TO COMPLETE YOUR DEGREE

Step one – bringing together your thoughts and information

The first task in creating a solid plan is to focus the plan. This is where you bring all the things you've been considering together in one place and make, depending on where you are in the process, either a tentative or more firm decision about when and how you are going to work on them. Some areas to consider are the goals to be achieved with this plan and how far out you're going to plan. For illustrative purposes, we will be creating a long-term plan to complete your bachelor's degree so that you can move in one of two directions: employment or graduate school yet, keep in mind, you can and should adapt this to meet your goals. Remember to make your goals SMART goals!

The next step is to gather the information you've been collecting about your career values, skills, and interests, including interesting subfields, potential directions for your career, degree requirements for your psychology major, information about relevant minors, information you might have gathered about graduate school or employment, and information about your current life commitments and responsibilities. Examples of the information or notes that you might gather include: occupational directions like human resources, teaching psychology in the P-12 school system, or conducting research at a university or a research lab; college minors, such as biology, sociology, human resources, business management. These can be in the any form that works for you such as notes, documents, or websites however, make sure that they are easily accessible as we move through the planning process.

Step two – identify significant and/or re-occurring events and activities

Oftentimes we overestimate the amount of time actually available to work on tasks that move us toward our goals. It's easy to forget (or, otherwise underestimate) the amount of time it takes to prepare for an exam, for that big semester report that's due the last week of the semester, or how long it takes to prepare for a presentation. Likewise, we can easily overcommit "free" time, such as fall or spring break or weekends, overestimating how much time is available after we've completed those mundane yet often time-consuming tasks such as laundry, grocery shopping, and cleaning. There may be other commitments or responsibilities, such as hosting family and/or friends for a religious ceremony or holiday, that have either a single large effect or re-occurring effect on our time commitments. If we do not recognize the effect of these types of events or tasks on our time, we are likely to reach deadlines when we are insufficiently prepared to do our best.

Take a few minutes to make a list of the major one-time events or tasks that are planned or you expect to happen during the period covered by the plan. Similarly, don't forget to write down re-occurring events that require a time and/or effort commitment. Examples include events/parties related to holidays or sports, family get-togethers, work-related events (outside of normal work hours), and volunteer commitments.

BOX 6.2

Step 2: Example Significant and/or Re-Occurring Events

1. Annual family reunions, weddings, and other family ceremonies
2. Religious/spiritual/community holidays and observances.
3. Annual gatherings of organizations of which you are a member
4. Financial aid, income tax preparation, etc.
5. Employment, volunteer, and other regular commitments
6. Institutional, programmatic, or other academic deadlines

Step three – sort and organize!

Now we're going to organize your information – first, by deadline dates; then by precedence. Organizing this information by deadline helps you not miss critical points in your path toward your career. For example, if you or, if applicable, your parents/guardians do not submit the FAFSA form you won't be eligible for financial aid for the next academic year. Similarly, if you don't complete an application for a research assistantship or graduate school, you won't be considered for that opportunity. You might still ask "Why should I plan, since my life changes so quickly?". Well, that's exactly why a plan is so helpful – it helps us remain mindful of those things that are important in order for us to reach our goals, and, conversely, allows us to not worry about those things that we need to remember to do in the future, but don't need to keep in mind at the present. Thus, a long-term plan helps us to be present in the moment by freeing up our memory and attention to be with family and friends or learn new concepts or get that paper written. Think of it this way – you don't worry about learning the class material assigned for the last weeks of the semester on the first day of class, do you? No. At the beginning of the class you are concerned about the big picture. In other words, you're likely asking "What do I have to do to master this topic – what chapters or articles do I need to read? What assignments will allow me to demonstrate my mastery? What papers will need writing?" Then, most likely, you go home and figure out how you are going to organize your time to complete all of those papers that are due at about the same time. That's actually what we're going to talk about more in the next section of the text, however, these same principles and skills apply to longer time frames as well. So, if you already do a plan for a semester (or the equivalent time frame), what we're doing is transferring your skills to building a plan that reaches across years rather than months. If you can think of it this way, it may be easier to do. If you have not previously planned out your semester – don't worry, since we'll talk about that in the next section. By the way, we'll also provide thoughts on how to improve your semester planning in the next section, too. So, similar to the way you arrange your reading and work on assignments for a semester, you want to make sure that you complete preliminary or preparatory tasks before you work on the more complex tasks when you are creating a longer-term plan. This eliminates stopping in order to backtrack to complete a task that ideally would have been completed earlier.

On to creating your plan! If you haven't yet done so, this is the time to gather together information about the classes you need to take to complete your degree (often called a *program of study* or *degree plan*), other graduation requirements (such as, completing a senior paper or exit examination), and information related to volunteer or professional development tasks (such as application deadlines), and other time commitments. When you've done all that, the next step is to make sure that you make a list of any "hard" deadlines. "Hard" deadlines are those with serious consequences if missed. For example, if you miss applying for a summer internship or for graduate school, you must wait a year to apply again. The consequences of that might be that you are "on hold" until the next application cycle, thus, delaying your progress toward your goal, or you might have missed that window of opportunity. We all make mistakes. When that happens, the best thing to do is learn from it and move on. Don't beat yourself up over it – and don't make it worse by staying stuck. Other times, delays are unavoidable. For example, you or a family member are in an accident or come down with a serious health issue right before the deadline, preventing you from finishing the application. Similar advice applies – learn, move on, and use your resources (e.g., consult with an advisor or mentor about next steps). "Soft" deadlines have fewer or less serious consequences – and some groups will work with a potential applicant with extenuating circumstances. It rarely hurts to ask. And it's definitely a good idea to ask when, for example, there are discrepancies in posted due dates or a problem with the software to maximize the likelihood the responsible organization will work with you to make it right.

So, make a list for those things with deadlines or due dates. Do the same thing for non-academic/career-related tasks. As an example, if your psychology program requires you to complete a project or exam in order to graduate, note what the project is and any deadlines related to completing portions of the project or applying to take the required exam. Similarly, if you are a co-founder of a community non-profit organization to encourage young students to engage in science, technology, engineering, and/or mathematics (STEM) activities, you will want to include time commitments for board/staff meetings, major events, and similarly large tasks that take a significant amount of time and energy to complete. Once you've gathered together as much of this information as you can, you'll want to organize them by date. Notice that our focus here is on larger events – events that have a significant impact on your time, such as events that take more than a week to accomplish when we take into account the planning, preparation, and implementation. We'll work on smaller events and activities when we speak to the semester and weekly plans.

Step four – build your plan to reach your goal

Now it's time to build your plan. To do that, let's pull out the Career Development plan forms included with the text. The first, Form 6.1, is an *Organizing my Career-Related Information* form. On this form, you can gather relevant information related to your career goal into one place for easy reference. We also developed the next two forms, Forms 6.2 and 6.3, to help you lay out your Career Plan to complete your bachelor's degree in four and six years, respectively. These are the actual forms to sketch out your plan with recommendations for action each semester. If you're currently enrolled in a bachelor's degree program or considering one, we encourage you to use whichever form most closely fits how long you think it will take you to complete your degree. If you've already completed your bachelor's degree, then adapt this plan to meet your current goals. We'll talk more specifically about modifying the plan later – once you've got the hang of how to do this.

As you engage with the forms, you'll notice that we've done some of the organizing for you. For example, we've included our recommendations for the best times to accomplish specific career-related tasks. If you missed those, don't worry – but do attend to them as soon as possible. The tasks included in the plan are the larger tasks that move students through toward successful completion of their degrees. These were sorted and organized just as we are going to do here with the additional and/or more specific tasks that you will need to add in for your plan.

At this point, we want to add into this document important events that you know will take up time, based upon the deadlines and ordering that you previously completed. For example, if you've received a "save the date" notice for a wedding that is a year off, you will want to make a note of it during the semester that it is planned to occur. Other activities or tasks, such as volunteer activities and busier times at work should also be included, as they affect the time available for coursework and therefore your decision-making about academic progress and career development activities. These types of activities and tasks go into the right-hand column. Note that these forms are available online as MS Word documents, so you can add large tasks identified by your program as necessary for degree completion by inserting a new row in the appropriate year and typing in the task. After you've developed a draft, share it with your partner, academic advisor and/or mentor for feedback. This will make sure that you haven't left out anything important and/or relevant to your particular situation. It's also helpful to identify accountability buddies who will encourage and support you in meeting your goals and celebrate important milestones with you!

BOX 6.3

Step 4: Example Completed First Year-Plan

1st Year (first 30 credit hours)

Career/Professional Career Development Activities	Major Events/Tasks/Activities Beyond School
Adapt to the University/Program and build strong GPA	Work 20 hours/week

(Continued)

BOX 6.3   (*Continued*)

1st Year (first 30 credit hours)

Career/Professional Career Development Activities	Major Events/Tasks/Activities Beyond School
Talk w/more advanced students to learn about opportunities and how to succeed	Volunteering 5 hours/week
Explore organizations related to major (join at least one when eligible)	Religious commitments
Talk with advisor every semester (accomplishments, plan, and how to best benefit from opportunities)	Shanice's wedding
Find Psychology- related summer job/ or research/lab experience	

Additional notes: Update reading and study skills to free up time for professional development activities, such as department colloquia.

Several final thoughts as we wrap up this topic. As a reminder, there are two Career Plan forms for creating a plan to complete your degree. One is focused on completing your degree in four years, while the second is focused on completing the degree in six years. If you compare the two documents, you'll note we simply spread out the activities from the four-year plan to cover six years – recognizing that it's likely that someone taking six years to complete their degree has other commitments and responsibilities that do not allow the time for completion in four years. That's OK. If you are thinking of completing your degree in more time than this, recognize that most of the tasks and activities on the forms are placed in specific semesters because they are best accomplished before those in the subsequent semesters. Each semester is its own table on the form, so you can copy/paste and adjust as will work best for you. Finally, we've included in the Advanced Move section, Form 6.4, titled *Post-secondary 10-year career plan*, to lay out a plan to complete your degree(s) and enter into the workforce when you are ready to build a more extensive long-term plan.

CREATING A PLAN TO COMPLETE A SPECIFIC SEMESTER SUCCESSFULLY

Now that we've reviewed and organized the information needed to complete your degree, it will be easier to create a plan for the current semester (Rockquemore, 2014). Why? Because you have a draft of the important tasks and projects that need to be completed by the time the semester ends already at hand. We've provided you with a form to help you organize this information as well. Once you've opened the *Semester Plan* form (Form 6.5), transfer the information about the tasks that you have to accomplish by the end of the current semester from your plan to complete your bachelor's degree (Forms 6.2 or 6.3) to the appropriate category on page 1. Then, add in the information from course syllabi such as due dates, research team assignments, work, volunteering, and other responsibilities. You now have a complete list of tasks and goals for the approximately four months around the semester (or, three months if your school is on the quarter system). It may seem a bit overwhelming at this stage, however, don't stop. The next page of the form helps you to organize this into a do-able set of tasks for each week.

On the second page of the semester plan form (Form 6.5), we encourage you to break down each task, assigning it to a specific week. That will help you make the tasks more manageable and seem much less overwhelming. If a task will take more than one week to complete (such as a major paper for a course), break the task down into smaller pieces. Let's take the major paper as an example. You could assign the task of identifying a topic to one week. However, identifying a topic requires either prior knowledge (meaning you already have read some of the literature) or that you have a task of doing a literature search to see if the topic might be interesting. If you're in the latter category, you might assign conducting a brief literature search to identify a topic to your first week, followed by conducting a more extensive literature search during your second week. Regardless of your starting point, it might also be helpful to give yourself weeks three to seven to read, say a minimum of ten articles a week, in preparation for writing the paper, followed by two weeks (weeks eight to nine) for additional reading that you didn't anticipate. In this example, some of the assigned tasks for the next few weeks would likely include outline the paper, draft several sections, edit the paper, check for grammar and formatting, then finalizing and submitting your paper on or before the due date. You'll notice that each week there is only one focused task related to completing the paper, rather than the large complex and overwhelming task of "I've got to get that paper done!".

BOX 6.4

Semester Plan: Example Career Development Weekly Goals

Week		Academic Goals	Professional/ Career Dev.	Work/ Employment	Volunteering /Other	Personal Goals
1	8/17	Attend class and obtain syllabi and assignments	Review syllabi for career-related assignments	Work scheduled hours	Bake cookies for school bake sale	Exercise Organize study space

(Continued)

BOX 6.3   (*Continued*)

Week		Academic Goals	Professional/ Career Dev.	Work/ Employment	Volunteering /Other	Personal Goals
2	8/24	Complete readings and get clear on major assignments	Consider how your interests relate to your classes	Work scheduled hours		Exercise Hang out w/ new friends
3	8/31	Complete readings; Review earlier readings and notes to deepen understanding; Literature searches for major papers	Ask advisor for name of upper- level student for success discussion	Work scheduled hours	Psych Club volunteering	Exercise Explore city
4	9//7	Study for tests; Then review articles for papers	Meet with upper-level student	Work scheduled hours	Take car to garage	Exercise Attend event

Once you've assigned everything to a specific week, review it to see if there are weeks that are over- or under-loaded. Make adjustments while keeping in mind that this is version 1.0 or take 1 of your semester plan. Plans change to accommodate new circumstances – if they are to be successful. A plan that does not adapt to changing circumstances becomes outdated and does not support your movement toward your goal. Feel free to update it as things change. By the way, the first time or two that you use this process, it is likely to take more time than it will when you become comfortable with it. In addition, your plans will improve as you become more aware of how much time you realistically need for different tasks and activities. As a result, your decision-making about the things that you are committing yourself to do or be responsible for, as well as your decision-making about your academic course load, will become more effective. This will help you to ensure that you achieve your degree goal at the quality level that you desire.

CREATING A SHORT-TERM PLAN TO COMPLETE A WEEK SUCCESSFULLY

If you've been working along with us; Congratulations! You now have a written plan to guide you through your undergraduate education experience and one to help you complete the semester successfully. These are foundational for keeping you focused and on track – and are easily adaptable for other life and career goals. These two plans allow you to see the big picture related to how you will achieve your goal. Now we get down to the nitty-gritty! We've included a weekly *Time Schedule Form* (6.6) for you to use to make the plan for the semester real. By taking the time to try out how you will fit everything that needs to be done into a slot in your available time, you eliminate the indecision time that stalls us out and demoralizes us when we look back at what happened (or, didn't happen) during a week.

Let's get started by opening up the Time Schedule Form (Form 6.6). You can be as simple or as fancy as you would like to be with this. Using colors can assist in seeing similar activities across the week. Different fonts can also be used although in our experience, using more than three different fonts can actually be more confusing than clarifying. In addition, it is usually most helpful to put the information into the spaces before highlighting or changing styles/fonts.

First, let's write in any of those "immoveable objects" – things that must happen at a specific time and cannot be moved. Your class times or times for religious observances would be examples. Next, put into the form time for activities that have some flexibility and take up time. Examples here would be driving to campus or work, or exercising. You should also block out time for sleeping, dressing, eating, and other maintenance tasks (like grocery shopping and laundry). If someone else does those things for you – you've just gained time to spend on doing tasks to meet your goals! Yeah!

By now your weekly schedule should be starting to fill up. Before it gets too full, let's put in the time for your academic work and professional/career development goals. Starting with your academic goals, let's block out time for studying and preparing for class. As we shared earlier, the general rule is that undergraduate students should plan to spend about three hours reading, reviewing and preparing for class per credit hour for that class. This is an average, as some courses are more complex, dense, or otherwise challenging, and therefore, require more time to absorb and make meaning of the information. The content of other courses is more easily absorbed into our mental framework – in other words, it is easier to make meaning of the information. However, three hours per weekly class hour (or, credit hour) is a good estimate to use. Go ahead and block off study/reading time for each class. Depending on various factors, you may want to block off another three hours each week to work on larger projects, such as papers or group projects. These types of activities generally require specific, focused work that is different from the reading and learning of text material and so need their own time slots. Later, you can come back and label these with the specific work you plan to accomplish during each time period. For now, we are just creating a "place holder".

At this point, you are likely to find yourself with little to no time left over for other things. That is a typical experience for individuals just starting to use plans to help them achieve their goals. What is happening is that, instead of coming to a critical point in the semester and recognizing that you can't complete everything that needs to be done, you are seeing ahead of time how you have overscheduled or overcommitted yourself – in time to make decisions about your priorities and, if relevant, negotiate for assistance so that you can achieve your goals to the best of your ability. If you are running out of time, it often helps to brainstorm ways to be more efficient with your time. This might include creating a study group where participants share responsibility for learning specific chapters and related information and "teaching" the other group members. This type of sharing responsibility can lighten everyone's load while ensuring that everyone learns all the material as efficiently as possible. Other examples would include learning to speed read or use known study formats such as SQ3R (Survey, Question, Read, Review, Recite). Check out your campus learning or academic support/center for resources for improving your reading speed and/or other learning skills. In addition to finding ways to be more efficient, there are other methods to increase the time available to achieve goals. One way is to use waiting time to read small chunks of material or complete a quick task. You may also be able to engage your network – family and friends – to help support you achieving your goal. Using this option requires understanding why that individual may want to assist you, as well as the potential limits to their ability to assist. Thus, recognizing that someone may only be able to assist you during specific times or at a specific point in the semester will help you to negotiate support that you need, while not overtaxing the relationship that you have with the individual. The topic of maintaining relationships is discussed in greater depth in Chapters 7 and 8.

Once you've placed your tasks in a timeslot, you've completed the planning phase. Next, we implement that plan by using the weekly plan to keep us focused and on track. In addition, if you find that you need to change things up due to changing demands, then you can easily identify things you can "switch around" so that you don't miss a task that needs to be done that week. If you've never used a weekly or even daily plan before, this is likely to seem awkward. We encourage you to try it out for a few weeks – making adjustments and learning how you actually need to spend your time – before abandoning it. Finally, recognize that, if you can accomplish the work in less time than you put into your plan, you've just gained some additional time to spend as you wish.

CHAPTER SUMMARY

In this chapter, you learned how to create plans to achieve your goals at three levels: across multiple years, across a semester, and across a week. At each level, the tasks and activities become more specific and focused as you move from a multi-year plan to a weekly schedule, with tasks and activities in the weekly schedule being assigned to a specific timeframe for completions. For each of these levels of planning, care must be taken to ensure that tasks are placed in the plan in order that the action needs to take place – for example you can't interview for a job or graduate school program before submitting an application and being invited to an interview.

Two other points are important to reiterate before we leave the chapter. First, plans change. Numerous factors and events can affect the flow of our work, such as illness, weather, and delays in obtaining resources. Having a plan makes it easier to adapt and keep moving forward, so expect to have a "version 2.0" or even "3.0". Second, having a plan can help you communicate with important people in your life who might want to know why you are not as available as you were before you started back to school. It also helps you to see where the demands for a particular week will not fit and allow you to solicit assistance and support to enable you to accomplish the required tasks. This assistance and support can range from improving your reading and learning skills to collaborating with others to facilitate each other's learning to negotiating with important others to take over some tasks while you attend to your learning.

EXERCISES

1   Using the handouts provided, complete a plan to complete your degree. Once you have a draft, take it to your advisor (or, favorite faculty member) and ask for their feedback. Make sure that you state your career goal on your plan so that the faculty member can give you the best feedback possible.

2   Using the handouts provided, complete a plan for the semester. Once you have a draft, take it to your advisor (or, favorite faculty member) and ask for their feedback. Make sure that you state your career goal on your plan so that the faculty member can give you the best feedback possible.

3   Using the handouts provided, complete a plan for an example week. Once you have a draft, take it to your advisor (or, favorite faculty member) and ask for their feedback. Make sure that you state your career goal on your plan so that the faculty member can give you the best feedback possible.

Next steps: the advanced move

1   Take a week and track how you spend your time – use either 15- or 30-minute intervals. Note what you are doing, where you are doing it, how long it takes (or, you spend working on it), and what you accomplished. Review how you spent your week. Consider the following questions:

a.   Consider how much time you spent on each area of your life. How did you spend your time?

b.   Using a broad definition of "productive", were some time(s) more productive than others?

c.   What would you have liked to do more of in order to reach your goal(s)?

d.   What would you have liked to do less of in order to reach your goal(s)?

e. What might you do better or have done differently to support you in your work to reach your goals?

f. What resources might you access to help you learn or develop new skills to help you reach your goals?

2 Using the ten-year career planning form (Form 6.4), plan out your career for the next four–ten years, beyond your bachelor's degree. Remember – it's version 1.0 at this point in time!

REFERENCES

Covey, S. R. (2013). *The 7 habits of highly effective people: Powerful lessons in personal change* (25th anniversary). Simon & Schuster.

Covey, S. R., Merrill, A. R., & Merrill, R. R. (1994). *First things first: To live, to love, to learn, to leave a legacy*. Simon & Schuster.

Doran, G. T. (1981). There's a S.M.A.R.T. way to write managements' goals and objectives. *Management Review, 70*, 35–36.

Fielding, M. (1999). Target setting, policy pathology and student perspectives: Learning to labour in new times. *Cambridge Journal of Education, 29*(2), 277–287.

Gortner Lahmers, A., & Zulauf, C. R. (2000). Factors associated with academic time use and academic performance of college students: A recursive approach. *Journal of College Student Development, 41*(5), 544–556.

Korstange, R., Craig, M., & Duncan, M. D. (2019). Understanding and addressing student procrastination in college. *Learning Assistance Review, 24*(1), 57–70.

Krumrei-Mancuso, E. J., Newton, F. B., Kim, E., & Wilcox, D. (2013). Psychosocial factors predicting first-year college student success. *Journal of College Student Development, 54*(3), 247–266. https://doi.org/10.1353/csd.2013.0034

Locke, E. A., & Latham, G. P. (2019). The development of goal setting theory: A half century retrospective. *Motivation Science, 5*(2), 93–105. https://doi.org/10.1037/mot0000127

Macan, T. H., Shahani, C., Dipboye, R. L., & Phillips, A. P. (1990). College students' time management: Correlations with academic performance and stress. *Journal of Educational Psychology, 82*(4), 760–768. https://doi.org/10.1037/0022-0663.82.4.760

MacCann, C., Fogarty, G. J., & Roberts, R. D. (2012). Strategies for success in education: Time management is more important for part-time than full-time community college students. *Learning and Individual Differences, 22*(5), 618–623. http://dx.doi.org/10.1016/j.lindif.2011.09.015

Misra, R., & McKean, M. (2000). College students' academic stress and its relation to their anxiety, time management, and leisure satisfaction. *American Journal of Health Studies, 16*(1), 41–51.

Mpofu, E., D'Amico, M., & Cleghorn, A. (1996). Time management practices in an African culture: Correlates with college academic grades. *Canadian Journal of Behavioural Science/Revue canadienne des sciences du comportement, 28*(2), 102–112. https://doi.org/10.1037/0008-400X.28.2.102

Rockquemore, K. A. (2014). *Every semester needs a plan* (webinar). National Center for Faculty Development & Diversity.

Schippers, M. C., Morisano, D., Locke, E. A., Scheepers, A. W. A., Latham, G. P., & de Jong, E. M. (2020). Writing about personal goals and plans regardless of goal type boosts academic performance. *Contemporary Educational Psychology, 60*.

Trueman, M., & Hartley, J. (1996). A comparison between the time-management skills and academic performance of mature and traditional-entry university students. *Higher Education, 32*(2), 199–215.

van der Meer, J., Jansen, E., & Torenbeek, M. (2010) 'It's almost a mindset that teachers need to change': First-year students' need to be inducted into time management. *Studies in Higher Education, 35*(7), 777–791. https://doi.org/10.1080/03075070903383211

Wade, D. T. (2009). Goal setting in rehabilitation: An overview of what, why and how. *Clinical Rehabilitation, 23*(4), 291–295. http://dx.doi.org/10.1177/0269215509103551

Walker, P. (2008). What do students think they (should) learn at college? Student perceptions of essential learning outcomes. *Journal of the Scholarship of Teaching and Learning, 8*(1), 45–60.

PART **III**

The role of relationships in your educational and career success

CHAPTER 7

Relationships in your professional life

ORIENTING QUESTIONS

1. What types of advisors are available to assist you as a college or university student?

2. What are some good ways to work with advisors and mentors?

3. How can building a relationship with one or more faculty members help your career?

4. How can you build a professional relationship with one or more faculty members?

5. What are some ways to form and sustain healthy professional relationships with classmates and peers?

DOI: 10.4324/9780429296413-10

INTRODUCTION

Despite the importance of individual effort (and planning) and persistent myths about people who are "self-made" and achieved success "on their own", none of us succeed or fail on our own. As we discussed in earlier chapters, our career – and indeed life – success is intricately connected with other people – and the contexts, both seen and unseen, in which we have developed, been socialized, and operate today. Humans are social animals (Aronson & Aronson, 2012). We need and benefit from healthy human relationships throughout our lives, including professional relationships. Although professional relationships are similar in some ways to other human relationships, they also have some unique characteristics that we'll explore in this chapter. Moreover, given the importance of professional relationships in careers in general and, more specifically, careers in psychology, this chapter provides both a practical and unwritten rules perspective on developing and maintaining a range of healthy professional relationships, with a focus on advisement and mentoring, working with professors and peers, and building and maintaining a professional support network.

ADVISEMENT AND MENTORING

Some of the most important professional relationships you will likely have the opportunity to develop in college and beyond are with advisors and mentors. Advisement and mentoring are associated with student success (Crisp & Cruz, 2009; Kirp, 2019; Sedlacek, 2004; Walker et al., 2001) as well as professional and personal growth (Crisp & Cruz, 2009; Moss et al., 1999; Vaccaro & Camba-Kelsay, 2018; Walker et al., 2001). Whether formally assigned or not, advisors and mentors can be excellent sources of information, guidance, and, at their very best, serve as role models and active supporters of your educational, career, and life success. We'll explore a little more about advisement and mentoring next as well as how you can make the most of these special professional relationships.

About advising

Most colleges and universities offer academic and other forms of student advisement. There are many forms of advisement such as academic advisement that often includes course selection, meeting other requirements for graduation, and preparing for success in your career and career advisement to assist you in making informed career decisions and, sometimes preparing materials for field placements, summer, and other employment. There are also institutional, departmental, programmatic, and, often, individual advisor differences in how advisement is defined, implemented, and accessed. For example, as an undergraduate student, you may be assigned and/or have the option of working with professional full-time staff advisors, faculty advisors, peer advisors, career, or other special services advisors. You may also be assigned or have the option of working with an advisor with a different title such as director, assistant director, dean, assistant dean, coordinator, intern, graduate assistant, or counselor (Kuhn et al., 2006). In general, advisors' roles are to provide information and support to assist you in reaching your academic and often, career goals. Given the variety of advisor types and functions, it's important to find out, as early as possible in your academic career, how advisement works for students pursuing *your* degree/career plan at *your* institution, as well as what's recommended and expected (e.g., to see your advisor before registration), and any additional advisement opportunities.

Advisors are most often found through contacting the relevant office (e.g., academic advising, career advising) or at events that are designed to introduce students to various institutional services. Most institutions have some type of orientation – whether a meeting, event, or class – that introduces you to all these offices. Advisors and others who work or volunteer at orientation events are often very student-centered and willing to help. Of course, orientation typically comes at the very beginning of the program of study however, if you missed that, you can always search your institution's website or ask someone (ideally associated with your program or department) to help you. In addition to learning about academic advisement for your degree program at your institution, it's to your advantage to learn whether your institution offers specific services for career advising, mental health advising, and more, or if one office (or person) performs all these roles. Where are all these services located? Do you need appointments to see these various types of advisors? If so, how do you set up appointments? These are all essential questions to consider, find answers to, and follow up – so you don't miss out on these important professional relationships!

Academic advising is so very important to your progress and success that it's important to know and understand how advisement and related services are organized at your college/university. Do faculty members in the various departments perform the academic advising function, or do you need to work with a professional academic advisor for at least part of your undergraduate studies? Is there a centralized or decentralized advising office? Are advisors located in one main office or different academic departments? Do individuals have access to multiple advisors/advising offices or are they assigned to one specific office and/or advisor? There are multiple easy ways to learn about this – you can check the website for information about academic advising or ask a professor or another knowledgeable person in your academic department.

BOX 7.1

Reflection on Good Advisement

Reflection: Think about one or more good advisement experience(s) you experienced or heard about.

Questions to consider: What was most helpful? What was the role of the relationship you had with this person in making the experience a positive one? How did you help the advisor to understand what you needed and provide effective support? What type of advisement would be helpful to you now or in the near future? How might you seek out that type of advisement or mentoring? If you had that – or a similar opportunity – again, what, if anything, would you do differently?

About mentoring

Mentoring is, in many ways, similar to advisement yet to some degree, distinct. For example, mentoring, like advisement is defined and carried out in diverse ways (Benishek et al., 2004; Crisp & Cruz, 2009; Moss et al., 1999; Vaccaro & Camba-Kelsay, 2018; Walker et al., 2001). In addition, you can have multiple advisors and mentors. However, mentoring is typically broader in scope with the potential to develop into a deeper professional relationship (Jones et al., 2018). You may be assigned and will often have additional opportunities to work with mentors and potential mentors such as advanced peers, librarians, and others with institutional and/or professional knowledge, while pursuing your education and at various points during your career. Perhaps the most important distinction between *student* advisement and mentoring is that mentoring is not limited to students. Many highly successful people in business and related fields work with mentors to further develop their competencies (Crisp & Cruz, 2009). Similarly, some highly successful people volunteer to serve as mentors as a way of sharing their expertise and experience (Moss et al., 1999; Vaccaro & Camba-Kelsay, 2018; Walker et al., 2001). Despite the frequently reported positive outcomes of mentoring, the most effective mentoring relationships are informal (Jones et al., 2018), voluntarily develop (Benishek et al., 2004; Farrelly, 2008), and are mutually rewarding and reinforcing (Benishek et al., 2004), respecting power differentials (Albana, 2021; Benishek et al., 2004; Cook et al., 2018), including race, gender, and other human differences (Albana, 2021; Benishek et al., 2004; Moss et al., 1999; Sedlacek, 2004; Vaccaro & Camba-Kelsay, 2018).

Finding mentors

How do you find mentors? Or advisors who might take that role? We recommend starting with those individuals around you. Faculty members, in particular, take mentoring the next generation of professionals in their field seriously. In addition, we encourage you to investigate advisement/mentoring opportunities offered by your academic program or college/university; student and/or professional organizations (such as APA, APS, and divisions); and, when relevant, your employer. It's also helpful to ask professors and advanced peers, who are also potential mentors, for additional referrals and, overall, tap into your social/professional support system – including relevant online professional networking sites (if you are already a professional or working). Seek out people with shared interests – and don't be afraid to branch out and make your own connections or contact an individual you believe may be better positioned to help you. Similar to other professional relationships, the prospect of rapport and a mutually rewarding relationship are keys to developing and maintaining effective advising and mentoring relationships.

Making the most of mentoring relationships

In working with advisors and mentors, it's important to consider the outcomes you want to achieve – and do your part. As an advisee and mentee or protégé (Ng et al., 2020; Schlosser & Gelso, 2001), it's your responsibility to prepare for meetings and other interactions, reflect and act on the feedback you receive, and maintain open communication with your advisor and mentor. In short, these and similar relationships work best when you show your willingness to engage and follow through. Beyond the basics of advisement, some advisors and many mentors, formal and informal, are happy to support your educational as well as professional development. Many will share information, provide guidance, and help you think through complicated decisions. Some may also serve as a confidant and sounding board, helping you tap into multiple perspectives, and otherwise increase your professional opportunities, including network.

BOX 7.2

Reflection on Good Mentoring

Reflection: Think about one or more good mentoring experience(s) you experienced or heard about.

Questions to consider: How did you become connected to this individual? What was most helpful about the mentoring relationship? What was your role? If you had that – or a similar opportunity – again, what, if anything, would you do differently? What type of mentoring would be helpful to you now or in the near future? How might you seek out that type of advisement or mentoring?

PROFESSORS

Students often approach faculty members through the lens of their prior experience in high school, not realizing that there is a difference in the roles and expectations of these two types of instructors (Cox, 2009). Getting to know faculty members as advisors, mentors, and instructors can help you to be more effective in moving toward your career goal. In fact, faculty mentoring is associated with educational and career success (Barnett, 2008; Jones et al., 2018). Moreover, professors and other instructors generally appreciate common courtesies such as letting them know when you need to miss class or might have difficulties with an assignment. Remember, they don't read minds. Moreover, most professors in this area are more than happy to help you and are actually quite patient and inventive in working with you to promote understanding – and your success.

So, let's talk a bit about who these people are and some of the benefits of engaging with your professors in a more positive manner. Professors come in all shapes, sizes, backgrounds, demographic characteristics, and personalities, although in many U.S. institutions they are still predominantly European American and male. They also have diverse interests – even though psychology faculty tend to have an interest in some aspect of psychology, and often, the human mind and functioning. Most also enjoy working with and getting to know students!

If you want to learn a bit about full-time (and some adjunct) faculty members' interests, find your institution's website for the department and look for the link that says faculty, faculty and staff, or something similar. This page typically contains basic information about the faculty – their office addresses, phone numbers, and emails. In many instances, it contains information about their educational backgrounds, research interests, and perhaps a link to their curriculum vitae (CV), webpage with more information about their research, or to their lab website.

Typically, full-time faculty engage in teaching, research, and service. Many consider advisement and mentoring a major part of their teaching role. Faculty members advise in a number of ways. First, they may provide direct academic advising to students, depending upon the way advising is set up at the institution. Second, they may serve as faculty advisors to student organizations. Third, they may have a research team on which students can volunteer or work to gain research experience and receive both advising and mentoring in addition to developing their research and critical thinking skills. Lastly, you may meet a faculty member in class or stop by their office to chat (that's one of the purposes of office hours) and benefit from some impromptu advising (and, often, mentoring, too!).

On a related note, many students confuse the role of an adjunct faculty member with that of a full-time professor (or other teaching faculty). Although there are exceptions, most adjunct faculty are hired to teach one or more specific classes on a semester-to-semester basis. As such, they rarely have formal responsibility for advising, mentoring, or other student services. So, anything beyond teaching they do is a bonus – and not to be expected.

BOX 7.3

Mini-Exercise – Learning About Your Professors

1. Using your favorite internet browser, click over to the department in which your major can be found (e.g., Psychology Department).
2. Look for the link on that page that takes you to a list of Faculty members and click to go to the Faculty listing page.
3. Look for the name of your instructor, advisor, or another faculty member about whom you'd like to learn. When you find their name, look for information about that professor. See if the departmental listing includes a link to an additional website or the professor's CV.
4. Review the information and consider what it tells you about the faculty member's interests, research, and teaching. How might this information help you to see how you might be able to learn from them, obtain advice from them, or receive assistance and/or mentoring from them?

Faculty roles and you

We'll start with teaching, since the primary reason many people enroll in a college or university is to take classes and learn from faculty members. Faculty members must have expertise in the field for which they are hired to teach (e.g., psychology). In addition, they often teach courses in their subfield or area of expertise (e.g., developmental psychology, forensic psychology) and are there to help you learn and master the course content and, when applicable, develop skills. They can best do that when you are prepared for class, ask thoughtful questions, and engage in the activities and assigned tasks. Your instructor can assist you through conversations during/after class or during their office hours. Professors can be helpful even if you aren't having difficulties with the class. For example, if the topic is interesting to you, we suggest meeting with the professor to discuss your interest and asking for ideas about how to learn more about whatever interests you. If this is within their area of expertise, they may have a lot to say and they may help you to learn more about the topic.

Most full-time faculty members also provide service work to support the institution, the community, and/or their profession. While some of these service activities are focused on their profession (e.g., reviewing journal articles for publication), others are more student-centered. Two other examples might be helpful. First, if you look around, you will see many student organizations on campus. Each one is required to have a faculty sponsor to support students and help them achieve the goals of the organization. Second, the psychology department may sponsor opportunities to engage in community service. A faculty member may be responsible for coordinating and organizing these experiences so that the student can make the most of them. There are often opportunities to engage with or assist faculty as they conduct these tasks and provide opportunities to develop leadership and management skills that will serve you long after you've graduated.

Faculty members tend to be curious and so often have research projects – the type and quantity often depend upon the type of institution. These are opportunities for you to learn more about a particular topic, learn how to do research, and/or increase your critical thinking and analytic skills. Helping a faculty member with their research is an opportunity for you to develop skills that will be important in both the workplace and in graduate school. Volunteering on a faculty member's research team can also open opportunities for attending conferences, presenting, and, yes, might even lead to publishing an article in a professional journal. Moreover, as we've shared in other places, research experience is generally a plus if graduate school is in your future.

BOX 7.4

Mini-Exercise: Getting to Know Your Professors

1. Choose a professor with whom you feel comfortable.

(Continued)

BOX 7.4 *(Continued)*

2. If you have them for class, stay after class for a few minutes, or, if not, go to their office (physically or virtually) and chat with them for a few minutes. As an aside, that's what office hours (which almost all full-time professors post) are for!
3. Here are some topics you might use to start a conversation:
    a. You could ask them how long they've been at this institution and what attracted them to working here.
    b. Is this course in your specialty area? If so, ask how they became interested in it. If not, ask what their specialty area is and how they became interested in that area.
    c. You could ask them about what they did at your current or planned level of education that helped them to be successful.
    d. You could ask them to recommend ways to learn more about the topic (or, a subtopic) that the class is covering.
4. Don't forget to write a thank you note/email and/or let them know the results of following up on their suggestions.

To summarize, faculty members typically have many roles in colleges and universities. A significant number of those roles provide opportunities for students to interact with and learn from faculty members. In particular, you can make the most of advising and mentoring opportunities by choosing to interact with faculty members in one or more ways. While this may seem obvious to some of you, others of you might be less comfortable with this idea, so the next section will help you to become more comfortable with the idea of interacting with and developing professional relationships with your faculty members.

Overcoming fear: understanding professors

We often fear that with which we are least familiar – and many students fear (and therefore avoid) talking with faculty members (Cox, 2009). Often students put faculty members up on pedestals – seeing them as "all knowing". This couldn't be further from the truth. While psychology faculty generally have a broad and general knowledge of the field, they often have specialized knowledge in one subfield, such as cognitive psychology, physiological psychology, or child and adolescent development. They likely know much less about other fields or topics, for example, the human–computer interface. Similarly, they bring varying degrees of interpersonal skills, different styles of teaching (often learned from the teachers they admired), and theories about student learning to their job. Faculty enter academia knowing that they will be working with students in many roles and many keep in mind the importance of preparing students for the world of work, while supporting students' growth and development. This balancing act is affected by the roles and expectations of their institution discussed earlier. So. . .

1   Faculty members are not your parents or your boss – those are different roles.
2   Faculty members are generally not privy to the workings of the administration – likewise, these are two very different roles.
3   Faculty members do not know everything about psychology or their specialty. There is so much to know that most faculty members continue to study and learn long after they obtain their degree.
4   Faculty members have lives outside the institution that requires their attention (e.g., families).
5   Faculty members have a commitment to helping students develop their knowledge, skills, and abilities related to psychology – often in very different ways from one another.
6   Faculty members must monitor where they put their time in order to ensure that they can do their job (i.e., fulfill the institutional expectations and agreements that were made when they were hired).

Overcoming a fear can be accomplished in several ways. We'll list them first and then we'll talk further about them.

1   Allow yourself to recognize that your faculty members were once in your very place – an undergraduate (or other) student trying to figure out how to be successful and how to interact with their faculty members.
2   Reflect on what might be disconcerting you about faculty members, then speak with someone who can assist you in better understanding the situation so you can decide your next steps.
3   Find a way to interact more with one or more faculty member.
4   Learn more about what it takes to be a faculty member.

Let's take the first suggestion – recognizing that faculty members weren't born as they are now. Faculty members were once students, like yourself, who have chosen this position as their occupation or career and are trying to do the best they can – just as you are trying to do the best you can at learning about psychology. It's not that they don't know more than you – they do because they've been studying psychology and related topics longer than you – it's that they are just as human as you. They may make snap judgments like you, or mis-remember things in the heat of the moment like you, or forget things like you. If you can recognize that someone is more like you than not, then it's easier to connect with them. Once you've become comfortable with the fact that faculty members are like you in some ways, you can begin to incorporate the ways in which they are different. This includes the fact that they have responsibilities to you, their department, the university, and their profession that often affect their interactions with you, specifically, or students in general.

The second suggestion, reflecting on what is disconcerting you about one or more faculty members, allows you to separate out a fear or concern that may be affecting your interactions with all faculty members – in other words an assumption or belief that may be affecting your ability to build a relationship with faculty members – or, something about a specific faculty member that is affecting your ability to connect with that specific faculty member. If you find that it seems to be a more global reaction to faculty members, you might want to reflect on the specifics and evaluate the confirming or disconfirming evidence – is this belief true of the sample of professors to whom I have access? Speaking with upper-level students or friends, or even someone at the counseling center may give you enough information to help you to see faculty members both more realistically and/or more individually. If your concern is with a particular faculty member, the previously mentioned options also may be helpful. In addition, consulting with your advisor or other trusted faculty member may help generate new ideas and solutions.

With regards to the third suggestion, many times, exposure to someone unknown can help you to better understand that person and develop a relationship with that individual. You could take a class that they teach, volunteer on their research team, or even make an appointment to learn more about that faculty member, to ask for their thoughts about succeeding in your studies, or to learn more about their area of expertise and/or research efforts. These suggestions all put you in a position to engage with the faculty member in a structured way that should result in you learning more about that individual and, hopefully, beginning to develop a professional relationship with that individual. These suggestions are also relevant for the fourth suggestion mentioned earlier.

Before we leave this topic, we'd like to make two further suggestions. First, don't forget that faculty members have their own intersecting identities and cultural backgrounds. Depending upon the institution, you may find greater or lesser diversity, as well as different kinds of diversity among faculty members. This will also impact the way they interact with you. A respectful inquiry to see if the faculty is interested in sharing information about their unique backgrounds can be another way to connect with a faculty member and reduce your fears or anxieties. Second, if you are curious about the role or occupation of being a professor or faculty member, you can learn more about this occupation from the career counseling or career services office who generally maintain materials about different occupations. You can also find occupational information from the Bureau of Labor Statistics' O*net online (www.onetonline.org).

Benefits of building relationships with professors

Why should you take the time and energy to build a relationship with any of your faculty members? Faculty members may be able to provide opportunities to develop skills and obtain experiences that employers and graduate programs value. They are able to provide letters of recommendation attesting to your knowledge, skills, and abilities to enhance your employment and/or graduate school prospects. They often have a network in the field as well. In short, they can provide opportunities that will assist you with your future – both educational and employment-related.

An additional benefit of talking with your professors is that they begin to know you and see you as someone who is committed to your career in this field. That's really important and helpful for several reasons. First of all, faculty see students who take the time to ask questions and develop a clear understanding of a topic, whether through visiting with the professor or engaging with the professor in class or in their research team/lab, as committed to that major. Faculty are on the lookout for students like that, as these are the students most likely to benefit from additional mentoring and support. Thus, as you demonstrate your interest in learning in your major, they may let you know about different opportunities, whether for scholarships or grants, or special trainings, or even invite you to consider gaining experience through volunteering or working on their research team. In addition, when you need those letters of recommendation to apply for a summer internship, job, or graduate school, you now have someone who knows both how committed you are to your field and who has had experience of your academic work. Thus, they can write you a strong and authentic letter, which often makes a true difference in the opportunities that come your way. So, displaying motivation and persistence can result in support and mentorship to help you be successful in your chosen field. This is further augmented by your efforts to develop advanced professional behaviors, which we'll talk about next.

Building professional relationships with professors

Before we discuss what a healthy relationship with professors looks like, it is important to note that relationships with professors vary. Just as some professors are outgoing and gregarious, while others are quiet and reserved, faculty members have their own conceptualization or understanding of advising and mentoring, as well as their own interpersonal style. Professors may be focused on supporting you through your degree, helping you to develop skills to support your education, and/or helping you to prepare for the next step in your career. These are all legitimate foci for grounding this type of relationship. These foci might be considered the "content" around which the relationship revolves. In addition, some faculty members will want to learn all about you and may share a lot about their own personal lives. These faculty members work on the belief that they are helping you to see how you can be both a person and a professional. Other faculty members prefer to keep their personal lives separate from their professional lives and believe that you should have that option too. In working with them, you will likely find they are aware that some people are more selective with whom they share personal information, so they attempt to respect their own as well students' boundaries. Both types of faculty members (and those in between) have your best interests at heart, while having a different style of building relationships (Hale et al., 2009; Jordan, 2000). In addition, some faculty members define their relationships with students more narrowly or more clearly with regards to the scope of the relationship, for example, approaching an academic advising relationship differently than a mentoring relationship or research team supervision relationship. Thus, unless your professor explicitly establishes the boundaries of a particular the relationship, feel free to ask. The goal is to be clear about how to work best with your professor.

That said, a healthy professional relationship with your professor is one in which both individuals understand the parameters of the relationship and have respect for each other's roles and responsibilities in that relationship (Hoffman, 2014). Such a relationship is one in which both parties feel heard, their viewpoints taken into account, while both external realities and the expertise of both parties are acknowledged and incorporated into the relationship. Both individuals have a degree of commitment to the relationship and intend to put in effort to sustain it. So, what does all this mean for you? It means that you will benefit most from the relationship if you and the professor are defining the relationship in the same way. You can ask a question such as, "I know that professors work with students in different ways. So that I can be most effective, I'd like to know how you see us working together." Mentioning that you are aware that faculty members engage in advising, mentoring, supervision, and teaching relationships with students and would like to better understand how that professor prefers to engage with students will also help them to understand where you are coming from and, thus, better respond to your initiation of this conversation.

Setting appropriate boundaries is important in all relationships. It's about respecting each other, understanding the context, and practicing the art of being a professional. Let's start with the basics – time. Both you and your professor only have so much time, due to the 24-hour limit imposed by our world and by the additional responsibilities that both of you carry. It should be noted that while both of you have responsibilities, they are likely different and limit each of you in different ways. That means that neither you nor your faculty member will be available to each other at the snap of a finger. This means that you should not wait until the last minute to try to meet with your professor. Also, when you and your professor set a time to meet, both of you should have the professionalism to keep that appointment unless a true emergency intervenes. Should that happen, letting the other know as soon as possible is only polite.

One of the most challenging situations faced by both students and professors is negotiating how and how much they will work with each other. This is most often the case when the student engages in mentoring or research with the professor, although it can happen with academic advising, too. Your faculty member often presents opportunities they think will advance your career and development. They may even be specific in letting you know about opportunities that may benefit your career long after you finish your degree. The faculty member expects you to discuss the opportunity with them, evaluate it and your time commitments, as well as its impact on your career goals. The decision is yours. However, if you say "no" to too many things, the professor will stop bringing you opportunities, as you have made it clear that you are not interested in them. So, how do you decide? First, be realistic about what you need and want from your degree. A student who needs a degree to keep their job is very different than the student who is looking to go on to graduate school and have a research career. Second, being clear about your priorities and goals helps you align your actions and commitments with those goals. This also gives you a basis for having a conversation with your professor about how to develop the abilities, knowledge, and skills to move to the next level of your career.

Working with a faculty member as a research team member, work-study assistant, and the like can assist you in getting to know the faculty member, as well as the faculty member getting to know you. A good relationship, especially one in which the faculty member has had time to observe your work and skills can help when recommendations are needed, as well as building your skillset. The more a faculty knows about your interests, goals, and objectives, the more they can assist you in moving your career forward.

CLASSMATES AND PEERS

Don't underestimate the potential of positive relationships with classmates and peers. Those who do, miss out! They miss potentially rewarding relationships, learning opportunities, and, long-term, professional network possibilities. Let's start with the potential for rewarding relationships. What brings – and keeps – people together? Yes, you're right. They generally have something in common, most often shared interests and/or goals. Back to classmates, people taking the same class(es) as you – what do you have in common? Yes, that's a basic question – but you're taking the same class. Could you help each other with that class? Share notes when one of you has to be absent? Clarify the requirements for an assignment? Prepare for class? Study together? You get the idea. Here's a suggestion: when you start a class, take the risk to introduce yourself to a classmate, offer your contact information (your college/university email is safe), and welcome the other person's (you could even ask). Get to know your classmates and peers, what they do well, their interests, and, if relevant, particular expertise. Beyond the immediate benefits, classmates and peers are your potential future professional peers – and potentially a key part of your professional resources and network.

Beyond class-related interactions, positive relationships with classmates and peers (people at your level in similar circumstances, both broadly defined) have the potential to enrich your college experience – and life! As just one example, classmates and peers understand the challenges and opportunities inherent in your shared experience such as taking the same classes, pursuing the same or a similar degree, and/or career paths. Shared experiences are more likely to lead to meaningful and mutually beneficial relationships than other types of interactions (Lester et al., 2019). In fact, some of our longest standing friends (that we're intentionally not calling *old* friends), are friendships that grew from shared experiences. Moreover, classmates and peers can put challenges – and opportunities – into perspective, letting you know that you are not the only person who's intimidated, scared, happy, excited, or fill in the blank, or otherwise being human (Yalom & Lezscz, 2005). Classmates and peers can also empathize with challenges, offer perspectives you might not have considered – and, perhaps the most fun, help you put your accomplishments in perspective – and celebrate with you! And you can do the same for your classmates, peers, and friends. For example, you could say (or hear) "What do you mean you 'only' got a B? That was a challenging project, you learned a lot doing it, and you earned that B. Let's go celebrate!" How could you turn that down?

Moreover, as discussed earlier, humans are social animals (Aronson & Aronson, 2012), who need to feel we belong (Maslow, 1943, 1968) that we *fit* in with our environment and the organization as a whole (Holland, 1997; Holland & Holland, 1977; Tinto, 1993, 2007). Most, if not all of us, to one degree or another, also want to feel we *matter*, to be recognized and appreciated, by people and institutions (made up of people) who matter to us (Anderson et al., 2012). Overall, healthy professional peer relationships, from college through professional life, offer a sense of belonging and mattering with associated benefits such as reduced stress (Anderson et al., 2012). Peer relationships can also inspire healthy competition and thus enhance your – and your peers' – performance. Friends have a dynamic way of uplifting your spirts while simultaneously pushing you to be the best version of yourself. In addition, professional relationships with peers are often less formal and structured – and can evolve into friendships.

Friendships, like peer and other professional relationships, take time, respect, self- and other-awareness, mutuality, and communication to develop. However, some people try to short circuit this process in their attempts to belong, fit in, matter, and get ahead. Some try too hard, for example coming on too strong, which can have the effect of turning off the very people they are trying to impress. Others present a false version of themselves and, in so doing, lose part of themselves. Still others may egregiously violate their own value systems. Less overtly, some college students and professionals fall into the trap of choosing short-term benefits, like social popularity, over the long-term benefits of dedicated work and planning, in their attempts to fit in with their peers. The long-term consequences of such patterns, as illustrated by Armstrong and Hamilton's (2013) ethnographic study of socio-economically diverse college women in their aptly titled book, *Paying for the party*, are particularly pronounced for students with fewer social and economic resources to cushion and support a recovery. The lesson is clear – think long-term, plan, and work your plan!

STARTING YOUR PROFESSIONAL SUPPORT NETWORK

Much like your family, friends, and neighbors have supported you growing up, professional networks support your development and success in psychology. Below are suggestions for developing your professional network:

Building relationships with your peers

Other students majoring in psychology with you are likely to continue on into the field, or, at least take other classes with you. Take opportunities to engage in group discussions, projects, sharing notes, group study sessions and the like to build relationships with those whose interests are similar to yours as discussed earlier. In addition, there are advantages to joining and actively participating in student psychology clubs, professional organizations, and, when you qualify, professional honor societies such as Psi Chi. To illustrate, these organizations often provide a forum to connect with like-minded people to discuss topics of shared interest, and work with each other toward shared goals, and otherwise engage in professional development. Some also offer opportunities to present, apply for grants, engage in community service and/or advocacy work, and more. Check them out!

Attending workshops and conferences . . . and possibly presenting

Workshops and conferences are another excellent way of meeting others and learning more about various aspects of psychology. These can be at the local, state, regional, national, or international level. To get started, consider attending one or more local conferences to get a sense of how they work. There may even be opportunities to present (usually your research work) on your campus. This is another area in which good relationships with advanced peers, your advisor, professors, and/or research team leader can be helpful. They're often happy to share information and resources.

How do you do this when you have a family and/or other obligations?

Managing competing priorities for those with family or other care-taking relationships is challenging – to say the least. Having a supportive family and/or organization can make all the difference in the world. Thus, helping your family, in particular, to understand what it takes to obtain a degree and be successful in the field requires intentional and ongoing conversations so they better understand your commitments and goals. Sometimes, those who only see that you are gone or locked in your office or other work space may be having difficulty understanding what it will take to reach those goals. We encourage you to continue reading the next chapter to learn more about this topic.

CHAPTER SUMMARY

In this chapter we've discussed four types of professional relationships: those with advisors and mentors, faculty members, peers, and taking the first steps toward building your professional network outside of the university. In all types of relationships, your authentic engagement can both enrich your life and help you move forward in your career path. In discussing these relationships, we've also tried to share methods for building and thinking about those relationships. We encourage you to use the exercises and reflections included here to deepen your understanding of how relationships have supported and enhanced your life to date.

EXERCISES

1   Introduce yourself to a classmate you'd like to know better.
2   Review your academic and career plans (from Chapter 6), identify one professional organization to join or become more active with, and make a commitment to introduce yourself to someone you haven't yet met at a meeting/gathering this semester. Do that and follow up with a "nice to meet you" email.

Next steps: the advanced move

1 Introduce yourself to someone whose career you admire, and ask, politely of course, for an informational interview.

REFERENCES

Albana, H. F. (2021). *Faculty perceptions of dyadic advising relationships, power, and cultural consciousness on college student learning outcomes* (Unpublished doctoral dissertation). Seton Hall University.

Anderson, P., Goodman, J. P., & Schlossberg, N. K. (2012). *Counseling adults in transition, linking schlossberg's theory with practice in a diverse world* (4th ed.). Springer.

Armstrong, E. A., & Hamilton, L. T. (2013). *Paying for the party: How college maintains inequality.* Harvard University Press.

Aronson, E., & Aronson, J. (2012). *The social animal* (11th ed.). Worth.

Barnett, J. E. (2008). Mentoring, boundaries, and multiple relationships: Opportunities and challenges. *Mentoring & Tutoring: Partnership in Learning, 16*(1), 3–16. https://doi.org/10.1080/13611260701800900

Benishek, L. A., Bieschke, K. J., Park, J., & Slattery, S. M. (2004). A multicultural feminist model of mentoring. *Journal of Multicultural Counseling and Development, 32*, 428–442.

Cook, R. M., McKibben, W. B., & Wind, S. A. (2018). Supervisee perception of power in clinical supervision: The power dynamics in supervision scale. *Training and Education in Professional Psychology, 12*(3), 188–195. https://doi.org/10.1037/tep0000201

Cox, R. D. (2009). *The college fear factor.* Harvard University Press.

Crisp, G., & Cruz, I. (2009). Mentoring college students: A critical review of the literature between 1990 and 2007. *Research in Higher Education, 50*(6), 525–545. https://doi.org/10.1007/s11162-009-9130-2

Farrelly, M. J. (2008). The relationship between the advisory working alliance and the ability to cope among psychology doctoral students. *Dissertation Abstracts International: Section B: The Sciences and Engineering, 69*(2-B), 1322.

Hale, M. D., Graham, D. L., & Johnson, D. M. (2009). Are students more satisfied with academic advising when there is congruence between current and preferred advising styles? *College Student Journal, 43*(2), 313.

Hoffman, E. M. (2014). Faculty and student relationships: Context matters. *College Teaching, 62*(1), 13–19.

Holland, J. L. (1997). *Making vocational choices: A theory of vocational personalities and work environments* (3rd ed.). Psychological Assessment Resources.

Holland, J. L., & Holland, J. E. (1977). Distributions of personalities within occupations and fields of study. *Vocational Guidance Quarterly, 25*(3), 226–231. https://doi.org/10.1002/j.2164-585X.1977.tb00945.x

Jones, H. A., Perrin, P. B., Heller, M. B., Hailu, S., & Barnett, C. (2018). Black psychology graduate students' lives matter: Using informal mentoring to create an inclusive climate amidst national race-related events. *Professional Psychology: Research and Practice, 49*(1), 75–82. https://doi.org/10.1037/pro0000169

Jordan, P. (2000). Advising college students in the 21st century. *NACADA Journal, 20*(2), 21–30.

Kirp, D. (2019). *The college dropout scandal.* Oxford University Press.

Kuhn, T., Gordon, V. N., & Webber, J. (2006). The advising and counseling continuum: Triggers for referral. *NACADA Journal, 26*(1), 24–31.

Lester, A. M., Goodloe, C. L., Johnson, H. E., & Deutsch, N. L. (2019). Understanding mutuality: Unpacking relational processes in youth mentoring relationships. *Journal of Community Psychology, 47*(1), 147–162. https://doi.org/10.1002/jcop.22106

Maslow, A. H. (1943). A theory of human motivation. *Psychological Review, 50*(4), 370–396. https://doi.org/10.1037/h0054346

Maslow, A. H. (1968). *Toward a psychology of being* (2nd ed.). Van Nostrand Reinhold Co.

Moss, P., Debres, K. J., Cravey, A., Hyndman, J., Hirschboeck, K. K., & Masucci, M. (1999). Toward mentoring as feminist praxis: Strategies for ourselves and others. *Journal of Geography in Higher Education, 23*(3), 413–427.

Ng, Y. X., Koh, Z. Y. K., Yap, H. W., Tay, K. T., Tan, X. H., Ong, Y. T., . . . Krishna, L. (2020). Assessing mentoring: A scoping review of mentoring assessment tools in internal medicine between 1990 and 2019. *PLoS One, 15*(5), 1–18. https://doi.org/10.1371/journal.pone.0232511

Schlosser, L. Z., & Gelso, C. J. (2001). Measuring the working alliance in advisor – Advisee relationships in graduate school. *Journal of Counseling Psychology, 48*(2), 157–167. https://doi.org/1 0.1037//0O22-0167.48.2.157

Sedlacek, W. E. (2004). *Beyond the big test: Noncognitive assessment in higher education.* Jossey-Bass.

Tinto, V. (1993). *Leaving college: Rethinking the causes and cures of student attrition* (2nd ed.). University of Chicago Press.

Tinto, V. (2007). Research and practice of student retention: What next? *Journal of College Student Retention: Research, Theory & Practice, 8*(1), 1–19.

Vaccaro, A., & Camba-Kelsay, M. J. (2018). Cultural competence and inclusivity in mentoring, coaching, and advising. *New Directions for Student Leadership, 158,* 87–97. https://doi.org/10.1002/yd.20290

Walker, K. L., Wright, G., & Hanley, J. H. (2001). The professional preparation of African American graduate students: A student perspective. *Professional Psychology: Research and Practice, 32*(6), 581–584. https://doi.org/10.1037/0735-7028.32.6.581

Yalom, I. D., & Lezscz, M. (2005). *The theory and practice of group psychotherapy* (5th ed.). Basic Books.

CHAPTER 8

Relationships in your personal life

ORIENTING QUESTIONS

1. What are some things you can do maintain healthy personal relationships while you're working toward your career in psychology?

2. Who are the most important people in your personal life? Who matters to you?

3. How can you maintain relationships with your family and friends while pursuing your career goals?

4. What are some other ways to expand your personal network?

DOI: 10.4324/9780429296413-11

INTRODUCTION

This chapter focuses on building and maintaining effective relationships in your personal life. This includes family, friends, and other important people in your life. If you're wondering why this book on careers in psychology includes a chapter on personal relationships, the short answer, as we shared in Chapter 7, is that humans are social (Aronson & Aronson, 2012). To one degree or another, we need to belong (Maslow, 1943, 1968), to fit in (Holland, 1997; Holland & Holland, 1977), to matter (Anderson et al., 2012), and to be in *relationships* with other people.

Personal relationships are both deceptively simple and complicated. On one hand, we all have relationships. On the other hand, there are many types of personal relationships, with varying degrees and levels of connection, commitment, as well as differences in the ways they develop, are maintained, and so much more. Then consider the incredible number and array of possibilities when diverse, complex, and unique people interact!

Given these possibilities, personal relationships can inspire the full range of human emotion – and artistic expression from joy through pain and despair. We can learn from our own as well as others' relationships and our perceptions of them. We can grow, heal, and enhance our self- and other-understanding in a full range of healthy relationships with others (Comstock et al., 2008; Yalom & Lezscz, 2005). Relationships can also be perfunctory, obligatory, disappointing, and harmful in many ways and at various levels.

Psychologists contributed to significant theoretical and empirical advances in the understanding of personal relationships over the last few decades (Vangelisti & Perlman, 2018) – so personal relationships are another specialty area in psychology to consider! As a full review of the literature on personal relationships is beyond the scope of this chapter, we've focused this chapter on practical guidance and unwritten rules of developing and maintaining important personal relationships as well as preventing and mitigating challenges many people experience while developing and maintaining careers, including as students.

HEALTHY PERSONAL RELATIONSHIPS

Personal relationships, for the purpose of this chapter, are those that, at least to some degree, are developed or maintained outside your professional roles and responsibilities. We use the phrase *to some degree* intentionally. For example, most familial relationships are personal, even if you work with or for family members. At the same time, professional peer relationships have the potential to become more personal, sometimes developing into long-standing friendships and romantic relationships. Social, including family, relationships are associated with career and life satisfaction and, by extension, success (Chan et al., 2020).

BOX 8.1

Reflection on Healthy Relationships

Reflection: Think about your healthy relationships. What makes (or made) them good? How can you build on that success?

Healthy relationships are characterized and enhanced by "effective communication and the expression of positive emotions and sentiments such as appreciation, gratitude, and admiration" (Cannon & Murray, 2019, p. 310). As such, personal relationships, like all relationships, require a range of positive behaviors, in evolving social, cultural, and political contexts (Cannon & Murray, 2019; Comstock et al., 2008; hooks, 1984). Given this tall order, healthy personal relationships are founded on self- and other-awareness, respect, and an ongoing commitment to personal development, all of which are integral to careers in psychology, particularly graduate training in health service psychology and professional practice in psychology (APA, 2017) as well as many related fields (e.g., ACA, 2014). At its best, this includes enhancing your awareness of your inner world, attending to your own racial/ethnic and other identity development (Helms, 2004, 2017; Ponterotto et al., 1995), and committing to the ongoing process of acknowledging and addressing hidden biases (Jackson et al., 2003; Malinen & Johnston, 2013). Overall, self-awareness, which is foundational to developing and maintaining healthy relationships, generally benefits you, your relationships, and your community in the long term. It also has the potential to make a positive difference in the larger society.

If you have experienced positive relationships in whole or in part, you have a significant advantage in life (Lachman et al., 2015; Sedlacek, 2004), which is something to celebrate and share. However, you may have had – or still have – challenging experiences that don't have to continue. Regardless of your past and current experiences, we encourage you to invest in your own well-being. This can include building upon, expanding, and, when helpful, changing your support system. If you find you need or want to build your interpersonal skills or otherwise would like additional support, consider engaging the services of a licensed mental health professional or psychologist. If you're a student, your campus counseling will be an excellent resource. Furthermore, if you (or someone you know) is in danger, please get away and get help (not necessarily in that order).

As philosophers have observed for millennia and more than a few psychologists have observed over the past century, we change others and are changed through our relationships. Relationships are at the heart of psychotherapy and counseling (Comstock et al., 2008; Kottler, 2017; Yalom & Lezscz, 2005) so much so that recent advances in psychotherapy outcome theory and research builds on what we know about authentic personal, real relationships (Comstock et al., 2008; Fuertes et al., 2019; Gelso, 2002; Gelso et al., 2018; Yalom & Lezscz, 2005) associated with improved psychotherapeutic outcomes (Gelso, 2018).

"The meeting of two personalities is like the contact of two chemical substances. If there is any reaction, both are transformed" – C. G. Jung

Personal and professional relationships

Some people prefer or feel that it's in their own best interest (e.g., as self-protection) to maintain a clear separation between their personal and professional relationships. Others are open to the potential for friendship with professional peers. Still others actively invite or encourage the development of professional into personal relationships. For most students and early career professionals without supervisory responsibility, this is an individual choice, taking into account the recommendations for professional relationships in Chapter 7.

For example, having a friendly lunch with a professional peer is generally positive. It might also be positive for your relationship to develop into a friendship or even romantic relationship. At the same time, it's smart to proactively set boundaries consistent with your values and relevant institutional policies. For many people, the college and early career years offer unprecedented opportunities to meet many new people, concurrently with the responsibility of making good decisions about who you'll spend your time with – and how. It's smart to plan ahead, and when applicable, set up a mutually supportive buddy system and consult with trusted and knowledgeable mentors before making important decisions or doing things (like changing your major or dropping out) that you might later regret (Armstrong & Hamilton, 2013).

In addition, as you begin to take on supervisory and similar roles, it's particularly important to more fully consider the ethical and political implications of blurring the boundaries between professional and personal relationships. That is one of the reasons many people rightly caution against mixing business with pleasure. Similarly, if you have supervisory or other evaluative responsibilities, you also have the responsibility to act in accordance with relevant law as well as your, your employer's, and your profession's ethical principles. For example, the *APA Ethical Principles of Psychologists and Code of Conduct* (2017) explicitly prohibits psychologists from engaging in exploitive behavior and calls upon psychologists to use their power and professional positions for the good of all.

In addition to professional and expert power held by many in supervisory roles, it's also important to recognize the often-unacknowledged power differentials associated with different racial/ethnic, gender, ability status, and class identities or perceived identities – and the ways in which power affects or could affect relationships. Power is also relative and contextual. What this means is you may have, or perceive that you have, more or less power than another person, and this may change depending on the context. As an example, college students generally have less power to decide course content and delivery than their professors – yet they always have power to make the best of those relationships, as shared in Chapter 7, and do their part to prevent abuses of power, seek help, and, when necessary, work to ameliorate any harm. Moreover, in the best-case scenarios, that both of us are grateful to have experienced (from both sides), graduates develop their own professional and expert power with the potential to become professional peers and, occasionally friends, with former professors.

FAMILY AND FRIENDS

BOX 8.2

Reflection on Maintaining Connections

Reflection: What are some ways you can keep connected with your important people? With everything you need to do? As you develop and change?

There are at least as many ways to define family and friends as personal relationships, maybe more. Respecting the range of human experience and decisions, we encourage you to apply *your* definitions of family and friends, including those who've created their own family of choice, as you read, reflect, and engage in the recommended activities. Since these categories often overlap, we'll address personal relationships with family and friends first, then move, in the next section, to other personal relationships.

For some people, coming up with a list of their most important personal relationships is easy. For others, it's much more complicated. Regardless of your situation, we recommend making a list of your closest, most important, family and friend relationships, including the people you have responsibilities for (e.g., children) or otherwise count on you (e.g., spouse, parents). This list is for you alone. No one else has to see it (in fact, it's probably better if some don't) or know how you define closest, most important, family, or friends. It's also important to think of it as a work-in-progress, that you can adapt, revise, update, and otherwise change when helpful so it doesn't have to be perfect. The goal is to get this list out of your head into a format you can refer to and use as a springboard for next steps. Your journal (remember that?) might be a great place for this! The exercises at the end of this chapter offer additional ways to make meaning of your list.

A note about language and inclusion: Given the diversity, complexity, and range of personal relationships, we've primarily used the phrase *important people* to refer to the people on your important people list. We've also used the phrase *loved ones* to refer to close family (however you define that) and friends (and community members) on that list. If either or both of these phrases don't describe your relationships, please feel free to substitute your own.

Let's start with maintaining the positive relationships you currently have. It's generally more effective and takes less effort to prevent problems than to resolve them (Conyne et al., 2013). As an aside, prevention is another subspecialty in psychology to consider. To

maintain and enhance personal relationships and otherwise prevent relationship problems, it's important to take care of yourself *and* your important people.

We can demonstrate this care by considering and acting to meet, as much as possible,
both our needs and those of our loved ones. For most of us, this includes collaboratively
making the best choices for you *and* your loved ones, particularly those you have responsibility for and with loved ones such as children and spouses. When our loved ones feel
loved, appreciated, and respected, they're more likely to be understanding, supportive,
and happy (or at least ok) with shifts in the relationship (which will come – more on that
later). This is particularly important because, as we discussed in Chapter 7, healthy relationships with family and friends are associated with life and work satisfaction – and
success (Chan et al., 2020).

Some people will tell you, particularly if you're a woman, that healthy relationships
are incompatible with careers, particularly life-long personal relationships such as marriage and children. It is true that some people prioritize, some exclusively, one aspect of
life (i.e., career or family) over the other, for a season or their entire adult lives. Others
work to integrate these and other priorities into their lives. Regardless, work/life integration is a challenging, ongoing process for most of us. Those who succeed make realistic
plans, seek and accept help, and work their plans – all of which we're strongly encouraging and helping you to do. Those who do not succeed with work/life integration have often
attempted to do too much at the same time without the necessary planning and support.
Many people attempting to do too much suffer from stress and stress-related disease,
including burn out. They may also neglect important aspects of their lives such as personal relationships. Yes, some relationships end when one or more parties are pursuing
advanced study or a career. However, as more evidence that correlation doesn't equal
causation (a psychological and research principle), some relationships end, for the same
range of reasons as when neither partner is pursuing advanced study or a career.

At the same time, many people, including us, heard those warnings and, as a result,
committed to investing in our important relationships as well as our careers. We are very
happy to report that both are still working. It wasn't – and isn't – always easy – and your
experience may vary. However, as we've emphasized throughout this book, knowledge is
power. When you know the importance of healthy personal relationships, how to maintain
and develop those relationships, and prevent common challenges, as you will reading this
chapter, *and* commit to doing your best, you will be better positioned to attain your personal as well as professional goals. You can't always have it all at the same time, but you
can have it all sequentially, with good planning, support, work, and more than a little luck.

One of the most important things to consider, as we've emphasized throughout this
book, is being aware of and allocating your time, in accordance with your values, responsibilities, and goals. This is particularly important when you're considering or about to
embark on a new stage or level of work/school and/or relationships. In so doing, you will
have a better idea of how much time you have to share/invest in personal relationships.

We recommend reviewing the action plans you made in Chapter 6, considering if
your plans (long-term through weekly) continue to reflect your values related to relationships and, if not, revise them as necessary. Be sure to include time for the people on your

important people/relationships list, regular events (e.g., holiday gatherings, date nights), and leave room for unexpected opportunities (hey, let's get together), urgent needs, and emergencies. See the exercises at the end of this chapter for additional recommendations and suggestions.

When you've done this, you'll have a better idea of how much time you have (or will have) for each of your important personal relationships at different stages and phases, which for many of us (still) is a reality check. If the available time for personal relationships is insufficient for you, this is a good time to reconsider and, if necessary, revise your action plan. Keep in mind that when you're doing something for the first time (or even after that), it's easy to underestimate how long it will take you – and, as we discussed earlier, it's helpful to include extra time, padding, what one of our family members calls "oops time" so you don't overwhelm yourself and drop balls that are important to you. When you take all of this into account, you can start to figure out how your personal relationships might be affected by your choices – and what might work time-wise for each of them.

The next step is to communicate with the people on your important people list. When you do that, it's helpful to share your goals, important daily activities, challenges, and triumphs at the level of detail that interests each person or group of people. Don't fall into the trap of not sharing because you think your loved ones won't understand (when they might) or, at the other extreme, sharing too much detail and, in so doing, overwhelm or bore them. The best way to figure out how much information is helpful is to take into account the other person's style, your relationship with them, and their interests. You – and the other person(s) are the best judge of that.

As much as possible, it's helpful to sensitively communicate with close family and friends the ways in which your potential or actual decisions, particularly schedule changes, are likely to affect them. Some relationships require or benefit from daily connections, others weekly, and still others, are perfectly fine with much less frequent contact. For example, if you live with family or friends, they're probably in the daily connection category. Moreover, similar to the way you have expectations of family and friends, particularly those you live with or are otherwise close with, they likely have expectations of you – expectations that if left unaddressed (and even sometimes when addressed) can cause relational conflict. And, if you recall, the goal is to prevent relational conflict – and when that's not possible, to address (or begin addressing) your concerns as early as possible, to maintain and ideally enhance your personal relationships.

Ideally, you and your important family and friends have synchronized needs, wants, and scheduling. However, you might be out of sync, which might necessitate you reaching out; which is ok and perhaps better than waiting for others, particularly when you have a lot going on developing and maintaining your career on psychology. It might also necessitate recognizing your family and friends have different needs and interests in developing and sustaining relationships with you. If that's the case, your family member or friend might ask, encourage, or even insist you be available more than you're willing or able to be, which is challenging and often necessitates delicate negotiation and compromise, and highlights the importance of communication. It's also helpful to remember that it's OK, in fact, necessary, to set and uphold personal boundaries to protect your time, and sometimes yourself.

Common challenges and potential solutions

Some common challenges we've seen and experienced in decades of working with college students are when loved ones don't want you to go to school, away to school, take a job or internship, enter a particular field (psychology, what's that?), or something else that's important to you. They may also have a limited understanding of psychology, expect you to know more than you do, defend positions you don't understand (or agree with), or take on roles you're not (yet) qualified for, such as therapist. What are some good ways to respond if your family or friends, particularly those on the important people list, raise any of these concerns?

We recommend listening, particularly active listening to both their words and the emotions they're conveying or attempting to convey. Are they concerned about your safety? Their survival? Something else? Really listening with consideration and, when applicable, love (remember, these are your important personal relationships) will help you understand their concerns. The goal here is to listen to understand, not to respond or make your case in the moment, particularly if the moment is highly emotional. Understanding is the first step toward figuring out your best options for responding. You might respond by reflecting the other person's position – then answer honestly and respectfully. In our experience, these conversations generally take time, negotiation, persuasion, and sometimes compromise. It's also helpful to know that these, as well as the challenges that follow, are common challenges. As such, you wouldn't be the first person to experience this sort of challenge – and may have other personal and professional supports (e.g., an advisor) who can help you figure out your best options for responding positively, preserving the relationship, getting what you need, and ideally some of what you want (which is a win).

Another common challenge is the often-unrealistic expectations of students/new professionals and their loved ones. Sometimes these are matched unrealistic expectations in which both parties (or all, when more than one person is involved) have the same or similar unrealistic expectations. For example, some people naively believe that everything will stay the same when one person is embarking on a new adventure. More often, there's a mismatch between your expectation (e.g., that school and/or this new position will take a lot of time) and loved ones' expectations (e.g., that everything will stay the same). Otherwise, well-informed student/professionals may also experience this mismatch. The best way to address this common challenge is to review your realistic plan, prepare for, and have ongoing respectful conversations with your important people. Similar to our earlier recommendations, it's helpful to actively listen, know you're not alone, and reach out for social and/or professional support. And, as we previously suggested, clearly know and communicate your boundaries.

It's also important to recognize that social expectations, including hidden biases such as internalized sexism and racism, may play a part in your loved ones' expectations – and, if unaddressed, your response. For example, women are generally expected to take on the lion share of childcare and take on more household tasks – and do – than similarly situated men (Brenan, 2020; Hochschild & Machung, 2012; Richardson, 2012). Similarly, some people, perhaps including your important people (or even you), expect women to support men's education and careers at the expense of their own. Your response depends largely on your own values, level of awareness, style of communication, and the relationship. Some people are adept at negotiating these biases, asserting themselves, and/or setting boundaries, which are important skills! Others distance themselves as a self-protective measure. Still others choose to end the relationship if none of the other approaches are successful.

Mismatched expectations are particularly salient for first generation students and professionals. A parent, spouse, or other loved one may expect you to continue doing what you've been doing (or expect you to do) in any number of realms such as childcare and contributing financial support. They may also expect you to drop everything to help with family business, including situations they perceive as emergencies. They may beg you to stay or come home, or tell you that you can't do it, so you may as well drop out. They may also continue to urge you to do things that matter to them such as cooking or cleaning, participate in activities, or simply hang out with them – when you've already explained you cannot, often because you have work to do. If you find yourself in situations like this, remember you're not alone. Active listening is a good first step. It's also helpful to seek and accept help from both your social and professional networks (e.g., advisors or mentors) for suggestions and ideas toward coping with these challenging situations.

OTHER PERSONAL RELATIONSHIPS

As we discussed earlier, while some of us are fortunate to have the support of family and friends, some family members and friends may not know how to support you, others won't, and still others may undermine or otherwise sabotage your efforts. In any/all of these cases, it's important to know ways to identify other personal support systems for the various parts of your life. The short- and long-term benefits of social support include improved physical and mental health, which serves as a buffer to stress, increased opportunities for growth and learning, quality of life, and healthier communities (Cannon & Murray, 2019). Moreover, as we shared earlier, social support is associated with life and career satisfaction and success. (Chan et al., 2020).

One of the most common ways people connect with people with shared goals, values, and interests is through organizations and groups. In addition to social support, many of these groups provide opportunities, formally or informally, to develop interpersonal and social skills. Some also offer opportunities to develop leadership and other potentially transferrable professional skills. Given the vast array of organizations and groups, there's one (or more) for almost everyone – and, if there isn't, there is the potential to start a new one. However, since you're probably busy preparing for your career in psychology as well as developing your social network, we've organized some of the most popular organizations and groups into four broad categories to jumpstart your thinking about additional ways to build social support.

Faith and other spiritual communities offer people with shared values, goals, and often beliefs, opportunities to connect with each other both individually and in community. This category includes but is not limited to churches, synagogues, mosques, and other formal and informal spiritual communities, many of which also offer opportunities for self-development and service. The range of 12-step program groups such as Alcoholics Anonymous https://aa.org/, which are spiritually based mutual support and recovery groups, fall into this category as well.

The overwhelming majority of US adults consider religion and spirituality an important factor in their lives (Schlosser et al., 2010). Religion and spirituality are also associated with meaning, purpose, and a number of positive life outcomes, including career decision-making and satisfaction (Duffy, 2006; Hernandez et al., 2011). The subset of people who believe in a higher power, regardless of how they address or conceptualize that higher power, often find meaning in their relationship with that higher power.

Cultural/social organizations and groups such as African American sororities and fraternities, Sons of Italy, and the Hibernians, offer social and service opportunities in a culturally congruent environment. As a bonus, these organizations offer occasions for meeting and working with people who identify with and/or appreciate the group's culture. Furthermore, many of these groups promote knowledge and appreciation of the best of the identified group or groups, and some sponsor scholarships, mentoring, and professional development opportunities.

Community and civic groups are generally organized to promote a cause or attain a goal. Some are partisan such as the local chapter of your favorite political party, while others are decidedly nonpartisan such as the League of Women Voters. The diversity of groups in this category means that, like groups in general, there's at least one for almost everyone and, as mentioned, if you don't find one that works for you, all you need is an idea, some energy, and one other person to form your own group! Overall, the side benefit of bringing people with similar interests (and often values) together is the potential for personal relationships including friendship.

Social media, the web, and other technological advances have expanded opportunities for human connection – and challenges. On one hand, there have never been as many opportunities to meet people with shared interests, values, and goals. You can join or start a group for just about anything. On the other hand, the challenges include lower levels of interpersonal social skills, lack of privacy, and polarization.

While groups and associations such as those outlined here are good places to find and give social support, they're not the only way to expand your personal support network. Many people enjoy recreational activities and groups such as running, hiking, gardening, music, and book discussion clubs, all of which are good ways to meet people and unwind. As mentioned, if you don't find a group that interests you, see if you can start one! In addition, you may be able, in person or virtually, to connect with neighbors, people who share your interests, or those in a similar life stage or phase. As just one example of the latter, if you're a parent of one or more children in a specific age-range, that may make it easier to connect with similarly situated parents. Moreover, these other parents – as well as those who experienced this earlier (that is, to follow this illustration, have older children and were where you are now just a short while ago) – can be excellent sources of emotional, informational, and other support.

SETTING APPROPRIATE BOUNDARIES

Your success/attempts at success can be discomforting to others who are comfortable with your current relationship, also referred to as *relational homeostasis* (the status quo). Sometimes you can prevent undermining or other sabotage by communication; other times you might not be aware the other person is feeling threatened until they say or do something that suggests they aren't responding well to your success. If that happens, the best thing to do is to gently observe the other person's behavior, and ask what's going on – then listen, really listen and use your heart and head to work toward solutions that work for you, the important person(s), and the relationships. While sometimes sad, at the risk of sounding like a greeting card, some relationships are for a season, others are for a lifetime (and most are in between). If the relationship seems to be ending or drawing to a close sooner than you would like, communication is a helpful first step (notice the theme?).

SCHOOL/LIFE INTEGRATION

If the idea of *work/life balance* and its student corollary, school/life balance, is scary, you're in good company. Some people are intimidated by the popular idea of "balance", imagining work/school and life on opposite ends of a precariously balanced see-saw, on which only one can be up (or doing well) at a time, requiring constant vigilance. Others believe popular sayings such as "you can have it all", which, in our experience, rarely, if ever happens. For most of us, it's more accurate to say you increase the likelihood you'll be able to achieve some, perhaps most of your goals, when you thoughtfully *integrate* or infuse work and/or school *with* your life.

Given the fact that time is a limited resource (there are only 24 hours in a day), the best (perhaps only) way to integrate work and/or school with your life, is to make informed decisions, consistent with your values, priorities, context, and situation. As we discussed in earlier chapters, when your values include work, paid and/or unpaid, school, and the rest of your life, it's important to consider the relative importance of each area to you, now and in the future. When you've done this, you can refine your plans and allocate your time and energy in ways that matter most to you. Moreover, by attending to your values, priorities, context, and situation, you're more likely to reach your goals (and less likely to inadvertently get in over your head)!

To illustrate, full-time enrollment at the undergraduate and graduate levels is called full-time for the simple reason that it typically takes 35–40 hours per week to do well, so if you have another full-time commitment or the equivalent (e.g., work, family), you have choices to make. You might decide to defer one or the other, reduce your hours, or something else. Sure, you might, as some people do, think you're the exception, and pursue both full-time, which some truly *exceptional* people have done – and lived to tell the tale. However, far too many other people have found, in attempting to take on too much that they're human, and can't do what they unrealistically set out to do. Those folks often end up stressed, making excuses, dropping proverbial balls, sometimes shortchanging their health and other priorities. It's not pretty and can also have other negative consequences. The good news is that since you're reading this book, you will be better prepared. You will be prepared to make decisions based on good information that are aligned with your values, including your work values (Betz, 2002), that are both flexible and consistent with the plans you developed in Chapter 6 (if you missed that, go back to Chapter 6), which together are positioning you to be on your way to reaching your academic and career goals.

Moreover, keep in mind that while you can learn from and with others, your life, including your academic and career path is uniquely yours. Some of us are fortunate to attend college as full-time residential students. Others work while attending college part-time and still others, as we discussed in an earlier chapter, attend college part-time while working at one or more paid and unpaid caregiving jobs such as caring for young children. Although there are exceptions, women, including those engaged in paid work, generally have primary (sometimes sole) responsibility for the critically important yet often unrecognized, under-respected, and unpaid work of childcare, eldercare, and more.

Regardless of your personal, contextual, and socio-economic situation, the integration of school/work, and life offers both challenges and opportunities. In addition to the challenges noted here, it's a challenge to make the most of your opportunities, not using one opportunity as an excuse for not living up to another (particularly those that are freely chosen, like going to school). For example, some students use (or appear to use) family or work obligations as an excuse for not doing their school work. However, with the exception of real emergencies that can happen to anyone, most family and regular work obligations can be foreseen and worked with. If you've found yourself in a situation like this, it's helpful to consider if better planning, shifting or reducing your obligations (for example, taking fewer credits per semester), and/or tapping into your social network (peer and professional relationships!) would alleviate some of the stress, increase your effectiveness, and ultimately help you make a greater professional contribution.

Work and school/life enrichment

Although the challenges of work/school and life integration are more easily identified, another, often under-appreciated aspect of work/school and life integration are the protective factors associated with having multiple roles and outlets (Greenhaus & Powell, 2006; Powell et al., 2019). Although, as we discussed earlier, your professional peers are not necessarily your friends (and, we'll add here that your personal friends and family are not necessarily your professional peers), our professional and personal lives are dynamic, bidirectional, interdependent, and have the potential to be mutually reinforcing. This mutual reinforcement is conceptualized theoretically in Greenhaus and Powell's Work-Family Enrichment Theory (2006), recently re-conceptualized as Work Life Theory (Powell et al., 2019). Recent research lends support to this theory, showing that knowledge, skills, perspectives, and social support gained in one area (work or life) support development in the other (Chan et al., 2016, 2020; Nicklin et al., 2019). Moreover, this mutual reinforcement contributes to increased self-efficacy, work-life balance, and both work and life satisfaction (Chan et al., 2020). Overall, consistent with the goals of this book, the best way to make work and life mutually rewarding is to do your part to develop both.

CHAPTER SUMMARY

This chapter offers practical guidance and unwritten rules for building and maintaining effective personal relationships with family, friends, and others while you're pursuing your career in psychology. We also explored common relationship challenges and solutions, including setting appropriate boundaries, as well as school/life integration and enrichment.

EXERCISES

1 Draw a "psychological map" map of the important people in your life, putting yourself in the center of a series of concentric circles, with your important people in their appropriate places. Consider if there are people on that map you'd like to change your relationship with and, if so, how you might start that process (adapted from the Person-in-Culture Interview; Berg-Cross & Chinen, 1995).

2 Review and revise, if necessary, the Action Plans you developed in Chapter 6 to include professional and personal relationships (and if you haven't done them yet – do them, in writing, it does make a difference). In this review and revision, consider all levels of the Action Plans, long-term through weekly. It may be that there isn't sufficient time for more than a quick phone call, video chat, or meal with someone who's important to you during particularly busy weeks, but you could make time to get together, perhaps treating yourself and this loved one to a full day you'd both enjoy during a break or vacation. If so, that's something to know. Similarly, you might decide that you'd prefer to spend your time with important people in different ways than you're currently doing. There's something about having less of something (in this case time) to focus us.

3 Connect or re-connect with one or more people in your personal life. Share your goals, ask them about their goals, and share some ideas for mutual support. Check in at a mutually agreeable time interval (e.g., one week, one month, or longer).

Next steps: the advanced move

1 Reflect on and make a list of people you admire personally (i.e., not in your professional world). These can be people you know (or could potentially know), and/or people profiled in biographies or documentaries. What do you admire about those people? See if you can identify what they have done, how they act, and/or other attributes that you consider worth emulating. If that list includes one or more people you know personally – a family member, friend, or other acquaintance, count your blessings and consider reaching out to at least one of those people and sharing your reflections. This could be an opportunity to strengthen that relationship in a mutually reinforcing way.

2 If you're interested in personal relationships and want to learn more, Vangelisti and Perlman's (2018) *Handbook of personal relationships* is an excellent resource.

REFERENCES

American Counseling Association. (2014). *ACA code of ethics.*

American Psychological Association. (2017). *Ethical principles of psychologists and code of conduct.*

Anderson, P., Goodman, J. P., & Schlossberg, N. K. (2012). *Counseling adults in transition, Linking Schlossberg's theory with practice in a diverse world* (4th ed.). Springer Publishing Company.

Armstrong, E. A., & Hamilton, L. T. (2013). *Paying for the party: How college maintains inequality.* Harvard University Press.

Aronson, E., & Aronson, J. (2012). *The social animal* (11th ed.). Worth Publishers.

Berg-Cross, L., & Chinen, R. T. (1995). Multicultural training models and the person-in-culture interview. In J. G. Ponterotto, J. M. Casas, L. A. Suzuki, & C. M. Alexander (Eds.), *Handbook of multicultural counseling* (pp. 333–356). Sage.

Betz, N. E. (2002). The 2001 Leona Tyler award address: Women's career development: Weaving personal themes and theoretical constructs. *The Counseling Psychologist, 30*(3), 467–480.

Brenan, M. (2020). *Women still handle main household tasks in U.S.* Retrieved March 20, 2021, from https://news.gallup.com/poll/283979/women-handle-main-household-tasks.aspx

Cannon, J. L., & Murray, C. E. (2019). Promoting healthy relationships and families: An exploratory study of the perceptions of resources and information and skill needs among couples, single adults, and parents. *The Family Journal, 27*(3), 309–318. https://doi.org/10.1177/1066480719852357

Chan, X. W., Kalliath, P., Chan, C., & Kalliath, T. (2020). How does family support facilitate job satisfaction? Investigating the chain mediating effects of work – family enrichment and job-related well-being. *Stress and Health: Journal of the International Society for the Investigation of Stress, 36*, 97–104. https://doi.org/10.1002/smi.2918

Chan, X. W., Kalliath, T., Brough, P., Siu, O.-L., O'Driscoll, M. P., & Timms, C. (2016). Work – family enrichment and satisfaction: The mediating role of self-efficacy and work – Life balance. *The International Journal of Human Resource Management, 27*(15), 1755–1776. https://doi.org/10.1080/09585192.2015.1075574

Comstock, D. L., Hammer, T. R., Strentzsch, J., Cannon, K., Parsons, J., & Salazar II, G. (2008). Relational-cultural theory: A framework for bridging relational, multicultural, and social justice competencies. *Journal of Counseling & Development Development, 86*(3), 279.

Conyne, R. K., Horne, A. M., & Raczynski, K. A. (2013). *Prevention in psychology: An introduction to the prevention practice kit.* Sage.

Duffy, R. D. (2006). Spirituality, religion, and career development: Current status and future directions. *The Career Development Quarterly*, *55*(1), 52–63. https://doi.org/10.1002/j.2161-0045.2006.tb00004.x

Fuertes, J. N., Moore, M., & Ganley, J. (2019). Therapists' and clients' ratings of real relationship, attachment, therapist self-disclosure, and treatment progress. *Psychotherapy Research: Journal of the Society for Psychotherapy Research*, *29*(5), 594–606. https://doi.org/10.1080/10503307.2018.1425929

Gelso, C. J. (2002). Real relationship: The "something more" of psychotherapy. *Journal of Contemporary Psychotherapy*, *32*(1), 35–40.

Gelso, C. J., Kivlighan, D. M., & Markin, R. D. (2018). The real relationship and its role in psychotherapy outcome: A meta-analysis. *Psychotherapy*, *55*(4), 434–444. https://doi.org/10.1037/pst0000183

Greenhaus, J. H., & Powell, G. N. (2006). When work and family are allies: A theory of work-family enrichment. *Academy of Management Review*, *31*(1), 72–92.

Helms, J. E. (2004). The 2003 Leona Tyler award address: Making race a matter of individual differences within groups. *Counseling Psychologist*, *32*(3), 473–483.

Helms, J. E. (2017). The challenge of making whiteness visible: Reactions to four whiteness articles. *Counseling Psychologist*, *45*(5), 717.

Hernandez, E. F., Foley, P. F., & Beitin, B. K. (2011). Hearing the call: A phenomenological study of religion in career choice. *Journal of Career Development*, *38*, 62–88, http://dx.doi.org/10.1177/0894845309358889

Hochschild, A. R., & Machung, A. (2012). *The second shift: Working families and the revolution at home* (Rev. ed.). Penguin Books.

Holland, J. L. (1997). *Making vocational choices: A theory of vocational personalities and work environments* (3rd ed.). Psychological Assessment Resources.

Holland, J. L., & Holland, J. E. (1977). Distributions of personalities within occupations and fields of study. *Vocational Guidance Quarterly*, *25*(3), 226–231. https://doi.org/10.1002/j.2164-585X.1977.tb00945.x

hooks, bell. (1984). *Feminist theory from margin to center* (1st ed.). South End Press.

Jackson, M. A., Tal, A. I., & Sullivan, T. R. (2003). Hidden biases in counseling women: Balancing work and family concerns. In M. Kopala & M. A. Keitel (Eds.), *Handbook of counseling women* (pp. 152–172). Sage. https://doi.org/10.4135/9781452229546.n11

Kottler, J. A. (2017). *On being a therapist* (5th ed.). Jossey-Bass.

Lachman, M. E., Teshale, S., & Agrigoroaei, S. (2015). Midlife as a pivotal period in the life course: Balancing growth and decline at the crossroads of youth and old age. *International Journal of Behavioral Development*, *39*(1), 20–31.

Malinen, S., & Johnston, L. (2013). Workplace ageism: Discovering hidden bias. *Experimental Aging Research*, *39*(4), 445–465. https://doi.org/10.1080/0361073X.2013.808111

Maslow, A. H. (1943). A theory of human motivation. *Psychological Review*, *50*(4), 370–396. https://doi.org/10.1037/h0054346

Maslow, A. H. (1968). *Toward a psychology of being* (2nd ed.). Van Nostrand Reinhold.

Nicklin, J. M., Meachon, E. J., & McNall, L. A. (2019). Balancing work, school, and personal life among graduate students: A positive psychology approach. *Applied Research in Quality of Life*, *14*(5), 1265. https://doi.org/10.1007/s11482-018-9650-z

Ponterotto, J. G., Casas, J. M., Suzuki, L. M., & Alexander, C. M. (Eds.). (1995). *Handbook of multicultural counseling*. Sage.

Powell, G. N., Greenhaus, J. H., Allen, T. D., & Johnson, R. E. (2019). Introduction to special topic forum: Advancing and expanding work-life theory from multiple perspectives. *Academy of Management Review*, *44*(1), 54–71.

Richardson, M. S. (2012). Counseling for work and relationship. *Counseling Psychologist*, *40*(2), 190–242.

Schlosser, L. Z., Foley, P. F., Stein, E. P., & Holmwood, J. R. (2010). Why does counseling psychology exclude religion? A content analysis and methodological critique. In J. G. Ponterotto, J. M. Casas, L. A. Suzuki, & C. M. Alexander (Eds.), *Handbook of multicultural counseling* (3rd ed., pp. 453–465). Sage.

Sedlacek, W. E. (2004). *Beyond the big test: Noncognitive assessment in higher education.* Jossey-Bass.

Vangelisti, A. L., & Perlman, D. (Eds.). (2018). *The Cambridge handbook of personal relationships* (2nd ed.). Cambridge University Press. https://doi.org/10.1017/9781316417867

Yalom, I. D., & Leszcz, M. (2005). *The theory and practice of group psychotherap* (5th ed.). Basic Books.

PART **IV**

Career paths and options at different educational levels

CHAPTER 9

Bachelor's degrees

Career paths and options

ORIENTING QUESTIONS

1. How can thinking like a researcher or detective or journalist help you find your "best" career direction to start your career with your Bachelor's degree?

2. How can you find information about how psychology is used in different organizations and industries?

3. What are some ways to test your thinking about your career direction??

4. Who (or, what offices) can help you learn about experiential learning opportunities?

DOI: 10.4324/9780429296413-13

INTRODUCTION

You've learned a lot about education, work, and careers so far, as well as about making good decisions about achieving your career goals. Since psychology is a broadly construed degree, there are an infinite number of possibilities that you could take your degree. APA's Center for Workforce Studies reported (Stamm, 2020; APA, 2018) the results of an NSF survey. The report indicated that there were 3.5 million people with a bachelor's degree in psychology in 2017. Of those 3.5 million graduates, two million people did not move on to graduate studies – that's 56% of the graduates with majors in psychology! The report further indicated that the primary work activities for individuals with bachelor's degrees in psychology were professional service activities, teaching, research, management, sales and marketing.

If you think about this for a minute, we think you'll see this makes sense. How many people would be better at their jobs by understanding how people think and respond to others? You are probably thinking that there are few people that *wouldn't* be better at their jobs with an improved understanding of others. If this was your first thought, you would be right. In addition, the field of psychology provides students with a broad yet deep foundation including more training in research methods and statistics than most other college majors. Since learning research methods and statistics helps you to ask good questions and find the answers to those questions, psychology prepares you to move in many and varied different career directions. Since this can be overwhelming, let's start by focusing on how you think about using psychology in the world. To get into the swing of this, we encourage you to think about this as a researcher, detective, journalist, or lead in a mystery would. What do they focus on? Well, they look for who (you – we've got that down pat, right?), what, when, where, why, and how. Since we know the who – you – let's move on to thinking about the what, followed by the remainder of the list (where, how, and why).

WHAT DO YOU WANT TO DO TO CHANGE OR IMPACT THE WORLD?

Understanding the goal you want to achieve or the problem that you want to fix is always the first step to identifying good career directions. Throughout the previous sections of this text, we've explored psychology as a field with career options, the education necessary to engage in those options, and discussed tips for both planning your career and successful completion of the training necessary to engage in psychology as a career. As we've indicated previously, there are so many directions in which you can take a career in psychology that it was difficult to incorporate all that information in the earlier chapters. These last four chapters, therefore, are focused on providing an introduction to career directions in psychology at different educational levels as well as how to explore and discover more.

For those of you with experience in the world – whether it be paid or unpaid work – you already have some idea about the world of work and, most likely, about what you like and/or don't like about the workplace and how one collaborates to affect others in some way. This is helpful information in that you can use it to consider what may and may not work for you in psychology. For example, if you volunteered with Habitat for Humanity or worked for a major corporation (etc.) - what did you like about: 1) the people, 2) the setting, 3) the day-to-day flow of work and interaction, 4) the stated mission of the organization, and 5) the impact that you (through the organization) were having on the world? You want to make sure to think about what was missing, as well as what was present, as that, too, can be important information. Great clues to use in seeking out your new direction!

BOX 9.1

Applying Psychology to Work in Psychology and Related Fields: Website Resources

As a reminder about the different subfields in psychology (and closely related fields), check out their websites below. Many of these sites will have one or more listings of sub-fields for you to consider:

American Psychological Association – www.apa.org
Association for Psychological Science – www.psychologicalscience.org
American Counseling Association – www.counseling.org
National Association of Social Workers – www.socialworkers.org
Association for Talent Development (formerly, the Association for Training & Development) – www.td.org
Society for Human Resource Management – www.shrm.org

Let's start by taking a moment to either recall what brought you to psychology or, to go back to the notes that you've made as you've read this book about what drew you to psychology. This is where we want to elaborate, as much as possible, the picture in your head about how you see yourself changing the world, helping people, and making a difference. You can do this any way you wish – if you are a list-maker, you could make a list(s) of things you'd be doing and how the world would be different by the time you retire; if you are creative, you could write a poem, story, create a vision board/collage/mural/montage; you could even speak with a career counselor, as it is their job to assist you in clarifying your career direction. Another way to think about this is to imagine what your workday would be like. This is an imagery exercise. In this type of exercise, you allow yourself to recognize the usually unspoken thoughts about one's future life. Whether we realize it or not, we all have what might be called "expectations" about what our future will be. As with planning, bringing these thoughts into awareness permits us to look at them and begin to work toward implementing them.

BOX 9.2

Translating Meaning and Purpose to a Career Direction

So, let's try an example. Say that you struggled growing up and you don't want others to experience the same things that you did – you want them to have better "tools" and skills to deal with these things. You are the "who" and the statement includes both a "what" and a "why", so we need the "when", "where", and "how". You might have done some volunteering with a local organization to learn about how they work with younger children. You may have participated in a service-learning project at a nearby elementary school and had the chance to observe how school counselors work with children. Or, you may have participated in a research experience to study coping mechanisms in 5th grade students. Finally, you may have obtained a part-time job at a local residential facility for at-risk youth or for adolescents with substance abuse issues. Consider the questions below and then apply them to your real situation.

If this were you. . .

1. What would be attractive about working at these various places?
2. What would be unattractive about working in these places?
3. What would be attractive or unattractive about the issues being addressed in each place?
4. Do you have a preference for an age-group to work with?
5. Are there other characteristics that would make one option attractive or unattractive?

WHEN DO YOU WANT TO AFFECT THE WORLD?

Most students think about "starting" their career once they graduate, however, that is not your only option. Some of you may have developed an interest in doing a particular kind of work through knowing people who do that work, through volunteering, service learning, field experiences or some type of internship, while others may have been working in an industry and discovered the role of psychology in that industry. Thus, technically, you've already started your career. Good for you! Engaging in opportunities to explore the different ways of applying psychological knowledge to help the world is an important step toward finding your own niche in it.

Even if you do have a direction, we still encourage you to explore your options because you may not be aware of all the ways to achieve your goals. For example, we know of an individual (who lived back in the dinosaurs' age before high school psychology courses became available) and wanted to change the world by helping people understand and communicate more effectively across cultures. Because of their limited exposure and lack of access to information about careers, they chose language teaching as a career direction. It was only by happenstance (Mitchell et al., 1999) that this person encountered other students who were studying a particular subfield of psychology that focused on multiculturalism and was able to switch to that program. Had they not encountered these people; the individual would have been less effective at achieving their goal. This person benefited from their engagement with others and the role of happenstance in their life. You can more intentionally bring happenstance into your life by creating opportunities for happenstance to work for you (Valickas et al., 2019; Hagevik, 2000) by participating in activities that fit your thinking and schedule. Thus, you never know what you don't know if you haven't used all of your resources to explore your options.

BOX 9.3

Clarifying Direction and Building Experience Through Experiential Learning

Experiential learning is a broad term that covers volunteering, service learning, field/research experiences, internships, and other paid and unpaid opportunities to contribute to the community and "try out" a career direction. In some fields, such as engineering, it is more formalized, however, that doesn't mean that you can't take advantage of the benefits of this type of activity. So, how do you do engage in these types of programs? Well, here's a list of resources that can assist you in finding opportunities to "try out" your interests. Check them out:

- Volunteering – this is the broadest and, often, least organized. While some institutions have offices that coordinate volunteering in the community, others do not. However, that need not stop you. You can speak with your academic advisor or the department's field experience instructor to learn where other students (also not a bad resource) have volunteered. You can also check with the psychology department office – they may have a list of volunteer opportunities. You can also use the internet and other community resources, such as the local library, to begin to find volunteer opportunities.
- Service Learning – if your campus engages in service learning, there may be an office with that name – contact them for a list of courses that incorporate service learning (or ask your advisor) and then enroll in those that

(Continued)

BOX 9.3 *(Continued)*

fit your interests. It will provide you with a structured way to learn about a particular type of career direction.

- Field and Research Experiences – can be voluntary, however, many psychology departments have opportunities for you to earn course credit for engaging in activities that are related to a career in this field. If you know the instructor that teaches these courses, you will want to speak to them directly. If not, then see your advisor (in the department) or the psychology department office to find out who to speak with about these opportunities. In some institutions, a list may be maintained in the career services office.

- Internships – These are more structured work experiences that are designed to better acquaint you with the field and improve your skills. They are more formal experiences and may be embedded in a larger program, such as the Minority Access to Research Careers (MARC) program, the McNair Scholars program. You will need to speak to someone in the department – typically the person who coordinates the program, so check with your department advisor or the department office.

For those of you who haven't explored occupations or had the opportunity for experiential learning, it's not too late to start. Being able to speak knowledgeably about a career or your career goals, as well as experiences (volunteer, service learning, summer/part-time employment, etc.) is important for both employment and further study. Employers evaluate the types of experiences mentioned here in positive ways. These experiences indicate that you possess both basic employability skills (showing up when you are supposed to and dressing appropriately), as well as providing evidence of more advanced abilities, such as planning and strategizing to complete a project. If you are one of the many, many students who are working to support yourself (and, perhaps, a family) as you work toward your degree, consult with other students in your classes about how they engage, or speak with your advisor or instructors for ideas about how to work in some experience. We know of several faculty members who identified research tasks that could be completed at odd hours and without coming to campus so students who were employed full-time could participate and contribute effectively to the research team.

HOW DO YOU WANT TO AFFECT THE WORLD?

From a "how" perspective, we gain information about the process of the work that you want to do. For example, conducting equine therapy requires that you work, primarily, outside with horses and people who have psychological difficulties, while applying your understanding of developmental psychology to develop more effective playtime activities for four-year-olds is likely to be a combination of inside and outside activities. Both of these types of activities require thought, planning, anticipation of potential crises, and the application of one's knowledge of psychology, however, different people will be attracted to implementing their commitment to psychology in different ways. Perhaps another example will further clarify things. Many students that we've worked with want to make people's work lives as pleasant and productive as possible, so they focus on applying their skills in Human Resources (HR) departments. These departments help in the hiring process, onboarding new employees, paying them, dealing with benefits, and assisting when there are conflicts or difficulties. They also often provide support and/or training to managers so that they can be more effective in leading and guiding their department, team, or unit. Sounds like a big job, no? It is. So big that within most HR departments, you will find units or people that specialize in only one of these aspects of human resource management – such as providing training. For these positions, one is generally working inside – in an office or classroom and with adults of working age, rather than children, adolescents, or retired adults.

So, let's think for a minute about how one would combine psychology with work in another type of organization or industry. Some of you may have some ideas about this, as you may be a career changer, with significant experience in the world of work. This is an advantage, in that you already have ties and expertise that, should you choose, you can bring back to working in that industry from a psychological perspective. If you do not have such experiences – no worries! There are examples spread throughout the chapter to help you generate ideas, however, it might be helpful to spend a bit more time talking about combining psychology with another area. An easier way to start this process is to ask you to think back to high school, where you may have been exposed to something called the "Career Clusters" (Torpey, 2015), since not every high school utilizes the organization of industries and occupational groupings, it's reproduced in Table 9.1.

As you look at the clusters in Table 9.1, some are likely to appear as natural places to use your knowledge and understanding of psychology – Education & Training, Human Services, and Marketing in particular. Positions like teaching high school psychology and multicultural education courses, various community service positions, personal trainers, early childhood teachers, research lab assistants, and designing marketing materials may immediately come to mind in these particular areas. Similarly, you might be able to see links between your knowledge and skills in psychology and positions in the Law, Public Safety, Corrections & Security cluster. However, there are also careers that span across most clusters. This would include all of the human resource positions, managerial positions, trainers, and Equal Opportunity or Diversity office staff, to name just a few. It is beyond the scope of this text to list all the different ways to use psychology throughout the world of work, so I would like to suggest some ways to explore these combinations of psychology with another industry or field. Since many fields have equivalent "majors" in higher education, you might consider taking a course in an area to see if it seems interesting – or, at least talk to a professor in that department. Many students

TABLE 9.1 16 Career Clusters

Agriculture, Food & Natural Resources	Government & Public Admin. (cont.)
• Agribusiness Systems	• Public Management & Administration
• Animal Systems	• Regulation
• Environmental Service Systems	• Revenue & Taxation
• Food Products & Processing Systems	**Health Sciences**
• Natural Resources Systems	• Biotechnology Research & Development
• Plant Systems	• Diagnostic Services
• Power, Structural & Technical Systems	• Health Informatics
Architecture & Construction	• Support Services
• Construction	• Therapeutic Services
• Design/Pre-Construction	**Hospitality & Tourism**
• Maintenance/Operations	• Lodging
Arts, A/V Technology & Communications	• Recreation, Amusements & Attractions
• A/V Technology & Film	• Restaurants & Food/Beverage Services
• Journalism & Broadcasting	• Travel & Tourism
• Performing Arts	**Human Services**
• Printing Technology	• Consumer Services
• Telecommunications	• Counseling & Mental Health Services
Business Management & Administration	• Early Childhood Development & Services
• Administrative Support	• Family & Community Services
• Business Information Management	• Personal Care Services
• General Management	**Information Technology**
• Human Resources Management	• Information Support & Services
• Operations Management	• Network Systems

Education & Training
- Administration & Administrative Support
- Professional Support Services
- Teaching/Training

Finance
- Accounting
- Banking Services
- Business Finance
- Insurance
- Securities & Investments

Government & Public Administration
- Foreign Service
- Governance
- National Security
- Planning

Marketing
- Marketing Communications
- Marketing Management
- Marketing Research
- Merchandising
- Professional Sales

Science, Technology, Engineering & Mathematics
- Engineering & Technology
- Science & Mathematics

- Programming & Software Development
- Web & Digital Communications

Law, Public Safety, Corrections & Security
- Correction Services
- Emergency & Fire Management Services
- Law Enforcement Services
- Legal Services
- Security & Protective Services

Manufacturing
- Health, Safety & Environmental Assurance
- Logistics & Inventory Control
- Maintenance, Installation & Repair
- Manufacturing Production Process Dev.
- Production
- Quality Assurance

Transportation, Distribution & Logistics
- Facility & Mobile Equipment Maintenance
- Health, Safety & Environmental Management
- Logistics Planning & Management Services
- Sales & Service
- Transportation Operations
- Transportation Systems/Infrastructure Planning, Management & Regulation
- Warehousing & Distribution Center Operation

Source: Used with permission from Advance CTE. (n.d.). *Careers Clusters Pathways*. Advance CTE. www.careertech.org/sites/default/files/CareerClustersPathways.pdf

will not only have a major they will also have a minor when they graduate in order to strengthen their background to work in an area. For example, a student interested in human resources might major in psychology and minor in business or human resources, depending upon the available minors. Or someone interested in government might minor in political science. Another way to expand your awareness of ways to use your psychology degree is to visit the career counseling or placement office at your institution and peruse the materials there. By the way, placement offices sponsor career fairs in which employers visit campus and meet with students for both jobs after graduate and internships during your undergraduate training. However, you can also attend these events just to learn more about the types of jobs that are out there for you. Employers select the representatives that they send to these events for characteristics such as interpersonal skills, interest in people, and commitment to the organization (hint – does this sound like a job for a psychology major?).

As you can see from the previous paragraph, psychology can be applied in numerous settings. As you think about what you want to be doing, do not artificially restrict it to what you know, now, as psychology, since psychology is ever changing. For example, in the earlier part of the last century, who would have thought that psychologists would be used to help design job assignments so that people were actually using their skills and functioning better, or helping to reduce airline disasters by re-designing the airplane's cockpit so that it better aligned with how people actually process information? Who knows what problems and opportunities the future will bring us as this century progresses!

Employability skills

If you'll notice, in addition to discussing how you might use skills and knowledge in psychology to apply to a career field, we've also discussed the manner in which the skills in psychology support one's effectiveness in a different career or major throughout this text. Thus, one of our goals is to assist you in recognizing that various skills you learn throughout your education and experience in psychology will equip you for employment and occupations both in and beyond psychology. The most basic of these is termed *employability*, or *workforce readiness* skills (Crawford et al., 2011; Partnership for 21st Century Skills, 2009; Stone & Lewis, 2012). These include skills such as personal hygiene, punctuality, responsibility taking, professional dress and demeanor, teamwork, articulateness, critical thinking, and decision-making skills. These are the foundation for developing the transferable skills discussed earlier and will serve you well in whatever career direction you proceed. There are numerous resources on the internet related to developing these skills, however, if you think of experiences that you've had in the retail and/or hospitality industry, you are likely to begin to identify these skills. For example, contrast what you consider to be the best and the worst experiences that you've had in a fast-food, retail, or hospitality setting. What behaviors and attitudes were displayed by the employees that caused it to be a positive or negative experience? Then contrast those with your own behaviors.

Transferable skills

At a more complex level are *transferable skills* – in other words, skills that transfer to or are common across jobs and careers. In a recent survey of employers, NACE (2017) identified ten competencies that employers seek. These include critical thinking and problem-solving, oral/written communication skills, teamwork/collaboration skills, use of digital technology, leadership skills, professionalism/work ethic, career management, and global/intercultural fluency. One of the most important aspects of these skills is their focus on assisting the employer to solve the challenges they face in a manner that is respectful, collaborative, ethical, and professional. These ten skills are similar to the most frequently listed job skills in psychology job advertisements (APA, 2018). Similar to NACE, APA found that the most frequently mentioned skills, regardless of position type included: communication, computer and data analysis, critical thinking, cultural awareness, language, leadership, organizational, teamwork, and health records management.

Let's consider this for a minute. What we are suggesting is that not only are one's skills useful to conduct research, for example – these skills are transferable to other jobs (as discussed earlier) and equip you for occupations in other fields. You may be wondering why. Well . . . it's rather simple. Different fields use the skills, knowledge, and processes with a slightly different focus. Here are a few examples:

- Marketing and public relations departments in business, industry, education, and government conduct research ("polls") to learn about the public's opinions. Using research methods and statistical analyses you will learn in your classes with similar titles.
- Health care, education, and business organizations conduct research on two levels. First, they conduct research on the outcomes of their work – treatment outcomes, graduation outcomes, and sales are examples. However, they also often conduct "research" on the effectiveness of their programs and processes. This is the field of *program evaluation* mentioned earlier.
- Legislative bodies at the state and federal level (as also does the legal system) have offices that gather and synthesize information on various issues and proposals for laws or changes to laws. These offices are often called "Research" offices. They support the work of the legislators by providing information that will assist them in making more effective decisions for their constituents. In fact, many legislators and congresspersons have one or more individuals (often hiring undergraduate students as interns) in their offices who assist with synthesizing information and research with which they must deal.
- In particular, those with a background in Industrial/Organizational Psychology conduct research to develop processes and procedures to improve the ways in which organizations select and promote employees, while individuals with training in psychometrics may work for testing companies to improve the questionnaires, surveys, and tests that they publish.

As you can see, regardless of your career direction – within psychology or applying psychology in another field, the skills that you will be learning and practicing will transfer and support your career trajectory. This applies regardless of your focus – providing professional services, teaching, conducting research, managing organizations and processes, engaging in sales/marketing type work, or engaging in other work activities (Stamm & Fowler, 2019).

BRINGING IT TOGETHER – THE *WHY*

One of the reasons we've asked you to gather together all the information you've gathered about yourself is to help you see the patterns across all the different foci – who, what, when, where, and how. From our researcher/detective/journalist stance, we want to begin to identify information that will help you to not only see what part of psychology (or, related majors) you want to focus on, we also want you to be able to see the type of industry (e.g., health care, not-for-profit, education, policy-making, legislative, business, human resources, etc.) you would feel most comfortable in, as well as the type of work that you would find most rewarding (working with people, with data or information, with things or products, or with ideas; Holland, 1997; McIntyre & Graziano, 2019).

BOX 9.4

Imagining Your Future

This exercise will help you to bring into consciousness all those thoughts about how your future will look. It is likely to help you clarify your direction and may help you to become more aware of important values and goals. Below are the steps to implementing an imagery exercise:

1   Find a comfortable place where you can concentrate and work without distraction. Make sure that you have writing/drawing/sketching implements necessary to capture your thoughts and images, as well as any munchies or other supports that help you to focus and reflect. BTW, some people may prefer speaking their thoughts. If this is you, have a recorder handy – or, a friend who can take notes for you.
2   Close your eyes for a few minutes and shut out any noise or activity around you. If you are familiar with centering or meditation you should be familiar with how to bring your focus to yourself, rather than to everything going on around you. You want to calm your mind and relax so that those little, tiny thoughts that comprise your ideas about your future can come to the fore and coalesce.

(Continued)

BOX 9.4   (*Continued*)

3   Once you feel calm and focused, ask your mind to help you see a typical week or workday in the future. This day should be a typical day for you in your chosen career – a career in which you are satisfied and building a life.

4   Start with opening your eyes as you wake up in the morning. Where are you? What does the space look like? If you can see outside, what does the space outside look like? What are you wearing (or, not)? Who, if anyone, is with you? How many are there? What do they look like? What is their relationship to you? What do you do? Do you lay there reflecting, jump out of bed and start exercising, greet whomever is with you, start out any windows – what happens next after you open your eyes? Give as much detail as you can at this point.

5   Continue through the day in this same manner. As the ideas and thoughts flow, attempt to capture as many as possible since no detail is too small. Keep writing until you run out of thoughts, giving yourself permission to pick up the thread at another time to add more detail.

6   Then wind down and bring yourself back to the present. Depending upon your familiarity with imagery and self-reflection, this activity may require several sessions to obtain a clear picture, however, it is worth taking the time.

7   At some point you may want to refine the word picture that you've created and analyze it to see what it's telling you about how you see yourself contributing to and changing the world.

The purpose is to become as clear as possible about your vision of the future and your role in it. This will help you to connect your goals to specific career directions. For example, if you see yourself working in a research lab that uses MRIs, fMRIs, and other equipment to study the brain, that's a very different career direction from someone who envisions themselves creating effective developmental programs for at-risk youth or elderly persons with Alzheimer's disease. Similarly, those of you that envision yourself working in a business to create tools to help people with mental health issues, or to use your psychological knowledge to create a more equitable, effective work team, are different from those who see themselves working in a Human Resources department to ensure that employees are well-trained and receive the benefits and supports that they need to function well in the organization. Using psychology to help others is a very broad field – one can work for a state or federal legislative body and create law or work in the state agencies to assist those with mental illnesses, or, one can work with animals that help provide therapy – equine therapy to treat autism, therapy dogs for treatment of various disorders, trainers for mobility or service animals, etc.

NEXT STEPS

Once you have your who, what, when, where and why, it is time to make use of resources to formulate your plan for obtaining an employment post-baccalaureate degree. This is where the actions proposed in Chapter 6 are helpful, as they point you toward your career development center, career counseling center, placement office, local library, or workforce development office. These offices and organizations not only have information about careers, they actually have ways to link you to employers. This is particularly so for campus placement offices. They will also assist you with developing resumes, cover letters, interview skills, and other skills necessary for improving your ability to put your degree to use. We strongly encourage you to take the time to check out this important office and make the best use of their services – which may include helping you to find field experiences and/or internships that will help you develop skills and increase your attractiveness to employers.

Next steps can also include a *Plan B* (Schlossberg, 1996). Many people have more than one interest and will explore the most interesting to see which one works out the best – that's one form of a *Plan B*. Another form of a *Plan B* is to intentionally consider what you might do, should your original plan not work out. For example, graduate school is quite competitive, so many individuals have a plan to gain experience that will support their re-application the next year. Yes – people do apply to graduate school more than once. In fact, one of the authors was in the same doctoral class as an individual who had applied four previous times! The individual persisted and achieved their goal. In the meantime, they worked at jobs that gave them experience that would support their goals and increase their skills.

CHAPTER SUMMARY

In this chapter we discussed three major topics. First, we've discussed how to pull together all the information we've discussed throughout the book using the detective/journalist (*who, what, when, how, and why*) metaphor in order to chart a career direction in psychology with your bachelor's degree. We also discussed ways to gain valuable experience prior to, as well as after, graduation and highlighted the importance of the skills that are developed via these experiences. Finally, throughout the chapter we provided additional ideas and suggestions to help you explore your opportunities with a bachelor's degree in psychology. Recall that in previous chapters we have already pointed to resources for information and advice, so refer back to those chapters as needed to assist you as you work through this chapter. Third, we briefly discussed the value of a Plan B and/or alternative jobs that will support your skill development until you are able to obtain that "dream job" that jump starts your career. Finally, if you are reading this chapter and intend to further your education, you can still use your detective/psychology approach outlined in this chapter to gather and organize information to make good decisions.

EXERCISES

1   Accessing career information. As a reminder, if you haven't already, head to your career counseling and/or placement center (or, workforce development office) and learn about the information and resources they have to assist you.

   a.   You might contact your campus career counseling or placement services office to ask for access to the institution's occupational information system.

   b.   You can go online to the occupational information system developed and maintained by the federal government, called O*net. It can be found at Onetonline. org. There is no charge for using this system.

   c.   You may also purchase your own access to the Kuder career guidance and information system by going to their website: www.kuder.com

2   For those of you who have work experience and/or are changing careers, Richard Bolles' *What Color is Your Parachute?* has high quality information and resources. It's stood the test of time and remains relevant. Here's how to access this text:

   a.   The book is still being updated and published every year (with updates)

   b.   There are two websites: www.jobhuntersbible.com and eparachute.com

   c.   You can find his talks on YouTube – just search "Richard Bolles"

Next steps: the advanced move

1   Learn more about career paths in psychology by exploring the different subfields in psychology via the APA website, the Kuder Journey program, by visiting a career counseling or placement office, or through reviewing one or more of the following texts:

   a.   Hettich, P. (Ed). An eye on the workplace: Achieving a career with a bachelor's degree in psychology. Psi Chi. https://store.psichi.org/an-eye-on-the-workplace-achieving-a-career-with-a-bachelors-in-psychology

   b.   Kuther, T. L., & Morgan, R. D. (2020). *Careers in psychology: Opportunities in a changing world* (5th ed.). Sage.

   c.   Palladino Schultheiss, D. E. (2008). *Psychology as a major: Is it right for me and what can I do with my degree?* American Psychological Association.

   d.   Stenberg, R. J. (2017). *Career paths in psychology: Where your degree can take you* (3rd ed). American Psychological Association.

2   Learn more about how to succeed in your psychology major so as to better prepare yourself for the opportunities to come by learning from others:

   a.   Talk with your instructors and advisor – follow their advice.

   b.   Use the resources available on your campus, such as an academic support or student success office and the library.

   c.   Talk with people you know who have completed a bachelor's degree and learn from them what worked, what didn't, and what they would do differently, given the chance.

    d. Chickering, A. W., & Schlossberg, N. K. (2002). *Getting the most out of college* (2nd ed.). Prentice Hall.

    e. Geher, G. (2019). *Own your psychology major! A guide to student success.* American Psychological Association.

    f. McBurney, D. H. (2002). *How to think like a psychologist: Critical thinking in psychology* (2nd ed.). Prentice Hall.

    g. Silvia, P. J., Delaney, P. F., & Marcovitch, S. (2009). *What psychology majors could (and should) be doing: An informal guide to research experience and professional skills.* American Psychological Association.

3   Learn more about finding a job in psychology using resources such as the following:

    a. Your campus' career services or placement office and the resources they have available to you.

    b. The local Workforce Development office and library also have resources for learning about and finding employment.

    c. Landrum, R. E. (2009). *Finding jobs with a psychology bachelor's degree: Expert advice for launching your career.* American Psychological Association.

REFERENCES

Advance CTE. (n.d.). *Careers clusters pathways.* Advance CTE. www.careertech.org/sites/default/files/CareerClustersPathways.pdf

American Psychological Association. (2018). *Careers in psychology. [Interactive data tool].* www.apa.org/workforce/data-tools/careers-psychology.aspx

Crawford, P., Lang, S., Fink, W., Dalton, R., & Fielitz, L. (2011). *Comparative analysis of soft skills: What is important for new graduates.* Michigan State University and the University Industry Consortium.

Hagevik, S. (2000). Planned happenstance. *Journal of Environmental Health, 62*(9), 39–38.

Holland, J. L. (1997). *Making vocational choices: A theory of vocational personalities and work environments.* PAR.

McIntyre, M. M., & Graziano, W. G. (2019). A snapshot of person and thing orientations: How individual differences in interest manifest in everyday life. *Personality and Individual Differences, 136*, 160–165. http://dx.doi.org/10.1016/j.paid.2017.08.005

Mitchell, K. E., Levin, A. S., & Krumboltz, J. D. (1999). Planned happenstance: Constructing unexpected career opportunities. *Journal of Counseling & Development, 77*(2), 115–124. https://doi.org/10.1002/j.1556-6676.1999.tb02431.x

National Association of Colleges and Employers. (2017). *Career readiness competencies: Employer survey results.* www.naceweb.org/career-readiness/competencies/career-readiness-competencies-employer-survey-results/

Partnership for 21st Century Skills. (2009). *Framework for 21st century learning.* www.21stcenturyskills.org/documents/P21_Framework.pdf.

Schlossberg, N. K. (1996). *Going to plan B: How you can cope, regroup, and start your life on a new path.* Fireside.

Stamm, K. (2020, March 13). *Career pathways and the psychology major.* Presented at the Eastern Psychological Association Annual Conference.

Stamm, K., & Fowler, G. A. (2019, August 9). *Planning your career path in psychology.* Presented at the 2019 American psychological Convention, Chicago, IL.

Stenberg, R. J. (2017). *Career paths in psychology: Where your degree can take you* (3rd ed.). American Psychological Association.

Stone, J. R., III, & Lewis, M. V. (2012). *College and career ready in the 21st century: Making high school matter*. Teachers College, Columbia University.

Torpey, E. (2015, March). Clusters, pathways, and BLS: Connecting career information. *Career Outlook*, U.S. Bureau of Labor Statistics.

Valickas, A., Raišienė, A. G., & Rapuano, V. (2019). Planned Happenstance skills as personal resources for students' psychological wellbeing and academic adjustment. *Sustainability (2071–1050)*, *11*(12), 3401. https://doi.org/10.3390/su11123401

CHAPTER 10

Master's degrees

Educational options and career paths

DOI: 10.4324/9780429296413-14

INTRODUCTION

This chapter is focused both broadly and specifically on master's degrees (and their equivalent) in psychology. You may be curious about master's degrees in psychology in general and/or considering pursuing one yourself. To set the stage, we begin with a series of reflections then move to general information about master's education and career options and paths with a master's degree. This is followed by information and guidance to help *you* make (or confirm) decisions about pursuing a master's degree in psychology. The chapter concludes with practical guidance to make informed decisions about degree programs and ways to make the most of your master's level education and training.

Let's start this chapter with a set of reflection questions. The first reflection question for this chapter is: Would a master's degree help *you* reach your life/career goals? To answer that question, it's important to know that a master's degree is *optional* for a career in psychology. You may be able to reach your goals at the bachelor's degree level or skip this step entirely if you're admitted to a doctoral program with your bachelor's degree.

Why then, you might ask, would anyone earn a master's degree in psychology? More specifically, why might *you* (want to) earn a master's degree? This gets us back to the first reflection question: Would a master's degree help you reach your life/career goals? and the necessary follow up: Would a master's degree be a worthwhile investment for you?

Then, if a master's degree would be helpful and a good investment, the follow up questions are: What degree? and How do you choose a master's degree program?

We'll provide information and guidance to help you answer all these questions and more in this chapter. In addition, given the associations among psychology and allied fields (Brady-Amoon & Keefe-Cooperman, 2017; Worrell et al., 2018), we'll reference master's options in select related fields here, then explore those options more fully in Chapter 12. So, keeping in mind that this book is a choose-your-own-ending type of book – read on if you're interested in learning more about educational options and career paths in psychology with a master's degree!

MASTER'S DEGREES IN PSYCHOLOGY

Psychology, as we discussed earlier, is one of the most popular undergraduate majors (NCES, 2017, 2019). Although there are many ways to leverage your psychological knowledge at the bachelor's degree level (see Chapter 9), increasing numbers of people with bachelor's degrees in psychology earn graduate (i.e., master's and doctoral) degrees in psychology and closely related fields (NCES, 2017, 2019; Stamm et al., 2019). The first question here, however, is, would a master's degree help you? We believe the information presented here will help you answer that question.

Let's start with some basics. Psychology has long been a doctoral level profession. The doctoral degree was established as the entry-level credential for psychologists at the 1949 Boulder Conference (APA, 2011; Campbell et al., 2018). Sure, you may have (had) the opportunity to take psychology courses in high school and definitely do (or did) in college. Although on one level, a master's degree seems like a logical next step, it's not that simple. A master's degree in psychology is *optional*. You don't need it – but it might be helpful. You don't need a master's degree if you can reach your life/career goals with a bachelor's degree. You also don't need a master's degree if you're admitted to and earn your doctoral degree in a program that admits students with a bachelor's degree. In addition, as an aside, some doctoral degree programs award master's degrees en passant (on the way) to the doctorate. However, a master's degree might be *very* helpful to your life/career goals. It was (and still is, to some degree) to us – and many people we know.

Current status and trends

More than 25,000 people earn master's degrees in psychology in the U.S. each year; that's a little less than a quarter of all bachelor degree recipients, and significantly more than the number of doctoral degrees awarded (NCES, 2017). Master's degrees may be offered as a terminal (culminating) degree or, as noted earlier, en passant (on the way to) a doctoral degree. Unless otherwise specified, we're referring to both types when we refer to master's degrees. Many universities offer master's degrees in psychology (Hughes & Diaz-Granados, 2018) with majors ranging from general psychology to specialty areas within psychology such as industrial-organizational, experimental, and clinical, counseling, and school psychology, which individually and together are currently referred to as Health Service Psychology (HSP) areas (NCES, 2017). See Table 10.1 for a listing of the most popular master's degree majors.

The most common master's degree titles in psychology are the MA (Master of Arts) and MS (Master of Science) however, there are variations, often specific to a particular institution such as the M.Ed. (Master of Education). The title doesn't matter as much as major – and the quality of the education (and, if relevant, professional preparation) you'll receive. We'll also explore specialist and similar post-master's yet non-doctoral degrees (that are often categorized with master's degrees) in this chapter. Those degrees are typically more advanced than master's degrees with titles specific to a particular program or university such as the Ed.M. (Master of Education) degree offered by Columbia University's Teachers College and Ed.S. (Education Specialist) degree offered by Seton Hall University. But first, more on master's degrees.

Psychology master's degrees have outnumbered doctoral degrees in psychology by a ratio of more than 4 to 1 since 2004 (Hughes & Diaz-Granados, 2018; NCES, 2011, 2017). The highest number of master's degrees, representing more than a third of the total number awarded, have been in counseling psychology (Brady-Amoon & Keefe-Cooperman, 2017; Hughes & Diaz-Granados, 2018). The second highest number of degrees, representing almost 23%, were in general psychology (NCES, 2017).

As a group, the majority of master's degrees in psychology have been in HSP (Eisman et al., 2018; NCES, 2011, 2017), encompassing a 70% increase in these degrees between 2004 and 2013 (Hughes & Diaz-Granados, 2018). When master's level mental health providers from allied fields are included, there are almost six times as many master's level mental health providers as doctoral-level psychologists (Eisman et al., 2018) – and those are

TABLE 10.1 Master's Degrees Awarded by Major in Psychology

Master's Degrees Awarded by Major in Psychology	Total Degrees
Psychology, Total	26,773
Psychology, general	6,138
Psychology, other	1,981
Educational psychology	1,358
Industrial and organizational psychology	1,055
Forensic psychology	861
Applied behavior analysis	494
Developmental and child psychology	301
Community psychology	213
Experimental psychology	204
Applied psychology	195
Social psychology	173
Health Service Provider Subfields	
– Counseling psychology	9,160
– Clinical psychology	2,374
– School psychology	1,712
– Clinical, counseling and applied psychology, other	275

Note: Total degrees awarded 2015–2016
Source: NCES, 2017

just a few of the many master's level career paths in psychology! In fact, master's practitioners in Industrial-Organizational psychology and those with specialist degrees in School Psychology are much more common than doctoral level practitioners in those specialties.

Brief history and current context

As we have already noted, while popular and widely accepted, master's degrees are *optional* in psychology. In addition, there are still some questions about how master's degrees, particularly in the HSP subfields, fit into the larger profession. This is largely due to psychology's long history as a doctoral level profession, initially established at the 1949

Boulder Conference (Campbell et al., 2018). Interestingly, the report from that same conference included the first known recommendation to study master's degrees. Since that time, the master's issue, as this has come to be known, has been the focus of numerous APA task forces, working groups, and conferences (Campbell et al., 2018).

More recently, in response to changing social (Eisman et al., 2018) and professional contexts, APA took a series of historic steps to more fully recognize and support master's education and practice, with a particular focus on the HSP subfields. As of this writing, these steps include the adoption of guidelines for master's education (Hughes & Diaz-Granados, 2018) and development of standards and policies for APA accreditation of master's level education programs in the HSP areas that it currently accredits at the doctoral level (Campbell et al., 2018). Of the three HSP areas, school psychology has a long-standing unique association with APA as the only currently recognized specialty area for which a doctorate (although an option) is not required to practice as a school psychologist in school settings (Eisman et al., 2018). These advances are particularly relevant for counseling psychology, given its close alignment with master's level counseling and practice (Brady-Amoon & Keefe-Cooperman, 2017; Eisman et al., 2018; Jackson & Scheel, 2013a, 2013b). They also offer long-term opportunities for master's level clinical psychology practice (Worrell et al., 2018).

Accreditation

Why are educational guidelines and accreditation important? In short, accreditation is an indicator that an educational institution or unit (such as a degree program) meets the guidelines or standards established by a particular accrediting body, generally with input from experts in the field and the public. However, accreditation is more complex than that – particularly for master's programs in psychology and related fields.

At all levels, including master's education, regional accreditation (e.g., Middle States, Southern) is the most important – and essential – accreditation for higher education institutions in the U.S. to hold. As such, a regionally accredited college or university has demonstrated it meets the accreditor's and therefore the U.S. Department of Education requirements. It's important to make sure the college/university you plan to attend (or are attending) is regionally accredited. Colleges and universities may also have additional accreditations that may be helpful to you. For example, master's programs in school and counseling psychology may benefit from College or School of Education accreditation.

Many excellent master's (and bachelor's degree) programs in psychology are not eligible for – and therefore do not have program-level accreditation. At present, the *only* program-level accreditation option for master's programs in psychology is the Masters in Psychology and Counseling Accreditation Council (MPCAC; http://mpc acaccreditation.org/), which is limited to master's degrees in psychology and counseling with a practice component, otherwise known as the HSP subfields. However, as noted earlier, that may change as APA continues its work to expand its scope of accreditation.

CAREER PATHS WITH A MASTER'S DEGREE

Most people pursue a master's degree to increase their work and career options. Others leverage their master's degree to increase their options for admission to doctoral programs. In general, the advantages of earning a master's degree in psychology are advanced training, status, knowledge, and often, but not always, increased opportunities. The disadvantages are that a master's degree is a significant investment of time and money – that, like most investments, is only as good as what you put into it – starting with your decision to pursue a degree, and if so, what degree, where, and how. In the sections that follow, we list a few key categories of work typical of people with master's degrees in psychology and related fields.

Research oriented careers

Some people with master's degrees in psychology use their knowledge in research and other experimental ways. They may work as research assistants in a variety of areas such as market research or legislative analysis, occasionally rising to the level of being able to conduct their own research. (However, those interested in grant funding may find they're limited in the types of grants they can qualify for with a master's degree.) Some do this work to contribute to the advancement of knowledge either in general or in a particular area such as forensic, developmental, or social psychology. Others do this type of work during or after earning their master's degree to gain experience (as well as confidence and connections) to strengthen a potential (or eventual) application for admission to a doctoral program.

Administration and technical/practice assistants

Many people with master's degrees in psychology leverage their advanced knowledge in psychology to work in a variety of administrative roles in business, education, and other settings. They may also work as technicians or practice assistants, for example by assisting psychologists and other qualified administrators with psychological and neuropsychological assessments (Eisman et al., 2018).

Teaching and consultation

Another option for people with a master's degree in psychology work is teaching and consultation at the two-year and occasionally four-year college level and, with other relevant credentials, at the P-12 level. This extends into consultation, writing, and using social media to share your psychological knowledge.

Industrial-organizational psychology and career counseling

Industrial-organizational (I-O) psychology and career counseling are two master's level specialty areas in psychology that often practice at the master's level. I-O psychologists, as described earlier, typically engage in research, consultation, and work to improve employee satisfaction and the workplace. See the Society of Industrial Organizational Psychology website for more on specific career paths in I-O psychology (www.siop.org/Career-Center/I-O-Career-Paths). Career counselors may earn master's degrees in counseling psychology or counseling – and are often qualified for independent practice at the master's level. In most jurisdictions, a license is not required to work as a career or vocational counselor although that appears to be changing. See the National Career Development Association webpage for more on this specialty (www.ncda.org/aws/NCDA/pt/sp/home_page).

Health service psychology

As noted earlier, the majority of master's degrees in psychology are in the HSP subfields, principally counseling psychology, followed by clinical psychology, then school psychology. In addition, there are numerous related degrees (Eisman et al., 2018) such as counselor, marriage and family therapist, and social worker, that prepare practitioners for independent practice at the master's (or post-master's) level.

Licensure and school certification

We briefly considered accreditation earlier. In this section, we'll consider licensure, which is *not* required for most master's level career paths in psychology – and is not even an option in most states and jurisdictions. However, licensure is another important consideration if your career goals include independent practice in one of the HSP subfields or another area governed by licensure either now or in the future.

Almost one-third of states currently offer options for licensing in psychology at the master's level; however, there are significant variations in licensing requirements, title, and scope of practice (i.e., what licensees are authorized to do) from state to state (Buckman et al., 2018; Grus & Skillings, 2018). Only four or five of these states have master's level licensure in psychology that permits the independent practice of psychology. In others, master's level practitioners are called technicians or assistants – and their scope of practice reflects those titles (Buckman et al., 2018). So, what does all this mean? It means that in addition to clarifying your career goals, it's important to consider where you might want (or need) to work – and, if relevant, your options (and anticipated options) for licensure and practice in those jurisdictions.

If you're interested in psychology practice in a school setting, it's good to know that school psychologists are in a unique position. In most states and jurisdictions, the state education department credentials school psychologists with master's and specialist degrees to work in school settings (Buckman et al., 2018). In about a quarter of states, school psychologists who meet additional pre-doctoral requirements are also eligible to apply to the state licensing board for authorization to work as a school psychologist outside school settings (Buckman et al., 2018). In addition, school psychologists with an appropriate doctoral degree, who comprise less than 25% of school psychologists (NCES, 2011, 2017), are generally eligible for full licensure and practice as a psychologist (Brady-Amoon & Keefe-Cooperman, 2017).

Allied fields

If your life/career goals include independent practice as a counselor or therapist at the master's level, another option to consider is earning your master's degree in an allied field that offers a direct route to those goals. In this section, we'll briefly review the most popular options for licensure, independent practice, and school certification at the master's level: social work, counseling, and marriage and family therapy.

Let's begin with *social work*, the largest master's level specialty (HRSA, 2017; NASW, 2006). In most jurisdictions, a master's degree, typically the Master of Social Work (MSW), is required for licensure and independent practice. In a few, a person with a bachelor's degree in social work is eligible for licensure (ASWB, 2017). Given the variations in licensure requirements and scope of practice from state to state, it's always important to research and know your options. Furthermore, school social workers, who are typically credentialed by the state education department, are qualified to work in school settings. According to O*Net (n.d.a), the projected need for social workers, including those with related titles such as case manager, is expected to increase faster than average. We'll explore social work as well as other allied fields in greater depth in Chapter 12.

Similar to social work, *counseling* is a broad field with multiple specializations and work titles. People with master's degrees in counseling, counseling psychology, and closely related fields may not need a license for some specialties in some states (e.g., pastoral counseling) and settings (e.g., independent schools). However, similar to school psychologists and school social workers, master's level counselors with the appropriate coursework and supervised experience may apply for school counselor certification, which is required to work as a school counselor in most public schools. Similarly, with the appropriate coursework and supervised experience, master's level counselors may qualify for licensure and independent practice as a professional or mental health counselor, which is considered a growth career (O*Net, n.d.b). They may also qualify for licensure and to practice in other high need specialty areas such as substance abuse and addiction counseling (HRSA, 2017; O*Net, n.d.b).

At the same time, similar to other fields, there is wide variation from state to state in licensure title, scope of practice, and requirements for licensure, which makes it important to verify the degree you are considering will meet state licensing requirements in the state you plan to work in. It's also important to note that a few states restrict counselor licensure to graduates of counseling programs that are accredited by an accrediting body that takes the position that counseling and psychology are separate fields, which may limit graduates of psychologically oriented counseling and counseling psychology programs (Brady-Amoon & Keefe-Cooperman, 2017). There may also be other requirements. For example, the state of New Jersey requires applicants for licensure to have a master's or doctoral degree with the word "counseling" in the title – so even when applicants have met all the requirements with a master's degree with a different title, they are not eligible.

Marriage and family therapy is the smallest of the master's level direct service professions we'll consider yet, like social work and counseling, is an allied field to consider if you're interested in direct service and licensure at the master's level. Once again, the work and title vary state by state – yet this is another master's level profession with a bright employment outlook (O*Net, n.d.c).

FITTING IT ALL TOGETHER – DECISION MAKING (IS A MASTER'S FOR YOU?)

So – would a master's degree in psychology or closely related field help you reach your life/career goals?

To answer this question, it's often helpful to consider (and reflect on) ways in which your goals, interests, context, and situation align with some of the common ways people with master's degrees in psychology use their knowledge in the work world as outlined earlier in this chapter. The next question is how do you make decisions between and among psychology subfields and allied fields? That's similar to choosing one or more specialty areas. Once again, the short answer is to: 1) consider your values, needs, and goals, 2) explore the possibilities (read up, talk with people in the field), 3) consider how your values, needs, and goals align with the field, and 4) the likely return on investment (ROI), including what it would take, in terms of time, money, and other resources as well as what it would cost you *not* to pursue further formal education.

If you're not sure what's next, it may be helpful to know there are degrees of decidedness (and its corollary, undecidedness). In addition, graduate students (and prospective graduate students) often have similar variations in career decidedness as undergraduate students (Hammond, 2017) – yet graduate undecidedness is often at a higher level. For example, you may know for sure you want a career in psychology, but now that you know more about psychology, realize you have more choices. That can be both intimidating and exciting. You don't have to know exactly what you want to do to pursue a master's or other degree, but it's important to know what you want to accomplish with a master's degree, to inform your decision if a master's degree would be a good investment for you. Some questions to consider are: the timing of your degree, the time it will take, and the cost/benefit analysis of the degree. We'll explore each of these topics next.

Some people pursue a master's or a doctoral degree immediately or shortly after earning their bachelor's degree (sometimes with a little overlap), others pursue graduate degrees after a hiatus from formal education. If you're in the former group, you're in the swing of studying, learning, and making decisions – including your decision whether to pursue a terminal master's degree – or apply directly to a doctoral program. If there's been more time since your bachelor's degree, it may help to know you're not alone and your life experience can be an advantage! Many people earn a master's degree after some time away from formal education. Some have deferred their decision to pursue a master's to attend to other priorities such as work or family obligations. Others are making a voluntary or involuntary career transition, perhaps adapting after a career shock (Seibert et al., 2013), as so many people recently experienced during the pandemic.

Graduate education, including master's level education is often different than you've come to expect. Yes – there are classes, assignments, and projects, but more of the responsibility for learning and professional development shifts to YOU. As such, it requires more time and deeper levels of thinking and commitment than most undergraduate learning. To illustrate, while 12 credit hours are generally considered the minimum for full-time status at the undergraduate level, nine credits typically qualify for full-time status at the graduate level. What does this mean? It means that graduate students are expected to invest, dedicate, and put in more time outside of class per week – and therefore over each semester, than their undergraduate peers. Sure, some can do it with less, however, over time, those who do the minimum (or less) rob themselves, and to a lesser degree, their peers, of the learning/development they would have had.

Most graduate classes are intentionally designed to promote higher level learning, including the application, synthesis, and creation of knowledge, often with curated reading lists, to help students increase their knowledge and, often skills in a particular area. How cool! The master's level is aptly named – to promote the development of mastery in a particular field. Masters in a particular area, like *masters of the universe*, know the basics and go beyond. As such, master's level courses as well as more advanced work such as theses and other supervised research and field work, can be disquieting to students used to doing exactly what they're told to do or want to know *the* one right answer. Yes – it's important to be able to follow instructions and base your work on established evidence and facts, however, at the graduate level, starting at the master's level, the goal of education is to become a professional who is able to skillfully synthesize and apply knowledge in emerging contexts and situations. That's one of the ways psychology changes the world!

Similarly, most degree programs are carefully designed to help you reach the degree program goals. Sure, there are classes you'd rather not take – yet sometimes they open doors you might not have otherwise expected. In addition, some students find that courses that they might have otherwise avoided turn out to be exceptionally helpful – and enjoyable. Moreover, most graduate degree programs offer unique opportunities to work with professors with expertise in the field – and your participation/engagement in the degree program, with the professors, and in relevant extracurricular activities can help you make the most of your educational experience and beyond.

In addition to timing (the *when* of earning a master's degree), and time (how much it will take), it's important to consider both how much a master's degree would cost you – and what it would cost you not to pursue that degree. As with so much else in master's education, there's significant variation in tuition, other costs, and funding at the master's level. Some programs offer scholarships, grant aid, and/or Graduate Assistantships in which the graduate student works, sometimes as a teaching assistant (TA) or research assistant (RA), in exchange for partial to full tuition remission. Others rely on student self-financing, including employment income and student loans. No matter what – a master's program is a significant investment of time and, often money. In conclusion, we encourage you to consider the costs of a master's degree in conjunction with your current status including any outstanding student loans, your resources, available funding, and your goals.

BOX 10.1

Vignette – The Case of a Returning Student

Joan's first career (and college major) was in a very different field than psychology – and she wasn't all that serious about academics as an undergraduate. She was working full-time, raising a family, and although she earned her degree, she wasn't proud of her cumulative GPA. With the help of a career counselor, Joan decided that psychology would be a good field for her, but was concerned her low undergraduate GPA would be a barrier. So, she explored her options, worked to submit a very strong application, and was accepted to a master's program. She did very well in that program, made the most of her experience, and with her improved GPA, knowledge of herself, the field and her goals, and excellent recommendations, was admitted to her dream school, graduated, and is now a successful (on her terms) psychologist.

CHOOSING THE RIGHT PROGRAM FOR YOU

Up to this point, we've explored master's degrees in general and if a master's degree is for you. In this section, we turn our attention to the process of choosing a master's program that will work for you. As before, that goes back to your goals – and context. Another way of putting this question is – what degree/education/training will help you reach those goals? As before, you don't have to know the whole plan – however, the more you know, the better you can do your part to align (or better align) your actions with your goals.

For the purpose of this chapter, we'll assume you have decided to consider master's degrees in psychology or a closely related field. Great! That's a good first step. The next is to determine which master's degree. This is the *what* for your investigation – beginning with your answers to the following: Are you interested in advanced knowledge for its own sake? To improve your research competencies? To qualify for licensure or school certification? Is full-time study an option for you? Would part-time work better? Would a certain schedule (e.g., classes after normal business hours) work better for you? Your responses to those and related questions will help you narrow down the types of programs to consider.

We discussed the issue of *when* earlier, yet again for the purpose of this chapter, we'll assume you are considering a master's degree in the foreseeable future. However, if you're thinking longer term, the information that follows will also be helpful as long as you remain adaptable, for example, considering the possibility of relocation or other changes (e.g., licensure requirements) that will be important to consider before finalizing your plans.

The next step in this investigation is *where* you want to pursue this degree. Are you committed to staying in one geographic area? Some of us are – we have family, work, or other responsibilities or choices. Others are open to and might prefer relocating. The location of your prospective master's programs is an important consideration for campus-based programs. Your official residency (country and state or other jurisdiction) may also be important factors to consider. The latter can make a big difference in tuition costs at public universities. Your location may be less important (and potentially irrelevant) if you are interested in online learning. However, there are other important considerations. Do you have regular access to reliable high-speed internet services? Other equipment required/recommended by the program? Then there are other questions to consider, for example, is the program fully or partially online? If partially, what are the requirements and costs for the in-person component? Is the online aspect of the program offered synchronously or asynchronously? Synchronous online learning means classes meet on a set schedule, which is particularly important to consider if you're not in the same time zone as the university. You may be fine with that – as were a few students we recently taught – but then again, you may not. In asynchronous online learning, students participate on their own schedule within established parameters. For example, in the asynchronous online master's programs in counseling at Seton Hall, students and faculty interact by posting on an online message board Mondays through Wednesdays at times that work for them. Other programs have similar yet different requirements.

The second level of answering the question of *where* – and moving into *what* program/university – is doing more important research! Does the university have regional accreditation? This is essential as we shared earlier. Does it have other relevant accreditations? (See earlier section for more on this.) Is it a not-for-profit? Profit making enterprise? Most colleges and universities, public and private, are not-for-profits, meaning their primary purpose is to serve the public to whom they are accountable. However, the fastest growing sector for master's degree granting institutions is the for-profit sector (Worrell et al., 2018) which, by definition, serve and are accountable to institutional share-holders. That is a concern for many given some unscrupulous institutions however, if the institution and program meet your other requirements (e.g., regional accreditation and a good track record), then put that institution and program on your maybe list. A few other questions to ponder as you consider your potential programs are: How long has the program been around? What do graduates do? Can you verify that? Can you talk with any? If you're not already keeping a journal or other written record of your responses, this is a great time to do that. You might also find it helpful to set up a spreadsheet with your potential program list to keep that and your research findings organized.

In addition, if your career goals include licensure, it's essential to check with the training program(s) you are considering/enrolled in that the degree they offer meets the educational requirements for the type of licensure you want (e.g., psychology, counselor) in the jurisdiction you would like to be licensed in. It's helpful to verify this information with the relevant state or jurisdictional licensing board or agency by checking the requirements and scope of practice for master's level practitioners in that jurisdiction. Keep in mind that many licensing agencies are not able to verify eligibility of graduates from a particular institution or from out of state. For example, the New York State Office of the Professions only lists programs in New York state that qualify for licensure, not programs from other states that do. In addition, this is a reminder to carefully evaluate online information because, in our experience, there's far too much incorrect and misleading information about accreditation and licensure (and many other things) online. Finally, for now, when you're making these decisions, it's helpful to think ahead to where you'd like to be initially licensed as well as potential future locations.

Now we move to the nitty gritty of *what* – getting in and succeeding in your master's degree, with a nod and advance information for those keeping their options open for a future doctoral program. How's that list of potential master's programs coming? If you've been following this process, you've likely identified a short list of potential master's programs at regionally accredited institutions that, based on your research, will help you reach your career goals and work for you location and time-wise. If that's not the case, you might go back and revisit the steps in this section, use the services available through your college/university career center, or work with a career counselor.

Applying and getting in

Once you've decided where to apply, the next step is applying and getting in. The application process is fairly standard – submit the required materials by the application deadline and if required or recommended, interview well. That sounds easy – but is it? Well, there is a great deal of variation in admissions criteria among master's programs. For some, your undergraduate grades (particularly your cumulative GPA and sometimes psychology GPA) matter a great deal. Some programs may require specific undergraduate coursework, which, if you don't have, you may be able to complete before admission. Other master's programs have broader admissions criteria. Some even admit students with other undergraduate degrees. That's a wonderful opportunity for people who choose a career in psychology after they've already committed to or earned a bachelor's degree, like us!

In addition to transcripts, some programs require GRE or other standardized test scores, essays such as a personal statement, a resume, letters of recommendation, and sometimes a writing sample. Some are much more competitive than others. No matter what, it's important to submit all the required material and any optional material that would be to your advantage. For example, if your GPA or standardized test scores aren't at the level you'd like them to be (or worse, that your top program prefers), it would be to your advantage to demonstrate your interest, commitment, and ability in your essays and interview, and for your recommenders to emphasize your strengths. As with undergraduate education – and most jobs – you have your greatest leverage after an offer of admission has been extended. Of course, it's important to research the areas that matter most to you before applying however, once an offer has been extended, you can and should inquire about any other specifics that matter to you such as funding, assistantships, and the potential for waived or transfer credits.

Some master's programs will waive required courses based on prior academic coursework at the undergraduate or graduate level or documented experience. When one or more courses are waived, you may be able to substitute a more advanced course for a course with content you've already mastered (pun intended) or even graduate with fewer credits than indicated in the catalog for that degree. Transfer credits are typically limited at the graduate level. Some programs will not consider transfer credits, others will accept up to six graduate credits that meet specific requirements. Given the limits on waived and transfer credits, it's important to choose your graduate program carefully and, if you decide to transfer later (or already have graduate credits and are considering a new program), find out about your transfer credits, keeping in mind that it is a rarity at the graduate level, before you commit to your new program. In addition, if you're considering a doctorate (immediately afterwards or sometime in the future), it would also be helpful to check with prospective doctoral programs how their program treats transfer credits (some grant advanced standing, others don't).

Succeeding in master's level education/training programs

The best way to succeed in your master's program is to do everything that worked in your undergraduate program – go to class, take notes, meet with the professor, and complete assignments on time. Beyond this, as we discussed earlier, it's important to dedicate sufficient time to your course work, recognizing that most graduate classes and programs are designed to promote higher level learning to and master's level competencies in the relevant subfield. In addition, many master's programs offer additional opportunities (which are something to look for if this is important to you) to develop research skills, present or publish your findings, or develop other professional competencies.

As with other levels of education, careers, and life, there are often many invisible assumptions, expectations, and requirements in master's education and careers. Our recommendation is to recognize that unwritten rules, so to speak, often reflect dominant systems – so the best ways to address them is to acknowledge they likely exist – and seek support from knowledgeable advisors, mentors, and peers. Trust yourself as well. The goal, as we explored in greater depth in earlier chapters, is to be your best version of *you* as you earn your degree – and beyond. Keep in mind that your peers as well as your professors are your future professional colleagues – and can be a great source of mutual support for future career opportunities. The bottom line when you've made the decision to pursue a master's degree is to make the most of that opportunity – so you can make the most of your master's level career opportunities!

CHAPTER SUMMARY

This chapter is focused on master's and, to a lesser extent, relevant specialist degrees in psychology and allied fields. Beginning with a series of reflections about your career goals and life situation to set the stage, we provide information about the current status and trends in master's education as well as a brief historical context to help you make informed decisions about pursuing a master's degree. The next section outlines career paths with a master's degree in psychology including licensure and practice in HSP and select allied master's level professions. The third major section is designed to help you decide if a master's degree is for you – and the fourth, which follows immediately afterwards, is designed to help readers who've decided to pursue a master's degree how to choose a good program to maximize career success.

EXERCISES

1   Using your knowledge of research, explore the subfield(s) you are interested in. Compare your notes with a trusted advisor or career counselor.
2   Develop a list of questions you would ask in an informational interview. Share this list with a trusted advisor or career counselor to get their feedback. Identify potential people to ask to meet with you for a limited time for an informational interview. Follow up with a gracious thank you.

Next steps: the advanced move

Readers interested in learning more about the history and current status of the association among psychology, counseling psychology, and professional counseling are encouraged to read:

Brady-Amoon, P., & Keefe-Cooperman, K. (2017). Psychology, counseling psychology, and professional counseling: Shared roots, challenges, and opportunities. *European Journal of Counselling Psychology*, 6(1), 41–62. https://doi.org/10.5964/ejcop. v6i1.105

REFERENCES

American Psychological Association. (2011). Model act for state licensure of psychologists. *American Psychologist*, 66, 214–226. http://dx.doi.org/ 10.1037/a0022655

Association of Social Work Boards. (2017). *Compare license requirements*. http://aswbsocialwork regulations.org/jurisdictionLevelsReport.jsp

Brady-Amoon, P., & Keefe-Cooperman, K. (2017). Psychology, counseling psychology, and professional counseling: Shared roots, challenges, and opportunities. *European Journal of Counselling Psychology*, 6(1), 41–62. https://doi.org/10.5964/ejcop.v6i1.105

Buckman, L. R., Nordal, K. C., & DeMers, S. T. (2018). Regulatory and licensure issues derived from the summit on master's training in psychological practice. *Professional Psychology: Research & Practice*, 49(5/6), 321–326.

Campbell, L. F., Worrell, F. C., Dailey, A. T., & Brown, R. T. (2018). Master's level practice: Introduction, history, and current status. *Professional Psychology: Research & Practice*, 49(5/6), 299–305.

Eisman, E. J., Brown, K. S., & Martin, J. N. (2018). Marketplace and workforce issues. *Professional Psychology: Research and Practice*, 49(5–6), 314–320. https://doi.org/10.1037/pro0000215

Grus, C. L., & Skillings, J. L. (2018). Scope of practice considerations related to master's training and psychological practice. *Professional Psychology: Research & Practice, 49*(5/6), 311–313.

Hammond, M. S. (2017). Differences in career development among first-year students: A proposed typology for intervention planning. *Journal of the First-Year Experience & Students in Transition, 29*(2), 45–63.

Health Resources & Services Administration. (2017). *Behavioral health workforce projections, 2017–2030.* https://bhw.hrsa.gov/data-research/projecting-health-workforce-supply-demand/behavioral-health

Hughes, T. L., & Diaz-Granados, J. (2018). Master's summit: Quality assurance and accreditation. *Professional Psychology: Research & Practice, 49*(5/6), 306–310.

Jackson, M. A., & Scheel, M. J. (2013a). Integrating master's education in counseling psychology for quality, viability, and value added. *Counseling Psychologist, 41*(5), 717–723. https://doi.org/10.1177/0011000013493334

Jackson, M. A., & Scheel, M. J. (2013b). Quality of master's education: A concern for counseling psychology? *Counseling Psychologist, 41*(5), 669–699. https://doi.org/10.1177/0011000011434644

National Association of Social Workers. (2006). *Assuring the sufficiency of a frontline workforce: A national study of licensed social workers.* Executive Summary. www.socialworkers.org/LinkClick.aspx?fileticket=QKU6bvt6Rwc%3d&portalid=0

National Center for Education Statistics. (2011). *Digest of education statistics.* Table 290. Bachelor's, master's, and doctor's degrees conferred by degree-granting institutions, by sex of student and discipline division: 2009–10. http://nces.ed.gov/programs/digest/d11/tables/dt11_290.asp

National Center for Education Statistics. (2017). *Digest of education statistics.* Table 318.30. Bachelor's, master's, and doctor's degrees conferred by postsecondary institutions, by sex of student and discipline division: 2014–15. https://nces.ed.gov/programs/digest/d16/tables/dt16_318.30.asp

National Center for Education Statistics. (2019). Table 318.30. Bachelor's, master's, and doctor's degrees conferred by postsecondary institutions, by sex of student and discipline division: 2017–18. https://nces.ed.gov/programs/digest/d19/tables/dt19_318.30.asp

O*Net. (n.d.a). *Social work.* www.onetonline.org/link/details/21-1021.00

O*Net. (n.d.b). *Mental health counseling.* www.onetonline.org/link/summary/21-1014.00b

O*Net. (n.d.c). *Marriage and family therapy.* www.onetonline.org/link/summary/21-1013.00

Seibert, S. E., Kraimer, M. L., Holtom, B. C., & Pierotti, A. J. (2013). Even the best laid plans sometimes go askew: Career self-management processes, career shocks, and the decision to pursue graduate education. *Journal of Applied Psychology, 98*(1), 169–182. https://doi.org/10.1037/a0030882

Stamm, K., Christidis, P., Lin, L., & Conroy, J. (2019). Preparing for the future: The psychology workforce of the 21st century. *American Psychological Association Center for Workforce Studies.* https://www.apa.org/workforce/presentations/index

Worrell, F. C., Campbell, L. F., Dailey, A. T., & Brown, R. T. (2018). Commentary: Consensus findings and future directions. *Professional Psychology: Research & Practice, 49*(5/6), 327–331.

CHAPTER 11

Doctoral degrees

Educational options and career paths

ORIENTING QUESTIONS

1. What types of things can you do with a doctorate in psychology?
2. What types of degrees, programs, and majors are available?
3. Which combination of these will help *you* change the world?
4. How is training at the doctoral level different from that in a bachelor's or master's degree program?
5. Is a doctorate "right" for you?

DOI: 10.4324/9780429296413-15

INTRODUCTION

In Chapters 9 and 10, we explored career options for individuals with a bachelor's or master's degree in psychology. You've also learned a method for thinking through the decision as to your career direction. So, you may be reading this chapter out of curiosity – good for you – or, you may have decided that the way you want to change the world does or may require doctoral-level training. This chapter will discuss the types of education and, when applicable, training, and supervised experiences available to you and the directions in which they lead. We won't cover all of them, however, we will suggest ways of learning about career directions to help you reach your goals. We will also discuss (and provide references for further research) selecting and applying for doctoral-level training and what to expect once you arrive.

UNDERSTANDING DOCTORAL EDUCATION/ TRAINING: APPLYING AND GETTING IN

Take a moment to recall the processes that you followed (or will follow) in applying for admission to a college or university for your current or most recent degree. At the doctoral level, the process is similar, however, there are a few differences. We'll discuss those and then talk about tips for engaging the application process in the sections that follow.

Let's recall a few items before we move on:

1   Of the 3.5 million individuals who held bachelor's degrees in psychology in 2017, only 149,000 (4% of the total) obtained doctoral-level degrees in psychology (APA, 2020c). The take-away is that many people feel that they have obtained enough information about psychology (without a doctorate) to do the work they want to do.

2   The curriculum at the graduate level changes significantly from that at the undergraduate level. At the graduate level, there are no "general education" requirements. Most requirements are specific to the degree, major, and, if applicable, the role for which the program is preparing you.

3   Due to limitations in funding and space, no university provides training in all subfields of psychology, let alone the specialty areas within the subfields of psychology and the *new and emerging* fields in psychology. In addition, admissions to most doctoral programs is highly competitive.

4   Graduate training in psychology is often described by the field as "broad and general" with a focus on a specific content area. Thus, there are courses and training that are considered "foundational" as well as content-focused coursework.

These pieces of information are very important because they bind and explain much about graduate training in psychology. We'll try to explain here. First, you will find that most graduate programs focus on a subfield of psychology and have a particular group of faculty members who teach the core courses in that program. They are researching some aspects of the subfield, but not all. This means that, for a person who has identified a particular subfield and has research or practice interests in particular populations, disorders, topics, etc., just any old program will not work. Imagine yourself in a room full of psychologists who are all talking about eye-tracking movements in individuals who are 1) reading maps, 2) reading an airplane dashboard, or 3) reading the instrument panel on the hospital lab equipment to set up a blood test – and your interest is in learning to help children who have experienced trauma. Or, think of it vice versa. How much difficulty (or, ease) would you have joining the conversation, remaining interested in continuing the conversations, and/or thinking about making this your career? Exactly – it would likely be difficult. Thus, if you want to be a good researcher, practitioner, or applied psychologist, you would do well to pay attention not only to the subfield, but to the particular interests of the faculty within that program. As you might begin to see, doctoral study in psychology can get pretty focused. An easy way to identify potential programs that might be a good fit for you is to start to pay attention to the authors of journal articles or books that you find most interesting. If those individuals are writing what you find interesting, then maybe you should consider applying to study with them or other people doing similar work

When we say "study with them", we mean exactly that. At the doctoral level, you don't just apply to the institution for admission. You apply to both the institution (and often a graduate school) and the particular program – usually submitting one application through either the institution or through an admissions portal, such as PSYCAS. The way it works is that the application is forwarded to the faculty in the program to which you are applying and those faculty members review your application. How? They are looking at a number of things. In general, they will want to see that you

1   Have sufficient relevant undergraduate coursework so you will most likely be able to be successful in their program
2   Have interests aligned with the program and the experiences that specific program can provide in order to assist you in reaching your goals
3   Demonstrate a commitment to your career in this particular area/subfield in psychology

The second and third items are often confusing to prospective doctoral applicants, so we'll discuss them here. The easiest way to think about these pieces is to focus on your career goals. Say, for example, you wanted to become a researcher or therapist specializing in personality. Do you think that it would be helpful to focus your efforts on learning how to develop job selection procedures (I/O Psychology)? No, you would want to learn as much as you can about personality and related topics. Well, that's graduate school in a nutshell. So, the faculty in the program want to make sure that 1) they have expertise that will be valuable to you as you move toward your goal, and 2) that, due to limited resources on their part, that you are most likely to be committed to your career goal. Now, you can control the expertise item by selecting institutions that have faculty members doing research in the main area that you want to study and that fits your career goal. You can also affect their perceptions of your commitment by becoming engaged in your future career in psychology. This is demonstrated in letters of recommendation that attest to your commitment.

Note that you are likely to be required to submit both essays and a writing example. Both should be spell- and grammar-checked, as well as best demonstrate your capacity to be professional and produce a quality product. Remember, in graduate school you are likely to be asked to work with a professor to research and publish. More specifically remember the purpose of the essays – to provide enough information so the admissions committee (and often prospective faculty advisors) can decide whether or not you are a good fit for their program. So, keep focused on the purpose and utilize your resources to improve your communication. This can be challenging, as we live with ourselves all the time and we are trying to communicate who we know we are to people who never met us. There are several ways to improve this communication. First, ask people who know you to review your essays (it can be your family and friends), then take it to your campus writing center for assistance in improving the focus and organization, and finally, take it to your advisor or faculty member for their thoughts. Remember, they had to go through this process too, and may even have experience with the admissions committees/interviews for graduate programs in your department. We also encourage you to check with your library for texts on getting into graduate school in psychology (see exercise 1 at the end of the chapter). There are quite a few out there. Once you've reviewed several (or, gathered a group of friends to share the task by reading and summarizing different texts), the common (and, therefore, strongest) points will begin to emerge – pay special attention to them.

EXPECTATIONS AT THE DOCTORAL LEVEL

Let's start by talking about the difference between training at the graduate level versus training at the undergraduate level. Just to remind you, at the graduate level, education and training is more narrowly focused – no general education courses. It is expected that you have a commitment to the field and will put forth maximum effort to become competent in the area of study. As a result, in graduate school you typically take only 9–12 credit hours per semester. This doesn't mean that there is less work – on the contrary, there is more to learn and you need the time to learn it – however, this is why graduate studies are so focused. So, just as there was a shift of responsibility from the teacher to the student as you moved from high school to college so, too, another shift occurs at the graduate level. This shift is a shift to expecting you to apply critical thinking skills to the topics you will study in a different manner by directly applying the learning (for example, by designing a research study or utilizing the theory in work with clients) and critiquing the theories and knowledge so as to identify gaps that could affect interpretation or applications to particular situations. By the way, it's important to always remember that theories are just people's ways of making meaning of the world. They are limited by each individual's understanding and worldview, so it is important to recognize that bringing your worldview to bear on these issues is an important part of improving psychology's theories and practices. Think about how Dr. Mamie Clark's master's thesis on self-consciousness in African American children shifted our understanding of racism and was crucial in the Supreme Court case *Brown v. Board of Education* (*Brown v. Board of Education, 347 U.S. 483*, 1954) decision that ended legal segregation in public schools. There is an additional shift – one that is focused on socializing you into the profession. Here are some expectations that you will want to be aware of: that you will become active in the program, that you are open to mentoring from faculty to support your growth, and that you will take the initiative to find resources to support your development – including engaging with faculty and mentors to "learn the ropes" about being a professional in psychology.

Also, as you look at the curriculum, you may wonder why you need to take these courses – that some of them look like courses that you took for your bachelor's degree. Think back to the transition from high school to college for a minute. If you recall your high school courses, some of them had similar (or, the same!) titles as courses you took in your undergraduate degree. When you actually took those courses, did they just cover the same material? Or, did they go in deeper and more broadly? That's the same thing at this level – you will learn more about the complexities of the topics so that you can do a better job in your chosen career. Also, as a side note for those preparing to be a counselor or therapist, licensure requires this level of depth in order to be "minimally prepared" to function in these roles.

The biggest mistake that students make upon entering a graduate program is to think that they know how this all works. We guarantee you that the shift from undergraduate to graduate changes everything. Thus, engage and listen from the time you are offered a position in the next entering class. Read texts related to obtaining mentoring and succeeding in graduate school – see the advanced moves for suggestions. Engage, engage, engage. Once you are through your first year – if you've engaged and listened, you will have enough information to make effective decisions about opportunities and processes. Keep your goal in mind, but don't shut yourself off from new perspectives and opportunities – psychology is changing fast and so are the ways to implement it in the world.

BASIC INFORMATION TO CONSIDER

As you articulate your goal(s), the next step is to begin making decisions about the path to that goal. As you've learned throughout this book, there are many ways to prepare for a career in psychology. In order to best take advantage of the opportunities, you have to be informed – right? So, in this section, we try to give you an overview about graduate study in psychology – focusing on the doctoral-level training. Remember, the master's level training is discussed in Chapter 10, so if that's in your future, check it out.

Types of programs at the graduate level

Now, we'd like to give you an overview of how psychologists organize their subfields. At a basic level, there are two basic types of subfields in psychology – clinical practice and research. Fortunately for us, those two categories are too limited, and therefore, not as useful as a more detailed set of categories. We can start with the organizing system that the National Center for Educational Statistics (NCES, 2020) uses. The category of Psychology, as an educational major, is broken down into four groupings. The first grouping is General Psychology and while you may be most familiar with this label as related to your undergraduate degree (unless your program has "tracks"), there are graduate degrees that continue to support students who have an interest in psychology broadly. These degrees typically do not focus on the practice component, however, they often include practice-oriented courses, as well as courses related to the variety of subfields in psychology. There is another more general category, labelled "Psychology, Other". This category includes anything that doesn't fall in the other three categories.

The two larger categories of subfields are labeled as *Research and Experimental Psychology* and *Clinical, Counseling and Applied Psychology*. These two categories cover the major types of subfields in psychology. While we will discuss the contents of these two groupings further down in the chapter, for now, we'd like to focus on the differences in training that affect how you think about choosing, entering into, and graduating from programs. Let's focus first on the Research and Experimental Psychology grouping. The degree areas included here focus on psychology subfields such as Cognitive Psychology, Psycholinguistics, Personality, Social Psychology, Developmental Psychology, Psychometrics, Psychopharmacology, and Quantitative Psychology. As you can see, these subfields are focused on understanding and forming theories about particular aspects of psychology. As a result, there tends to be more training in theories, research methods, and a focus on increasing our ability to understand and make meaning of human beings and the systems in which they function from the perspective of that subfield. For example, Developmental Psychology (including both Child and Adolescent Development) contributes to our understanding of the process of psychological and psychobiological development of individuals across the lifespan, while Social Psychology focuses on how individuals behave in group contexts, the role of culture on individual functioning, etc. As you can see, they overlap when we start talking about the impact of culture and society on a child's or adolescent's development. As a result, you will often reach into another subfield's literature to support your understanding and theory-building – there's no absolute division. Rather, think of a subfield as a lens, way of thinking, or focused area in psychology. These fields are critical because they focus on what is typically called "basic" research that explains psychological phenomena.

Moving on to the Clinical, Counseling and Applied Psychology category, we are now turning our attention to those subfields in psychology that typically apply the research and theorizing from the previous grouping to actually working with humans. That doesn't mean that these subfields don't conduct their own research! However, more of the research in these fields focuses on things like understanding the impact of an intervention designed to help humans in some way. In other words, the program types represented in this group translate the theory and research to practice and extend its impact by demonstrating the theory's utility in the real world of helping people live better lives. The research that these fields do is sometimes called "translational" or "field" research, as it is often applying theory and knowledge to real-world situations. Some of the subfields in this group are very practice-focused, particularly Clinical Psychology, Counseling Psychology, and School Psychology, and, thus, require certification or licensure to practice in a particular state or jurisdiction. As a result, education in these areas typically includes training that differs from that in the previous category (Research and Experimental Psychology), as it includes supervised field work, most often in a mental health or psychological clinic. The remaining subfields in this category (e.g., Community, Industrial/Organizational, Forensic, and Performance and Sport Psychology) focus more on applied research or are so new licensure is not an option.

Differences in program structure

So, what do we mean by program structure? As we are using it here, we are focusing on the meta-level of how your graduate education is structured. At the graduate level, there are two primary structures, which sometimes exist in the same department – so it can be confusing. However, it's critical to understand the difference because you cannot easily transfer credits from one program/university to another. The first program structure is one in which you are admitted to a doctoral program, with only a bachelor's degree. These programs look like they take longer than the second variety because the coursework for the master's degree is embedded in the doctoral program. This means that you complete your master's degree along the way. Other programs only expect you to have completed a master's degree before you apply to the doctoral program. These programs look shorter because they don't include the courses for the master's degree (which you would have already completed). Of course, there's a third option. In this option the program is structured to admit students either with a bachelor's degree or with a master's degree. The former are required to take more courses than the latter, so they both end up with essentially the same number of required courses by the time they complete their doctorate. Thus, you have options and must pay attention to the structure of the program to which you apply.

Differences in degree type

You may or may not be aware that there are several types of doctoral degrees in psychology. These include the Ph.D., the Psy.D., and the Ed.D. The Ed.D. is most frequently found in programs situated in Colleges of Education and is less frequently awarded in recent years. This degree may be more practice-focused or research-focused, depending upon the program. Most, if not all degrees in the areas we've labeled Research and Experimental Psychology award Ph.D.'s, as these degrees are focused on training students to consume and produce research (among other things like teaching). However, when we are speaking about the Applied Psychology areas – and particularly those that are licensable, there is a wider variety of degrees to choose from. Degrees in the areas of Clinical, Counseling, and School Psychology may award the Ph.D., Psy.D., or Ed.D. With regards to these types of degrees, they have traditionally differed on the balance of their emphasis on research and practice, however, these distinctions are no longer as clear as they were when the Psy.D. was first created (Murphy, 2008). You can see that there is lots of room here for variation – and that is just what we find when we look at programs. These differences can open different opportunities post-graduation (Cherry et al., 2000) so it's important for you to be clear about your goals, and hence, the type of program that would best suit your needs. We encourage you to speak with your advisor or mentor to learn more about the degree types that are most relevant for your interests.

Financial support

Just as there is a shift in expectations and responsibilities, there is also a shift in funding. Many programs have graduate assistantships, where for teaching a course, working on someone's research, or helping out in the department you are provided with some combination of tuition waiver, and/or a stipend. There often are other sources of funding, such as grants, fellowships, loans, and scholarships. Due to the need for both researchers and practitioners in psychology, should you choose to take out loans to fund your education, there are *repayment* and *forgiveness* programs. For those choosing a career in one of the HSP subfields, there is an additional option for service in the military health corps for those who qualify (see Table 11.1).

TEXT BOX 11.1

Examples of Programs to Reduce the Cost of Graduate Study in Psychology

- Income-Based Repayment Programs: https://studentloans.gov/myDirect-Loan/index.action
- Public Service Loan Forgiveness (PSLF): https://studentaid.ed.gov/sa/repay-loans/forgiveness-cancellation/public-service
- National Health Service Corps Loan Repayment Program: https://nhsc.hrsa.gov/loanrepayment/
- NIH Loan Repayment Programs: www.lrp.nih.gov/
- Faculty Loan Repayment Program: www.hrsa.gov/loanscholarships/repayment/faculty/
- Other programs can be found on the APA Graduate Student Division's website: www.apa.org/apags/resources/loan-repayment.pdf
- U.S. Army's Health Professions Scholarship Program: www.goarmy.com/amedd/education/hpsp.html

DOCTORAL LEVEL RESEARCH OR EXPERIMENTAL PSYCHOLOGY OPPORTUNITIES

Many, if not most, treatments and interventions are driven by research. To use an example from biology/medicine, the treatments that you receive are based on 1) basic or foundational research to understand the nature of things (diseases, potential therapies or treatments); and 2) translational or clinical research that examines the effect of one or more particular treatments on a particular disease or problem. In other words, doctors (M.D.'s or D.O.'s) would have difficulty healing people if there weren't a large number of researchers (Ph.D.'s) in the background developing the knowledge and therapies that are used. However, we don't normally encounter these Ph.D.'s, since they often work behind the scenes – at universities, hospitals, research institutes (such as the National Institutes of Health), etc. This is very similar to the situation in psychology. You may know or have met a counselor or psychologist and decided that you wanted to help people in similar ways. That's cool – we need people to do that. However, we encourage you to reach deep into yourself to see if you might have that curious, questioning core that really, really wants to know, understand, and generate information that will lead to improved understanding of the mind and methods for treating psychological disorders.

Individuals trained in the research or experimental subfields in psychology conduct or manage research that helps other psychologists and the world to understand the mind better and helps develop methods to treat or work with humans and their contexts more effectively. Typically, they choose the subfield in which they are working because that population, or the particular type of problem they want to solve, is best viewed through the lens of that subfield of psychology. They design and implement research projects, collaborate with other researchers, manage their own research team, write grants to fund their research projects, and disseminate their results through presentations and publications. There are many more activities in which they engage, such as recruiting and supervising research assistants, interns, and fellows; or managing workflow on multiple projects. While many psychologists conduct their research as faculty members – research is a part of the job expectations for many faculty members – they also work in clinics, government, hospitals, and research institute settings to conduct research. As you think about a career that includes or focuses on research, remember that psychology research is conducted in order to understand the mind and how people use it. The theories and knowledge that are derived from that research are limited by the worldview brought to bear in creating it, thus, the greater the diversity of people conducting research, the more complete and more inclusive are the resulting products and applications. For example, women have continued to increase as a proportion of individuals in research faculty positions (APA, 2020a), surpassing 50% in 2015. Similarly, while research psychology (actually, most of psychology) remains predominantly White, in the ten years between 1995 and 2015 the proportion of individuals of color has increased from 8% to 22% and continues to rise (APA, 2020b).

DOCTORAL LEVEL APPLIED/HEALTH SERVICE PSYCHOLOGY OPPORTUNITIES

As you may recall from Chapter 9, we spoke about applied psychologists as both those who focused primarily on therapeutic interventions and were licensed, as well as those applied psychologists who may work with people, but in different ways (NCES, n.d.; Reaves, 2006). The applied psychologists we will discuss in this section generally work with people by providing therapeutic services – counseling, psychotherapy, etc. Health service psychologists (HSPs) apply psychological principles, methods, and procedures in the process of observing, describing, evaluating, interpreting, and modifying human behavior (APA, 2011). The practice of health service psychology includes a wide variety of tasks, including psychological testing or assessment; many different ways of conducting therapy; such as working with people with psychological disorders, disabilities, and career/work issues; providing supportive therapy, prevention or psychoeducational interventions; providing consultation to other health and legal professions; supervision of trainees and other personnel; as well as additional tasks that can be found either in the model licensure law approved by APA (2010) or in your state's legal code.

It should also be noted that there are not enough HSPs to meet current demand through 2030 (APA, 2020c). In other words, this is a growing field. However, you may not recognize this, as parts of the U.S. are currently well-staffed with psychologists (the northeastern and far southwestern portions), while other portions are significantly understaffed (the middle and southern states). In addition, some licensed psychologists have a general practice, in other words, they deal with a myriad of issues that clients present, while others specialize, that is they focus on treating specific issues, settings, or populations. Some examples of specializations include addictions, trauma, sleep, or vocational psychology; forensics, rehabilitation, or school psychology; and animal psychology, child psychology, geropsychology; school psychology, or sports psychology.

Licensure – what is it and why do we need it?

Many individuals in the Clinical, Counseling, and School Psychology, as well as the Applied Behavior Analysis subfields plan to do things like set up a private practice, work in a mental health clinic, or work in a hospital-based clinic or unit. To do this, they are required by the state in which they practice to be licensed. Doctoral training programs in psychology with this focus have a responsibility to train their students to practice in ways that don't harm people – similar to other fields that train students to provide health care services. As such, they often work to align their program requirements with both accreditation requirements and state licensure requirements in order to facilitate students moving into the practice workforce. However, licensure and licensure requirements, which are essential to protect the public by assuring minimum levels of competence, vary from state to state. Therefore, it's very important to fully investigate your prospective training programs – and licensure requirements in the jurisdictions in which you plan to work.

Some of the other subfields listed in the NCES Clinical, Counseling and Applied Psychology categories do not specifically require licensure, however, individuals may desire to apply the knowledge generated by research in this subfield to helping others – such as Geropsychology, Forensic Psychology, or Performance and Sport Psychology. As of this writing, these fields are not licensed specifically, however, those who are practitioners generally obtain licensure as a psychologist. If you are interested in fields such as these and want to practice, make sure that you start speaking to your advisor to obtain their assistance in understanding which programs would help you to meet licensure requirements – in addition to preparing you for practice in these specialty areas. To be clear, this means that if one's primary work is that of engaging in research and experimentation (those subfields primarily in the Research and Experimental Psychology categories), you would not be required to be licensed to practice (at least not at the time this text was written). Similarly, teaching at the post-secondary educational level does not generally require licensure.

OTHER WAYS AT THE DOCTORAL LEVEL TO USE YOUR KNOWLEDGE OF PSYCHOLOGY

Psychologists may also engage in work that crosses the boundaries or combines the two previously mentioned categories. They may or may not be licensed or, they may be certified either by the profession such as by the Behavior Analyst Certification Board or by state education agencies. Regardless of licensure, psychologists may engage in a wide variety of activities. For example, community psychology and environmental psychology focus on understanding and solving problems related to how communities function and/ or how their interaction with the physical world around them may have positive or negative consequences. Meanwhile, individuals focusing on performance or sports psychology, may work with everyone from members of the general public trying to improve their ability to engage in sports to professionals. As you can imagine, there are many ways of combining or sequencing the type of activities you engage in across your career in psychology. Some individuals in some circumstances combine different activities at the same time, while others do so sequentially. Their interests, goals, and the structure of the positions they hold all play a role in how their career moves and changes. Thus, psychology can be, although is not always, a flexible career. Several examples follow to stimulate your thinking.

Our first example is that of researchers. You can learn more about psychological research at the doctoral level by exploring the websites of research-oriented federal agencies such as the National Institute of Mental Health (NIMH), the Centers for Disease Control (CDC), the National Science Foundation (NSF), and the U.S. Department of Education (US DoE). Your research team leader is likely to also have information related to different career paths in research, as will the career center, career counseling center, and/or the library. By the way, librarians are great at helping you to dig up information!

You would think that HSPs would just sit in their offices and see clients all day. That might even seem boring to you. However, many HSPs work in settings where research is being conducted and participate in activities related to research, or they really like sharing their knowledge and experience, so they teach part-time at local post-secondary institutions or provide experiential learning opportunities for undergraduates, master's, and doctoral-level students. Another way that HSPs combine different types of career activities is their engagement in consulting or coaching activities. In these activities, HSPs apply their knowledge of psychology including psychological difficulties and challenges, as well as their understanding of how to create change, in order to help organizations, groups, or individuals change and/or achieve goals. Thus, helping a group to work together more effectively or to develop their skills in dealing with microaggressions would be examples of that might be addressed, usually through workshops, trainings, or individual consultations. HSPs may also collaborate with other groups to provide services to groups that are hard-to-reach or at-risk, such as people who are homeless or indigent, as well as taking therapy into the community so as to make services available to those who might have difficulty travelling to a clinic. In addition to providing different types of services in different places, HSPs may also become managers of groups of psychologists and/or run their own clinic.

Many of the activities from our other applied psychologist group highlight unique ways of combining career directions. For example, a geropsychologist, family psychologist, and school psychologist might work together with the local school system and local communities for older adults and nursing homes to find ways to increase interactions and the sharing of wisdom across generations. The combinations are limited only by your ability to imagine them.

CHAPTER SUMMARY

This chapter discussed doctoral-level education, particularly its structure and the opportunities afforded to those who complete the degree, as well as considerations for selecting a career direction or graduate program. A brief overview of the application process, with a focus on the unwritten rules was included. It also provides tips and resources for success in applying to and engaging in your doctoral-level studies. Due to the amount of available information through the Graduate Student division of APA and books (such as are listed in the following section), we strongly encourage students to read and discuss the information with their mentors, advisors, and peers so as to make the best use of available information.

EXERCISES

1   Start your own process of meaning-making by learning about being successful in both graduate school and graduate training in psychology. Here are some suggestions to get you started:

    a.   Demb, A. (2012). *Daring the doctorate: The journey at mid-career.* Rowman & Littlefield.

    b.   Giordano, P. J., Davis, S. F., & Licht, C. A. (2011). *Your graduate training in psychology: Effective strategies for success.* Sage.

    c.   Isaac, A. (1998). *The African American student's guide to surviving graduate school.* Sage.

    d.   Johnson, W. B., & Huwe, J. M. (2003). *Getting mentored in graduate school.* American Psychological Association.

    e.   Kuther, T. L. (2008). *Surviving graduate school in psychology: A pocket mentor.* American Psychological Association.

    f.   Phillips, E. M., & Pugh, D. S. (2008), *How to get a PhD: A handbook for students and their supervisors* (4th ed.). McGraw-Hill.

    g.   Privitera, G. J. (2014). *Getting into graduate school: A comprehensive guide for psychology and the behavioral sciences.* Sage.

    h.   Rittner, B., & Trudeau, P. (1997). *The women's guide to surviving graduate school.* Sage.

    i.   Rossman, M. G. (2002). *Negotiating graduate school: A guide for graduate students* (2nd ed.). Sage.

2   Learn more about graduate study in research-oriented psychology careers by exploring the website of the Association for Psychological Science (www.psychological science.org) and/or speak with a faculty member who teaches in that area and ask them about the associations that they belong to or participate in professionally.

3   Learn more about graduate study in psychology and divisions of interest to you at the following American Psychological Association Division websites:

    a.   Graduate Student Division web: www.apa.org/apags

    b.   See the full list at: www.apa.org/about/division

4   The goal of this exercise is to help you to identify research or practice areas of interest so that you can begin to focus in on the subfield in psychology that best fits you. Make a list of the courses that you've taken, then make two columns next to them. In the first column, indicate how interesting the topic was to you. Use a scale from 0 to 10, with 0 = no interest at all to 10 = so interesting that you'd like to take more courses on that topic. Now, rank all the courses. For the next step, we're going to focus only on the courses you ranked as "10" or, the highest number you ranked. Go to column 3. In column 3 list what topics or ideas or readings, etc. made that course so interesting. If it was "everything" – say that. You can continue to do this for all rankings, or you can stop at any point – your choice. The next steps are to take at least three of the most interesting and learn more about those subfields by talking with faculty, joining a research team that focuses in this area, reading in this area, and/or becoming a student member in the related organization.

Next steps: the advanced move

1 Ask an advisor or instructor
   a. To introduce you to a graduate student or the director or coordinator of the graduate program of your interest.
   b. For help (if the program of interest is not at your institution) in connecting with a faculty at another institution in that program.
2 Ask your advisor or one of your instructors to help you connect with some current graduate students so you can learn more about this important phase in your development.
3 Join the American Psychological Association's Graduate Student division and become active in the APA division that most closely aligns with your interests.
4 Read a book on succeeding in graduate school to increase your understanding of the educational process in which you will engage. Choose a book from the list in the previous section, Exercises (1) or ask your advisor/mentor for suggestions.

REFERENCES

American Psychological Association. (2011). Model act for state licensure of psychologists. *American Psychologist, 66*(3), 214–226. https://doi.org/10.1037/a0022655

American Psychological Association. (2020a). *Factsheet: Women's representation among the academic psychology workforce continues to increase.* www.apa.org/workforce/publications/academic-psychology/women.pdf

American Psychological Association. (2020b). *Factsheet: Racial/ethnic minority representation among the academic psychology workforce continues to increase.* www.apa.org/workforce/publications/academic-psychology/minority.pdf

American Psychological Association. (2020c). *Career pathways and the psychology major.* Retrieved January 31, 2021, from www.apa.org/workforce/presentations/career-pathways.pdf

Brown v. Board of Education, 347 U.S. 483. (1954). https://www.oyez.org/cases/1940-1955/347us483.

Cherry, D. K., Messenger, L. C., & Jacoby, A. M. (2000). An examination of training model outcomes in clinical psychology programs. *Professional Psychology: Research and Practice, 31*(5), 562–568. https://doi.org/10.1037/0735-7028.31.5.562

Murphy, M. J. (2008). *Factors associated with Ph.D./ Psy.D. Differences: Program content emphasis and instructional context.* Retrieved January 15, 2021, from www.apa.org/ed/accreditation/about/coa/assembly-differences.pdf

National Center for Educational Statistics. (n.d.). *Classification of instructional programs crosswalk: 2010 to 2020 conversion.* https://nces.ed.gov/Ipeds/cipcode/croswalk.aspx?y=56

Reaves, R. P. (2006). The history of licensure of psychologists in the United States and Canada. In T. J. Vaughn (Ed.), *Psychology licensure and certification: What students need to know* (pp. 17–26). American Psychological Association. https://doi.org/10.1037/11477-002

12

Specializations, allied professions, and using psychology in the world

---

ORIENTING QUESTIONS

1. What are specialties in psychology?
2. Why might you want to be a generalist or pursue another specialty?
3. What are some options for specialization in psychology and allied fields?
4. How can you decide or confirm your decision about a specialty area or allied profession?
5. How would your choice(s) help you use psychology in the world? To change the world?

DOI: 10.4324/9780429296413-16

INTRODUCTION

Some people know what they want to do early in life, others discover their career paths later in life (Encore, 2011; Foley & Lytle, 2015; Karlgaard, 2019) – and most of us are somewhere in between. The majority of people benefit from investing time and energy in career decision-making and planning (Hammond, 2017), some intuitively *know* and might even consider their career a calling (Duffy & Dik, 2013), while again, most of us are in between. Similarly, some people are generalists, others are clearly committed to a particular specialty, while others are interested in multiple specialties.

This chapter focuses on specialties, also referred to as specializations, in psychology, allied fields, and using psychology in the world. Consistent with the purpose of this book, we've intentionally defined specialty more broadly than is traditionally used in psychology (i.e., at the doctoral and post-doctoral level). We also want to emphasize that while many people build successful careers in general psychology, you may *need* an advanced degree and specialized training to reach your career goals.

GENERAL PSYCHOLOGY, SPECIALTIES, AND SPECIALIZATION

As a prelude to further discussion about specialties, let's consider the importance of general knowledge in psychology. The overwhelming majority – almost 90% – of bachelor's degrees in psychology are in general psychology (NCES, 2019). Those degrees, as we've discussed, are designed to promote graduates' foundational knowledge and critical thinking, research, and other life and career skills (APA, 2013). Although graduate programs typically build on general psychology (Zlotlow et al., 2011), more than three-quarters of graduate degrees in psychology are awarded in subfields, also known as specialty areas (NCES, 2017, 2019). The remaining graduate degrees are in general psychology, the second most popular category of master's and doctoral degrees in psychology (NCES, 2017, 2019). Many people appreciate the broad perspective a general degree offers. APA confirmed the importance of general psychology in 1946, when in setting up its divisional structure, it established the Society for General Psychology (SGP) as Division 1. SGP, which is open to generalists and specialists alike, is focused on the breadth and depth of psychology, including the integration of multiple perspectives in psychology (APA Division 1: SGP, 2021a). In sum, in a very real way, general psychology is both foundational – and a specialization – that is broadly applicable in careers and life.

There are also advantages to specialization, which by definition, builds on and extends general knowledge. At its most basic, none of us has to develop expertise in the vast array of specialties when we can consult with or otherwise learn from specialists in that area (e.g., by reading and research). This is true in many fields, including psychology, a diverse and quickly developing field, in which specialization that builds on general knowledge facilitates the development of knowledge and skills in specific areas (Neal, 2020; Roberts, 2006; Zlotlow et al., 2011).

Given the diversity within psychology, it would be impossible to describe – or even provide a full list – of the vast array of potential specialties in psychology. Such a list would continuously be developing. Moreover, it's very likely that new specialty areas will emerge. Perhaps you'll contribute to them! In addition, there are often specialties within specialties, sometimes called subspecialties, and other subfields. For example, we both identify as psychologists (a very broad professional term), counseling psychologists (a specialty), and vocational psychologists (a subspecialty within counseling psychology). Not to complicate matters more, both of us, like many psychologists (and other professionals) have additional informal specialties, some of which we intentionally worked toward and others which we acquired through making the most of unplanned opportunities, referred to in the vocational literature as *happenstance* (Krumboltz, 2009).

How then, can you explore potential specialties? In short, this process is similar to career exploration however, it's a little more in depth, and since specialization most often begins at the graduate level, might not be in your immediate future. As a reminder, you can explore the websites and publications of established professional organizations in psychology such as APA, APS, and others your professors or other academic advisors recommend. In particular, we suggest reviewing the current list of APA divisions (APA, 2020a), checking out the websites of those that interest you the most – and adding those that continue to interest you to your potential specialty list.

In addition to specialty information and as an added incentive to explore these resources, most divisions offer professional development resources and opportunities, including networking. Some divisions, like SGP, Division 1, offer free introductory memberships with no commitment (or credit card) required. Others, such as the Society for Teaching Psychology (STP) Division 2, which is affiliated with both APA and APS, welcome members interested in the goals of the society from both professional associations as well as the general public (STP, n.d.).

You may also be able to find good information about some specialty areas in psychology on O*net (onetonline.org) published by the Bureau of Labor Statistics (BLS) and other library resources. In addition, if you're considering or working toward a doctorate, you might find it helpful to explore APA's formally recognized specialty areas (APA, 2020a). Furthermore, if you're thinking longer term, to a doctoral degree plus experience, the post-doctoral specialties recognized by the American Board of Professional Psychology (ABPP, n.d.-a) and the Council on Specialties in Professional Psychology (CoS, 2020) may be worth investigating.

What are some other ways to explore potential specialties? One of the most basic is to use your research skills to find accurate, evidence-based information. This means identifying credible sources of information, critically analyzing that information, and checking your interpretations with people who are knowledgeable about the topic. Let's unpack that sentence as it applies to psychological specialties.

How do you know if a potential source of information about psychological specialties is credible? One simple way is to consider the source of the information. For example, does the source have experience or knowledge about careers in psychology such as your professor or advisor? Is your potential source working in one of the specialties you're considering? If so, they are more likely to have good information about potential specialties – and psychology – than others. In addition to your professors and advisors, who else do *you* know who might be able to help you explore potential specialties in psychology? Make a note of these potential resources to consult with after you've done your preliminary work, like reading further in this chapter.

How do you know if other sources of information (e.g., online) are credible? As mentioned earlier, it's important to consider the source. Who or what organization presented this information? What's the basis for their claims? Is it evidence-based? Verifiable? This is where your research and critical thinking skills come in – even when considering specializations and allied professions. Sadly, some websites that purport to give information (e.g., on accreditation and licensure) are misleading, incorrect, and even cleverly disguised advertisements. As such, we strongly encourage you to verify the information you need with trusted sources before you commit to any further training.

Key questions to consider as you read, reflect, and do the exercises in this chapter are: Do you need a specialization to reach your career goals? Would one be helpful? If the answer to either of these questions is "maybe" or "yes", let's continue with the process of making informed decisions about specializations in *your* career.

Are you ready for more research into potential specialties? If so, keep reading. In the next two sections, we've offered brief evidence-based descriptions of select popular and emerging psychological specialties and allied professions to inspire and guide further exploration and informed decision-making. Therefore, in addition to references (which, as a reminder, are generally good sources of information), we've provided recommendations for following up if you'd like additional or updated information about these – and other areas that interest you.

SELECT PSYCHOLOGICAL SPECIALTIES

Consistent with our earlier recommendations, this section offers brief overviews of the most popular psychological specialties as well as select emerging psychological specialties. We identified popular specialties by the number of graduate degrees reported by NCES and, when available, the number of practitioners in each area. We identified emerging specialties by reviewing the relevant professional literature, including O*net data and projections and reflecting on our experience advising thousands of people interested in careers in psychology.

We organized these brief overviews into categories by predominant career options (e.g., independent practice, research, and other) although there's some unavoidable overlap. In each of the sections, we offer suggestions for further exploration in these – and other related areas. As you read, explore, and reflect on potential specialties, we encourage you to continue refining your list of potential specialties, keeping in mind that specialties, while optional, can also be very rewarding. Sometimes you find *your* people and path in one or more specialty areas!

Clinical, counseling, and school psychology

Let's start with an overview of clinical, counseling, and school psychology, all of which are formally recognized specialty areas in psychology recognized by APA (2020b), CoS (2020) and ABPP (n.d.-b). Together, and individually, these specialties are health service psychology (HSP) areas. HSP has also been, and sometimes still is, known as applied psychology or professional psychology. As a whole, the HSP specialties represent more master's and doctoral level practitioners (and degrees awarded) than any other specialty in psychology. People with doctorates in HSP specialty areas are generally eligible for licensure as a psychologist and independent practice as a health service psychologist in all U.S. jurisdictions.

Clinical psychology is, by far, the most popular doctoral degree program in psychology. Based on data from NCES (2011, 2017), clinical psychology accounts for almost 40% of the doctoral degrees awarded in psychology each year. In comparison, counseling psychology, with the second highest number of degrees awarded each year, accounts for about 8% of the total number of doctoral degrees in psychology and 20% of clinical psychology degrees. School psychology is the fourth most popular doctoral degree in psychology, accounting for a little more than 5% of the whole. Stepping outside of the HSP group for a moment to fill in the top four, the third most popular doctoral degree is educational psychology, which is a good option for people interested in educational research, including the foundations of teaching and learning (APA Division 15, 2017). A doctorate in educational psychology does not generally meet the educational requirements for psychology licensure.

Similarly, despite the similarities between counseling psychology and professional counseling, which are explored in more depth in our discussion of master's level professions in Chapter 10, doctoral degrees in Counselor Education and Supervision (CES) do not, as a rule, meet the requirements for psychology licensure. The CES doctorate prepares the holder for faculty positions, specifically teaching and supervising master's candidates in counseling. People with doctoral degrees in CES generally qualify for licensure as a professional or mental health counselor (Brady-Amoon & Keefe-Cooperman, 2017).

At the master's level, the majority of HSP degrees are awarded in counseling psychology, followed by school psychology, then clinical psychology (NCES, 2017). Most people with master's degrees in counseling psychology and counseling are eligible for licensure as a professional or mental health counselor. In addition, people with a master's degree in counseling psychology, counseling, and school counseling may also be eligible for state education agency credentialing to work as a school counselor in most public schools. Similarly, people with a master's degree and often specialist (post-master's) degree in school psychology most often apply for state educational agency credentialing to work as a school psychologist. The greatest variability in degree and licensure options in HSP at the master's level is in clinical psychology, which we explored in greater depth in Chapter 10, with other information about master's degrees in psychology.

Research and experimental psychology

As a scientifically based profession, research is integral to psychology. It's also a psychological specialty. Regardless of your career status or aspirations, knowing how to find, critically evaluate, and apply research is essential. It's so important we're continuing to encourage you to do just that in life/career decision-making, including decisions about potential specialties, including research!

There are many ways to specialize in research ranging from working as a research assistant to supervising funded research labs or institutes as a principal investigator (PI). In addition, many college/university faculty members (aka academic psychologists) regularly engage in research – thus contributing to the fast-growing psychological knowledge base. There are many types of research (e.g., basic, applied), methods (e.g., quantitative, qualitative), and an almost unlimited array of potential concurrent specialty areas and topics to investigate. As a reminder, one of the best ways to find out more about specialty areas and topics is to explore the APS and APA websites, including relevant APA division websites and resources. As research, like science, typically develops incrementally, most researchers find their niche, sometimes intentionally, sometimes augmented by happenstance (Krumboltz, 2009; Krumboltz et al., 2013).

Cognitive and behavioral psychology

Some specialty areas have multiple tracks. For example, cognitive psychology is presented as a research, experimental *and* applied specialty area. The Society for Experimental Psychology and Cognitive Science, APA Division 3 (APA, 2021d) focuses on cognitive psychology and its subspecialties as research specialties. Moreover, to illustrate our recommendation to learn about specialties by reading journals in your area(s) of interest, Division 3 publishes five respected journals, all of which begin with *Journal of Experimental Psychology*, followed by a subtitle indicating the journal's focus, ranging from general, to more specific areas such as learning, memory, and cognition, and applied (APA, 2016).

Cognitive psychology is also an applied specialty area that informs our understanding of learning, memory, thinking, and related cognitive processes – and ideally best practice in numerous areas such as education and artificial intelligence. To learn more about the breadth and depth of applied cognitive psychology, check out the topics and articles published in the *Journal of Experimental Psychology: Applied*. In addition, as Behavioral and Cognitive Psychology (BCP) is a formally recognized specialty in psychology, all three specialty recognition groups (APA, 2020a; CoS, 2020; ABPP, n.d.-b) are excellent sources of further information about BCP and its subspecialties, perhaps the most well-known of which is cognitive behavioral therapy (CBT).

Applied behavior analysis (ABA), also called Behavior Modification and Learning Theory is another recognized BCP subspecialty – and a specialty in its own right. To illustrate ABA's status as a specialty as well as connections among specialties, APA's Division 25, Behavioral analysis, is focused on research, teaching, and the application of behavioral research, including behavior modification (APA, 2021b; BACB, n.d., 2020). This is, as you might have already surmised, related to educational psychology, school psychology, school counseling, and many degrees and career paths in education and human development.

Cognitive, behavioral, and other psychological research also opens up possibilities for future research and applications. For example, you may be interested in the intersection of psychology and technology. If so, there's a lot you can do with that, including cyberpsychology, an emerging field (Ancis, 2020). You might also want to explore integrative specialties such as cognitive neuroscience (Washburn, 2019), neuroeconomics, the integration of neuroscience, economics, and psychology (Miller, Sanger-Katz, & Wu, 2021), or behavioral economics (Kahneman, 2011). As an interesting aside, Daniel Kahneman's foundational work in behavioral economics was considered so important, he's the only psychologist to have ever been awarded a Nobel Prize, albeit in economics (Smith, 2002).

Social psychology

Social psychology is another popular example of a research, experimental, and potentially applied specialty in psychology. In general, social psychologists study human interaction with each other and their physical environments (APA, 2021e). The Society for Social and Personality Psychology (SSPP), the largest professional organization dedicated to social and personality psychology (SSPP, 2021a), is an APA division and an independent organization – so you don't have to be a member of APA to join SSPP (SSPP, 2021b).

Then, there's the Society for the Psychological Study of Social Issues (SPSSI), which like the others in this category is a well-regarded independent association, NGO member of the UN (SPSSI, 2019), and APA Division 9. SPSSI, established in 1936 in response to the social issues of that era has made significant contributions over the years promoting research and the application of research to promote positive social change and solve real world problems in a broad range of areas (Rutherford et al., 2011; SPSSI, 2019).

Other popular and emerging areas

Industrial-Organizational (I-O) psychology is an area of applied psychology and research with broad applications and a strong projected outlook (O*net, 2020a). I-O psychologists focus on organizational factors that contribute to employee satisfaction, productivity, and similar outcomes. Would you like to apply your psychological knowledge and skills in business? Do you enjoy administration, management, policy development, and/or consulting? Looking at systems, identifying areas of improvement, and making things better? If so, I-O might be for you. In addition to the resources discussed earlier, check out Chapter 10 if you're interested in I-O at the master's level.

Rehabilitation psychology is another specialty recognized by APA (2020b), CoS (2020), and ABPP (n.d.-b), all of which are excellent sources of information about this and other recognized specialties. Rehabilitation psychology is an area to consider if you're interested in research and/or applications to promote recovery from injury and well-being of people with disabilities and chronic health conditions. For more on rehabilitation psychology, see APA's Division 22 (APA, n.d.). Psychologists and aspiring psychologists with disabilities may also find common cause/solidarity/support in the division's section on psychologists with disabilities.

Psychiatric and vocational rehabilitation may be considered subspecialties as well as specialties in and of themselves with opportunities for people with varied levels of formal education. People who work in psychiatric rehabilitation and related fields at various levels, as well as in allied fields such as psychiatric nurse practitioners, help people recover from psychiatric illnesses and live meaningful lives. For more on this, we recommend exploring APA's *Psychiatric Rehabilitation* journal. Similarly, work in vocational rehabilitation focuses on finding, preparing for, and maintaining meaningful work in conjunction with recovery – just one of the many benefits of meaningful work. O*Net (2020b) projects a bright outlook for rehabilitation counselors and related job titles. Furthermore, as with many other areas, specialization is not necessarily limited. You (and many others) may specialize in one or more areas (e.g., clinical or school psychology) as well as rehabilitation psychology and/or other areas that work for you.

Forensic psychology is another triply recognized specialty (APA, 2020a; CoS, 2020; ABPP, n.d.-b). People with specialized training in forensic psychology at all levels contribute to research, including experimental research, and apply their knowledge as administrators and policy makers. They may also provide many forms of direct service such as case management, advocates, and testing and assessment to inform legal and other proceedings (Stutman & Brady-Amoon, 2011, 2015).

In addition to recognized specialties, APA also has a formal process for recognizing proficiencies – or supplemental subspecialties. The currently recognized proficiencies are sports psychology, addictions, biofeedback, and applied psychophysiology. The advantage of recognized specialties, proficiencies, and divisions based on shared interests are, in addition to shared interests, opportunities for professional development, networking, and opportunities to contribute to the development of the specialty. Furthermore, some psychologists appreciate and benefit from the professional accomplishments and recognition associated with Board certification (i.e., ABPP).

ALLIED PROFESSIONS

Some people interested in careers in psychology find their professional homes in allied professions rooted in or otherwise very similar to psychology. Although those career shifts can happen at any level, many are associated with increasing options for master's level education and career options, particularly those that lead to licensure and direct service practice such as social work and counseling (Brady-Amoon & Keefe-Cooperman, 2017; Campbell et al., 2018). Social work and counseling are just two potential allied fields you might consider, explore, and ultimately pursue. Similar to other life/

career options, it would be impossible to list, let alone describe, all the potential allied fields that are or will be available during your career – so research, and yes, you guessed it, reflection, are necessary.

To help you get started with your research, we've provided brief overviews of some of the most popular allied professions and suggestions for further exploration in these – and other – fields. In addition, as we've emphasized throughout this book, life/career decision-making, planning, and success is very personal. As a reminder, it's helpful to regularly reflect on your current situation, context, and goals, including current versions of the plans you developed in Chapters 3 and 6. With that information in mind, you can return to this iterative process of researching prospective fields and, when you identify one or more that might be a good fit for you, consider the degree to which a particular course of study and/or other professional preparation will help you reach your life and career goals.

In Chapter 10, we identified and briefly explored education and training, licensing and school certification, and career opportunities in three allied master's level professions – social work, counseling, and marriage and family therapy – that we'll explore further here. As a recap, all three are considered master's level professions because, with the exception of a few states that license bachelor's degree social workers, a master's degree is the minimum level of education required for licensure and independent practice. At the same time, although doctoral degrees in social work, counseling, and marriage and family therapy are options for those interested in advanced practice and, more often, teaching and research, licensure remains at the master's level in all three fields.

Counseling and counselor education

Counseling is a diverse field, encompassing multiple, often-overlapping, specialties. The largest of these specialties is mental health counseling, followed by school counseling, with addictions counseling (also known as alcohol and substance abuse counseling) coming in third (Health Resources Services Administration; HRSA, 2017). Professional counselors, regardless of specialty, typically perform a wide range of functions. They may work as administrators, researchers, or teachers. The majority engage in direct and indirect client service – counseling for prevention, early intervention, wellness, and career development – yes, that's a counseling as well as counseling psychology specialty. Moreover, O*net (2020c) projects increased demand for master's level counselors, both generally and in multiple specialty areas.

As noted earlier, professional counselors are generally eligible for counselor licensure in all 50 states and US jurisdictions, typically as Licensed Professional Counselors (LPCs) or Licensed Mental Health Counselors (LMHCs). Some jurisdictions offer additional licensure options for specialty areas such as New Jersey's Licensed Clinical Alcohol and Drug Counselor (LCADC). In addition, school counselors, sometimes also known as guidance counselors, may be eligible for state education department certification that qualifies the holder to work as a school counselor in a public school.

In terms of philosophy and approach, counseling and the recognized specialty of counseling psychology (APA, 2020b; SCP, 2021), including the ABPP (n.d.-b) specialty and certification in counseling psychology, and the CoS (2020) specialty of the same name, are more similar than different (Brady-Amoon & Keefe-Cooperman, 2017). We addressed counselor education, including doctoral degrees in CES in the earlier section on counseling psychology. We also recommend reviewing that section as well as the sections on counseling and counseling psychology in Chapter 10 in light of the close associations among psychology, counseling psychology, and professional counseling (Brady-Amoon & Keefe-Cooperman, 2017).

Social work and clinical social work

Social work is one of the largest health and social services professions (GWUHWI, 2017; HRSA, 2017). Social workers, like psychologists, work in a range of functions in a variety of settings. They are researchers, administrators, case managers, consultants, teachers, community organizers and more. Many work with marginalized and other vulnerable people (GWUHWI, 2017).

Although predominantly a master's level field (NCES, 2017), there are also career options in social work for people with bachelor's and, in some jurisdictions, less than a bachelor's degree. Regardless, psychology is good preparation. To illustrate, in a recent survey of master's level social workers, the two most frequently reported undergraduate majors were social work (25.3%) and psychology (17.9%). In addition, psychology was the most frequently reported second major, accounting for 14% of those reports (GWUHWI, 2017, Table 6).

Social workers with the requisite training and supervised experience may also qualify for licensure as a social worker. Most of these licenses are at the master's level however, some jurisdictions offer licensing options for people with less than a master's degree. Approximately 50% of social workers with a master's or doctoral degree are licensed (GWUHWI, 2017), often as clinical social workers. For the most part, licensed social workers are eligible to provide mental health services including therapy. However, similar to other professions, there are significant jurisdictional variations in title, scope of practice, and eligibility by jurisdiction. As such, if you're considering licensure in social work, it's important to check the requirements with the licensing agency in the jurisdiction(s) you're considering. Social workers may also qualify for state education agency certification to work in public schools as school social workers. As mentioned earlier, if you see yourself working as a social worker with children in a school setting, it's important to check those requirements.

Marriage and family therapy

Marriage and family therapy (MFT) is another license-eligible master's level practitioner degree and profession with high anticipated growth (Bureau of Labor Statistics; BLS, 2020). MFTs are licensed in all 50 states and most US jurisdictions. As the title indicates,

MFTs typically help people improve marriages, couple relationships, and families. They frequently work from a systems perspective, helping people understand themselves in the context of their family and other systems such as community and culture.

In terms of philosophy and approach, MFT is similar to the psychological specialty of Couple and Family therapy (APA, 2020b) and the CoS (2020) and ABPP (n.d.-b) specialties in couple and family therapy. The Society for Couple and Family Psychology, APA Division 43, works to advance research, education, public policy, and practice from a family-systems approach (APA, 2021c).

Human development and family studies

These broad areas of advanced training and specialization are often attractive to people interested in careers in psychology. Similar to MFT and couple and family psychology, these specialty areas focus on human development and behavior as individuals and family members. This includes the study of lifespan development and family systems. People interested in human development and family studies are frequently employed in health departments, agricultural extensions, and more (NCES, 2020).

Psychiatry

If you're interested in the biological underpinnings of human functioning and psychiatry research, administration, and/or practice, then psychiatry, the medical specialty most closely aligned with psychology, is a good allied field to consider. As medical doctors with an MD or DO degree, psychiatrists typically diagnose and treat people with mental illnesses. With their biological as well as psychological training, psychiatrists understand the interrelationship between mind and body, can order and interpret medical as well as psychological tests and assessments, and prescribe and monitor medication. Psychiatrists may also pursue further specializations such as child and adolescent psychology. For more on this, see the link to the American Psychiatric Association (2020c) website in the references.

How do you get from psychology to psychiatry? Well, although many medical schools require undergraduate coursework in biology, chemistry, and other natural sciences, a specific major is not required for admission to most medical schools. Some people complete a post-baccalaureate pre-medical program, colloquially called a post-bac, to strengthen their medical school applications.

SPECIALTY AREA DECISION-MAKING PROCESS RECAP

Keep in mind that specialization is, by definition, advanced – so we encourage you to develop a strong basis for your future specialization by committing yourself to life-long learning, including doing your best in your current stage and phase. For example, if you're currently an undergraduate student, recent graduate, or otherwise early in your career in psychology, this is a great time to master the basics – knowledge and skills, including research and critical thinking skills. However, at the same time, we encourage you to use the process embedded in this chapter to explore specialties that will help you reach your goals. In addition, it may be helpful to consider that specialty area decision-making and development, like other aspects of life/career decision-making and development, are often continuous processes with short-and longer-term goals. You have to start somewhere and sometime – how about right where you are, today?

BUILDING YOUR CAREER IN PSYCHOLOGY: USING PSYCHOLOGY IN THE WORLD

This chapter, like the rest of the book, is based on psychological principles. It's also based on our specialty areas of counseling psychology and vocational psychology, as illustrated by our emphases on reflection to promote self-knowledge in context, and – you got it – life and career development. Overall, our goal in this final chapter, like the rest of this book and, in particular, the chapters in Part IV of this choose-your-own next step section of this book, is to empower *you* to make informed decisions now and whenever you want or need to – to build your career in psychology and use psychology in the world.

In so doing, we encourage you to commit to life-long learning and professional development consistent with your own personalized blend, unique combination of interests and goals. In addition to considering and pursuing potential specializations, including general psychology as you build your career in psychology, we encourage you to consider what sets you apart from the thousands of people with a bachelor's degree in psychology or closely related fields – and how you can make the most of your knowledge, skills, and opportunities. In short, we encourage you to invest the time and energy to apply the lessons in this book to create a life and career that works for you, the people you serve – and makes a positive difference in the world!

CHAPTER SUMMARY

This chapter explores psychological specialties and allied fields. In keeping with the goal of this book, we defined specialty broadly while recognizing formally recognized psychological specialties at the doctoral and post-doctoral level. We briefly reviewed general psychology, other popular, and a few emerging specialties in psychology as well as allied fields in conjunction with a guided process to empower you to make informed decisions about your potential specialties, allied fields, and life/career success. The chapter (and book since this is the final chapter) concludes with a reflection on ways you can use psychology in the world – in this case, consistent with your specialty!

EXERCISES

1   Create a chart or spreadsheet of potential specialties that you update regularly. Note what interests/intrigues you the most about them – and the level of formal education you need for each. List credible sources to find out more information, when you'll do that, and leave a space to indicate when that task is complete.

2   Explore the top three potential specialties on your list on the APA website, O*net, and, if you're considering one or more graduate degrees, the National Center for Education Statistics (NCES). What new information did you discover? Who can you verify/share that with?

Next steps: the advanced move

To learn more about cognitive processes and behavioral economics for which Kahneman received the Nobel Prize in economics (there is no Nobel in psychology at present), we recommend reading his best-selling book, *Thinking Fast and Slow*. Bonus: Find someone to read this with you (or who has already read it) and discuss your impressions.

REFERENCES

American Board of Professional Psychology. (n.d.-a). *About ABPP*. www.abpp.org/About.aspx
American Board of Professional Psychology. (n.d.-b). *Application information. Learn about Specialty Boards*. www.abpp.org/Applicant-Information/Specialty-Boards.aspx
American Psychological Association. (2013). *APA guidelines for the undergraduate psychology major, Version 2.0*. www.apa.org/ed/precollege/about/psymajor-guidelines.pdf
American Psychological Association. (2016). *Society for experimental psychology and cognitive science: Division 3. Experimental journals*. www.apadivisions.org/division-3/publications/journals
American Psychological Association. (2020a) *APA divisions. View all divisions*. www.apa.org/about/division
American Psychological Association. (2020b). *Recognized specialties, subspecialties, and proficiencies in professional psychology*. www.apa.org/ed/graduate/specialize/recognized
American Psychiatric Association. (2020c). *What is psychiatry?* www.psychiatry.org/patients-families/what-is-psychiatry-menu
American Psychological Association. (2021a). *APA division 1: Society for general psychology*. www.apadivisions.org/division-1
American Psychological Association. (2021b). *Division 25. Behavior analysis*. www.apadivisions.org/division-25?_ga=2.76837013.1438150613.1610552895-1129173216.1544894124
American Psychological Association. (2021c). *Society for couple and family psychology*. www.apa.org/about/division/div43
American Psychological Association. (2021d). *Society for experimental psychology and cognitive science. Division 3*. www.apadivisions.org/division-3/index?_ga=2.43408805.1438150613.1610552895-1129173216.1544894124
American Psychological Association. (2021e). *Society for social and personality psychology*. www.apa.org/about/division/div8

American Psychological Association. (n.d.). *Rehabilitation psychology*. https://division-rehabpsych.squarespace.com/

American Psychological Association Division 15. (2017). *What is the difference between educational psychology and school psychology?* https://apadiv15.org/2017/02/05/what-is-the-difference-between-educational-psychology-and-school-psychology/

Ancis, J. R. (2020). The age of cyberpsychology: An overview. *Technology, Mind, and Behavior, 1*(1), 1–15. https://doi.org/10.1037/tmb0000009

Behavior Analyst Certification Board. (2020). *BACB fact-sheet_200122*

Behavior Analyst Certification Board. (n.d.). www.bacb.com/about/

Brady-Amoon, P., & Keefe-Cooperman, K. (2017). Psychology, counseling psychology, and professional counseling: Shared roots, challenges, and opportunities. *European Journal of Counselling Psychology, 6*(1), 41–62. https://doi.org/10.5964/ejcop.v6i1.105

Bureau of Labor Statistics. (2020). *Occupational outlook handbook. Marriage and family therapists.* www.bls.gov/ooh/community-and-social-service/marriage-and-family-therapists.htm#tab-6

Campbell, L. F., Worrell, F. C., Dailey, A. T., & Brown, R. T. (2018). Master's level practice: Introduction, history, and current status. *Professional Psychology: Research & Practice, 49*(5/6), 299–305.

Council on Specialties in Professional Psychology (CoS). (2020). www.cospp.org/

Duffy, R. D., & Dik, B. J. (2013). Research on calling: What have we learned and where are we going? *Journal of Vocational Behavior, 83*(3), 428–436.

Encore. (2011). *Encore career choices: Purpose, passion and a paycheck in a tough economy.* https://encore.org/wp-content/uploads/files/EncoreCareerChoices.pdf

Foley, P. F., & Lytle, M. C. (2015). Social cognitive career theory, the theory of work adjustment, and work satisfaction of retirement-age adults. *Journal of Career Development, 42*(3), 199–214. https://doi.org/10.1177/0894845314553270

George Washington University Health Workforce Institute. (2017, October). *Profile of the social work workforce.* www.cswe.org/Centers-Initiatives/Initiatives/National-Workforce-Initiative/SW-Workforce-Book-FINAL-11-08-2017.aspx

Hammond, M. S. (2017). Differences in career development among first-year students: A proposed typology for intervention planning. *Journal of Tthe First-Year Experience & Students in Transition, 29*(2), 45–64.

Health Resources & Services Administration. (2017). *Behavioral health workforce projections, 2017–2030.* https://bhw.hrsa.gov/sites/default/files/bureau-health-workforce/data-research/bh-workforce-projections-fact-sheet.pdf

Kahneman, D. (2011). *Thinking, fast and slow*. Farrar, Straus and Giroux.

Karlgaard, R. (2019). *Late bloomers: The power of patience in a world obsessed with early achievement*. Currency.

Krumboltz, J. D. (2009). The happenstance learning theory. *Journal of Career Assessment, 17*(2), 135–154.

Krumboltz, J. D., Foley, P. F., & Cotter, E. W. (2013). Applying the happenstance learning theory to involuntary career transitions. *Career Development Quarterly, 61*(1). https://doi.org/10.1002/j.2161-0045.2013.00032.x

Miller, C. C., Sanger-Katz, M., & Wu, K. J. (2021, January 10). After vaccinations, keep your guard up. *The New York Times*, Review section, p. 5.

National Center for Education Statistics. (2011). *Digest of education statistics*. Table 290. Bachelor's, master's, and doctor's degrees conferred by degree-granting institutions, by sex of student and discipline division: 2009–10. http://nces.ed.gov/programs/digest/d11/tables/dt11_290.asp

National Center for Education Statistics. (2017). *Digest of education statistics*. Table 318.30. Bachelor's, master's, and doctor's degrees conferred by postsecondary institutions, by sex of student and discipline division: 2014–15. https://nces.ed.gov/programs/digest/d17/tables/dt17_318.30.asp

National Center for Education Statistics. (2019). *Table 318.30*. Bachelor's, master's, and doctor's degrees conferred by postsecondary institutions, by sex of student and discipline division: 2017–18. https://nces.ed.gov/programs/digest/d19/tables/dt19_318.30.asp

National Center for Education Statistics. (2020). *Detail for CIP code 19.0701. Title: Human development and family studies, general*. https://nces.ed.gov/ipeds/cipcode/cipdetail. aspx?y=56&cipid=90643

Neal, T. M. S. (2020). Generalist and specialist training in professional correctional psychology are compatible: Reply to magaletta and patry (2020). *American Psychologist, 75*(1), 106–107. https://doi.org/10.1037/amp0000567

O*net online. (2020a). *Summary report for: 19–3032.00 – industrial-organizational psychologists*. www.onetonline.org/link/summary/19-3032.00

O*net online. (2020b). *Summary report for: 21–1015.00 – rehabilitation Counselors*. www.oneton line.org/link/summary/21-1015.00

O*net online. (2020c). *Quick search for counselor*. www.onetonline.org/find/quick?s=counselor

Roberts, M. C. (2006). Essential tension: Specialization with broad and general training in psychology. *The American Psychologist, 61*(8), 862–870.

Rutherford, A., Cherry, F., & Unger, R. (2011). "Society very definitely needs our aid": Reflecting on SPSSI in history. *Journal of Social Issues, 67*(1), 1–7.

Smith, D. (2002). Psychologist wins Nobel Prize. Daniel Kahneman is honored for bridging economics and psychology. *Monitor, 33*(11). www.apa.org/monitor/dec02/nobel.html

Society for Counseling Psychology. (2021). *APA division 17*. www.div17.org/

Society for the Psychological Study of Social Issues. (2019). *Home page*. www.spssi.org/index. cfm?nodeid=1

Society for Social and Personality Psychology. (2021a). *Society for social and personality psychology*. www.spsp.org/membership/categories

Society for Social and Personality Psychology. (2021b). *Society for social and personality psychology. Membership categories and rates*. www.spsp.org/membership/categories

Society for the Teaching of Psychology. (n.d.). *Join or renew membership in STP*. https://teachpsych. org/join/

Stutman, G., & Brady-Amoon, P. (2011). Supporting dependant relatives of undocumented immigrants through psychological hardship evaluations. *Journal of Forensic Psychology Practice, 11*(5). https://doi.org/10.1080/15228932.2011.583909

Stutman, G., & Brady-Amoon, P. (2015). Assessing and redressing effects of second-class citizenship upon US citizen daughters of undocumented immigrants. In O. M. Espin & A. L. Dotollo (Eds.), *Gendered journeys: Women, migration and feminist psychology* (pp. 233–251). Palgrave Macmillan.

Washburn, D. A. (2019, June). Historian's column: Emanuel "Manny" Donchin. Remembering a longtime fellow and originator of cognitive neuroscience. *The Experimental Psychology Bulletin*. www.apadivisions.org/division-3/publications/bulletin/2019/06/remembering-donchin

Zlotlow, S. F., Nelson, P. D., & Peterson, R. L. (2011). The history of broad and general education in scientific psychology: The foundation for professional psychology education and training. *Training and Education in Professional Psychology, 5*(1), 1–8. https://doi.org/10.1037/a0022529

Appendices

Appendix 1

FORM 6.1: ORGANIZING MY CAREER-RELATED INFORMATION

Date of Completion: _____   Version #: _____

<u>Directions:</u> Fill in as many of the items as you are able. For those items that you lack information at the present, incorporate these items into your plan so that you can work to obtain this information. The spaces are expandable, so don't feel as if you need to be brief – put in all the information you need to help you make meaning of your information.

1. Currently, I'm majoring in psychology, emphasizing (check one):

   a. ____ Research/experimental (developmental, social, neuropsychological, etc.)

   b. ____ Applied/practice (clinical, counseling, or school psychology)

2. At this point in my education, my career goal is to become a(n):

3. The evidence I've gathered to support this decision to date is:

   a. Early occupational dreams:

   b. High School courses that I liked and/or was willing to work hard at:

   c. High School or college extracurricular activities to which I committed time and enjoyed:

   d. Internship activities (H.S. or college) I most enjoyed:

   e. Top 5 occupational matches based upon career decision-making questionnaire results:

      i. Interests (Self-Directed Search, Strong Interest Inventory, Kuder Journey, etc.):

  ii. Personality (Myers-Briggs Type Indicator, California Personality Inventory, etc.):

  iii. Values (Supers' Work Values Inventory, Kuder Journey Values Scale, etc.):

  iv. Skills (Skillscan, Kuder Journey Skills Assessment, etc.):

f. Work-related Certificates or Licenses I've obtained:

g. Educational data:

  i. HS GPAs: HS – Overall: ____/_____ HS – Focus Area: _____/_____

  ii. Post-secondary GPAs:

   1. Undergraduate: Overall: _____/_____ Major: _____/_____
Minor: _____/_____

   2. Graduate: Overall: _____/_____ Major: _____/_____
Minor: _____/_____

  iii. Assessments completed:

   1. PSAT/SAT/ACT: Total Score: _____
Other Scores: _____

   2. GRE/MCAT/LSAT/etc: Total score: _____
Subject Scores: _____

h. Feedback from employers or others that I respect about my strengths, skills, and "growing edges":

i. What I believe I have been most successful at doing:

j. What I value most about what I'm doing or have done:

k. What I am currently less successful at doing and/or does not align with my values:

Appendix 2

FORM 6.2: CAREER PLAN TO COMPLETE BACHELOR'S DEGREE IN FOUR YEARS

Instructions:

- Column 1: Each section contains a list of example activities and experiences beyond class-related work that facilitates your development as a professional in psychology and related fields, as well as space for specifics about courses to complete. Expand this area by adding rows.
- Column 2: In the right-hand column of each section is a space for you to add any additional activities or tasks that will take up time and affect your ability to engage in your coursework and career/professional development. Make sure to include any deadlines.

1st Year (first 30 credit hours)

Career/Professional Career Development Activities	Major Events/Tasks/Activities Beyond School (note any deadlines)
Adapt to the University/Program	
Talk w/older students to learn about opportunities and how to succeed	
Explore organizations related to major (join at least one when eligible)	
Talk with advisor every semester (accomplishments, plan, and how to best benefit from opportunities)	

1st Year (first 30 credit hours)

Career/Professional Career Development Activities	Major Events/Tasks/Activities Beyond School (note any deadlines)
Find Psychology-related summer job/ or research/lab experience	
Complete coursework (expand and list; add in details to make this a SMART goal)	

Additional notes: [Insert here]

2nd Year (31–60 credit hours)

Career/Professional Career Development Activities	Major Events/Tasks/Activities Beyond School
Identify faculty lab to work in to learn skills; develop research/lab skills	
Participate in Professional Student Organizations; learn about major/career	
Develop resume and have it reviewed by the Career Development Center	
Apply for research-based experiential programs (e.g., MARC)	
Attend career fairs to see what they are about and how they work	
Complete coursework (expand and list; add in details to make this a SMART goal)	

Additional notes: [Insert here]

3rd Year (61–90 credit hours)

Career/Professional Career Development Activities	Major Events/Tasks/Activities Beyond School
Work in faculty lab; help faculty present/ publish	
Participate in CDC workshops/activities to improve interviewing	

3rd Year (61–90 credit hours)

Career/Professional Career Development Activities	Major Events/Tasks/Activities Beyond School
Research graduate school programs; employers	
Prepare to take GRE; learn about funding for graduate study in your field	
Obtain interview clothes; Do mock interviews at CDC	
Complete coursework (expand and list; add in details to make this a SMART goal)	

Additional notes: [Insert here]

4th year (90–120 credit hours)

Career/Professional Career Development Activities	Major Events/Tasks/Activities Beyond School
Revise resume or CV; Complete GRE	
Attend Graduate School/Employment Fairs	
Apply for Jobs and/or Graduate School	
Continue Lab work, research, presentations	
Obtain letters of reference, transcripts, etc. for applications	
Attend Graduate School/Employment Interviews	
Finish research projects; present research at conference	
Complete coursework (expand and list; add in details to make this a SMART goal)	

GRADUATE! CONGRATULATIONS!

Additional notes: [Insert here]

Appendix 3

FORM 6.3: CAREER PLAN TO COMPLETE BACHELOR'S DEGREE IN SIX YEARS

Instructions:

- Column 1: Each section contains a list of example activities and experiences beyond class-related work that facilitates your development as a professional in psychology and related fields, as well as space for specifics about courses to complete. Expand this area by adding rows.
- Column 2: In the right-hand column of each section is a space for you to add any additional activities or tasks that will take up time and affect your ability to engage in your coursework and career/professional development. Make sure to include any deadlines.

1st Year (first 20 credit hours)

Career/Professional Career Development Activities	Major Events/Tasks/Activities Beyond School
Adapt to the University/Program and build strong GPA	
Talk w/more advanced students to learn about opportunities and how to succeed	
Check out resources for updating skills related to learning, writing papers, and taking exams	

1st Year (first 20 credit hours)

Career/Professional Career Development Activities	Major Events/Tasks/Activities Beyond School
Talk with advisor every semester (accomplishments, plan, and how to best benefit from opportunities)	
Explore the services of the career counseling and/or placement offices on campus	
Complete coursework (expand and list; add in details to make this a SMART goal)	

Additional notes: [Insert here]

2nd Year (21–40 credit hours)

Career/Professional Career Development Activities	Major Events/Tasks/Activities Beyond School
Explore organizations related to major and faculty research labs	
Explore opportunities for research skill development and mentoring	
Develop resume and have it reviewed by the campus career or placement center	
Apply for research-based experiential programs (e.g., MARC)	
Stay engaged with coursework and advisor	
Complete coursework (expand and list; add in details to make this a SMART goal)	

Additional notes: [Insert here]

3rd Year (41–60 credit hours)

Career/Professional Career Development Activities	Major Events/Tasks/Activities Beyond School
Volunteer in a faculty research lab	
Join psychology organization and become active	
Seek out psychology-related experiences – field, internship, or summer	
Attend a career or graduate school fair to see what they are about and how they work	
Stay engaged with coursework and advisor	
Complete coursework (expand and list; add in details to make this a SMART goal)	

Additional notes: [Insert here]

4th Year (61–80 credit hours)

Career/Professional Career Development Activities	Major Events/Tasks/Activities Beyond School
Work in faculty lab; help faculty present/publish	
Participate in CDC workshops/activities to improve interviewing skills	
If relevant, prepare to take required examination; learn about funding for graduate study in your field	
Remain active in professional organizations	
Stay engaged with coursework and advisor	
Complete coursework (expand and list; add in details to make this a SMART goal)	

Additional notes: [Insert here]

5th year (81–100 credit hours)

Career/Professional Career Development Activities	Major Events/Tasks/Activities Beyond School
Revise resume or CV; Complete relevant exams	
Participate in a field, internship or externship Experience	
Research Graduate Schools/Employment	
Begin to think about interview clothes and accessories	
Stay engaged with coursework, research experience	
Complete coursework (expand and list; add in details to make this a SMART goal)	

Additional notes: [Insert here]

6th year (101–120 credit hours)

Career/Professional Career Development Activities	Major Events/Tasks/Activities Beyond School
Draft essays for applications as needed; Re-take GRE as needed	
Attend Graduate School/Employment Fairs	
Obtain letters of reference, transcripts, etc. for applications	
Apply for jobs and/or Graduate School	
Attend Graduate School/Employment Interviews	
Talk to professors and alumni about transitions to grad school/work and develop a plan	
Complete graduation requirements and research work	
Complete coursework (expand and list; add in details to make this a SMART goal)	

GRADUATE! CONGRATULATIONS!

Additional notes: [Insert here]

Appendix 4

FORM 6.4: POST-SECONDARY TEN-YEAR CAREER PLAN WORKSHEET

Instructions:

- Column 1: Each section contains a list of example activities and experiences beyond class-related work that facilitates your development as a professional in psychology and related fields, as well as space for specifics about courses to complete and work/personal activities. Expand these last two areas by adding rows.
- In Column 2 list details about how you are going to complete the activity. For example, you might make a note about how to identify an older student to speak with and how you want to contact them.
- Column 3 allows you to celebrate the completion of this activity or provide a reminder of a deadline you need to meet. Fill in as much as you can, then realize that what you can't fill in becomes topics for research so that at some point you can fill in those sections with knowledge and awareness.

PART I: BACCALAUREATE DEGREE COMPLETION

Typical Activities (in addition to academic program requirements)	Your plan to complete this task:	Deadline or Date Completed
1st Year (< 30 credit hours completed)		
Talk w/older students to build relationships, learn about opportunities, and how to succeed		

Typical Activities (in addition to academic program requirements)	Your plan to complete this task:	Deadline or Date Completed
1st Year (< 30 credit hours completed)		
Talk with advisor every semester (accomplishments, plan, and how to best benefit from opportunities)		
Explore organizations related to major		
Engage as a participant in research projects		
Find Summer Job related to psychology or Research Experience		
Complete academic coursework		
[Insert Work/Personal activities here]		
2nd year (31–60 credit hours)		
Identify and join faculty research team or lab to develop research and group/collaboration skills		
Participate in Professional Student Organizations;		
Visit campus career office to learn about services		
Visit career counseling/ development center to learn more about careers in and related to your interests		
Develop resume and have it reviewed by the Career Development Center		

Typical Activities (in addition to academic program requirements)	Your plan to complete this task:	Deadline or Date Completed
1st Year (< 30 credit hours completed)		
Apply for research-based experiential programs (e.g., MARC)		
Attend career fairs to see what they are about and how they work		
Complete academic coursework		
[Insert Work/Personal activities here]		
3rd year (61–90 credit hours)		
Work in Faculty lab; help faculty present/publish		
Participate in CDC workshops /activities to improve interviewing		
Research graduate school programs; employers		
Prepare to take GRE; learn about funding for graduate study in your field		
Obtain interview clothes; Do mock interviews at CDC		
Participate in Conferences and off-campus internships		
Complete academic coursework		
[Insert Work/Personal activities here]		
4th year (90–120 credit hours)		
Revise resume or CV; Complete GRE		
Apply for Jobs and/or Graduate School		

Typical Activities (in addition to academic program requirements)	Your plan to complete this task:	Deadline or Date Completed
1st Year (< 30 credit hours completed)		
Continue Lab work, research, presentations		
Become a student member of your professions' organization		
Obtain letters of reference, transcripts,		
Keep up GPA and finish research projects; present research at conference		
Complete academic coursework		
[Insert Work/Personal activities here]		

PART II: TRANSITION TO EMPLOYMENT OR GRADUATE SCHOOL (SUMMER PERIOD)

Typical Activities (in addition to academic program requirements)	Your plan to complete this task:	Date Completed
Read program and institution handbooks		
ID Advisor and Potential Research Team		
Make sure GA application materials complete		
Find place to stay and move to new location		
Complete pre-requisites (if necessary) or employment paperwork and orientation		

PART III: WORLD-OF-WORK (OCCURS AFTER ANY OF THE DEGREE COMPLETION PERIODS)

Typical Activities (in addition to academic program requirements)	Your plan to complete this task:	Date Completed
Year 1:		
Get to know the expectations of the organization		
Learn about the parameters of your job		
Learn how to effectively present your ideas so others will hear		
Learn about the "promotion" structure and options		
Year 2:		
Evaluate your position and options in this organization		
Decide whether this is a good fit for your career		
Lay out a plan for making the most of your position or leaving		
Carry out your plan		

PART IV: GRADUATE DEGREE COMPLETION

Typical Activities (in addition to academic program requirements)	Your plan to complete this task:	Date Completed
Year 1:		
Talk with more advanced students about being successful in the program		
Join research team to improve skills		
Become active as a student member of your profession's association		
Begin to identify area of specialization; plan for thesis		
Build professional relationships with faculty and peers		
Complete academic coursework		
[Insert Work/Personal activities here]		
Year 2:		
Continue working in faculty's lab/research team		
Work with Chair on Thesis topic		
If in terminal program, apply for doctoral programs		
Begin job search if stopping with M.S. degree (see Part III above)		

Typical Activities (in addition to academic program requirements)	Your plan to complete this task:	Date Completed
If haven't already, begin attending conferences and presenting with Research Team		
Learn about grant writing and write a travel grant (to attend a conference)		
Complete academic coursework		
[Insert Work/Personal activities here]		
Year 3:		
Continue to build research and practice experience		
Begin work on publishing thesis and identifying topic for dissertation		
Continue to talk with faculty about career goals and seek feedback to increase skills		
Look for opportunities to present, and publish		
Attend conferences to network and build skills (CEU's)		
Stay active in professional associations and groups		
Find and write a grant to fund your dissertation research efforts		
Complete academic coursework		
[Insert Work/Personal activities here]		

Typical Activities (in addition to academic program requirements)	Your plan to complete this task:	Date Completed
Year 4:		
Continue to build professional relationships and connections		
Continue building skills and expertise through lab work		
Publish and engage in professional development activities		
Finish remaining coursework (as needed)		
Prepare for transition to internship, residency, or post-doctoral work		
Work on completing dissertation		
Complete academic coursework		
[Insert Work/Personal activities here]		
Year 5 and Beyond (May be optional, depending upon your program of study):		
Finish Dissertation and any tasks from year 4 that are not finished		

Appendix 5

FORM 6.5: SEMESTER PLAN FORM

For [insert semester label here]_
version 1.0 (insert date here)

Goals

Personal goals/projects

1. Exercise _ times/week
2. Sleep _ hours per night
3. Spend time with. . .
4. Attend. . .

Academic goals

1. Complete XXXX course at mastery/competence as demonstrated by. . . .
2. Etc.

Professional development/career goals

1. Related to increasing my learning effectiveness/efficiency:
   a. Learn how to speed read
   b. Learn how to use the SQ3R study method (Survey, Question, Read, Review, Recite)
2. Related to my professional development:
   a. Talk with my advisor/mentor about. . . .
   b. Read about YYY topic in psychology that has piqued my interest
   c. Attend a departmental colloquium or presentation

3   Career Plan tasks/activities
   a.   Insert from your degree completion plan for the semester here

Work, volunteering, and other commitments/goals

1   Insert information about your non-academic and non-psychology profession-related goals here

Accountability mechanisms

1   Time tracking on calendar
2   [insert the names of people who support you in getting things done here]

SEMESTER PLAN FOR: _____ **(v 1.0)**

Week		Academic Goals	Professional/ Career Dev.	Work/ Employment	Volunteering/ Other	Personal Goals
1	[insert date here]	[insert information about course requirements that you plan to do during this semester in the appropriate week]	[insert information about the professional/ career development activities that you plan to do during this semester in the appropriate week in this column]	[insert information about the work/ employment activities that you plan to do during this semester in the appropriate week in this column]	[insert information about the volunteering or other activities that you plan to do during this semester in the appropriate week in this column]	[insert information about the personal goals/ activities that you plan to do during this semester in the appropriate week in this column]
2						
3						
4						
5						
6						
7						
8						

Week	Academic Goals	Professional/ Career Dev.	Work/ Employment	Volunteering/ Other	Personal Goals
9					
10					
11					
12					
13					
14					
15					
16					

Appendix 6

FORM 6.6: TIME SCHEDULE FORM

Time Schedule for the Week of: _____

	Monday	Tuesday	Wednesday	Thursday	Friday	Saturday	Sunday
6:00							
6:30							
7:00							
7:30							
8:00							
8:30							
9:00							
9:30							
10:00							
10:30							
11:00							
11:30							
12:00							
12:30							
1:00							
1:30							

	Monday	Tuesday	Wednesday	Thursday	Friday	Saturday	Sunday
2:00							
2:30							
3:00							
3:30							
4:00							
4:30							
5:00							
5:30							
6:00							
6:30							
7:00							
7:30							
8:00							
8:30							
9:00							
9:30							
10:00							
10:30							
11:00							

Index

Page numbers in *italics* indicate a figure and page numbers in **bold** indicate a table on the corresponding page.

collaboration skills for 44; critical thinking skills for 44; definition 43; goal of 45; research skills 44; self-management 66; skills 43, 45; as a transferable skill 155

career planning 4, 32–33, 71, 104; goal setting and 51–54; *Integrative career planning for adults* 32; and placement center 72; time investment for 33; *What color is your parachute?* 32, 54, 159

career-related information 209–210

career shock 170

career transition 170

categories of work in psychology 23–28, 35; *see also* work categories

Center for Workforce Studies (CWS) 4, 11, 44, 146

Centers for Disease Control (CDC) 188

certificate 25, 30

challenging interactions 79

choosing the right program 172–175

Clark, Kenneth 5

Clark, Mamie Phipps 5, 182

classmates and peers 121–122; benefits of positive relationships with 121; *see also* peers

Clinical, Counseling, and School Psychology 23, 164, **165**, 184, 187, 196

clinical psychology/clinical psychologists 23, 29, **165**, 166, 168, 196

clinical social work 31, 201; *see also* social work

cognitive and behavioral psychology 197–198; cognitive psychology 29, 116, 197–198; therapy (CBT) 197

collaboration 131, 147, 155; benefits of 27, 84; in experimental psychology 186; of HSPs and other groups 189; in learning 62–63; of research teams and labs 84; skills 44, 155, 219

collectivist culture 84

communication 27, 62, 64, 65, 67, 113, 122, 128, 132, 134, 136, 152–153, 155, 181

community xx, 21, 26, 43, 48, 49, 80, 96, 115, 123, 128, 135, 149, 151, 188, 189, 201, 202

community and civic groups 135

confirmation bias 64

conscientiousness 77; *see also* responsibility

coping with bias and discrimination 64, 79–80, 128, 133–134; community 79–80; implicit bias 79; microaggressions 79, 189

Council on Specialties in Professional Psychology (CoS) 194, 196–199, 201–202

counseling xx, 4, 16, **22**, 23–24, 29–31, 48, 53, 56, 71, 72, 118, 128, 154, 158, 166–169, 173, 187, 189, 196, 198, 199, 200–201; counselor education 200–201

counseling and counselor education 200–201; *see also* counseling

counseling psychology/counseling psychologists 23, 27, 29, 48, 164, 166, 168–169, 194, 196, 200–201, 203

Counselor Education and Supervision (CES) 196, 201

Couple and Family **22**, 24, 202; *see also* Marriage and Family Therapy

Covey, S. R. 9, 10, 91

creativity **47**, 81–82, 85, 87

critical thinking xxii, 44, 63–65, 72, 78, 85, 114–115, 154–155, 181, 193, 195, 203; confirmation bias 64; feedback, openness to 44, 63–64; generalizability, limits of 64; information literacy and 65

cultural/social organizations and groups 135

curriculum 33, 179, 182; curriculum vitae (CV) 114; extra-curricular activities 42, 45, 171, 209; at the graduate level 179

Davis, Rosie Phillips 27

deadlines 94–97, 211, 214; "hard" deadlines 96, 99; "soft" deadlines 96; *see also* due dates

decision-making xix, xxi, xxii, xxiv, xxvii, 7–9, 23–24, 30, 32, 34, 38–56, 135, 154, 170–172, 193, 195, 197, 200, 202–203; choosing the right program 172–175; macro level 40; micro level 39; *see also* career decision-making; decisions

decisions: about education level and type 33; about path to goal 182; about priorities 102, 120; defining 42; fear 39; informed 33, 34, 52, 65, 71, 77, 136–137, 163, 175, 195, 203; life-career decision and plan 7–9, 23, 26–29, 30–34; on master's degree 170, 175; on over-commitment 93; to pursue a degree 167; on specialty area 202–203; uninformed 83; *see also* career decision-making; decision-making

degree type, differences in 184–185

developmental psychology 29, 115, 151, 183

discrimination, coping with 79–80

divisions, APA 29–30, 112, 183, 190–191, 194, 197–199; *see also* American Psychological Association

14; predominantly White 186; psychologists 25; psychology186, 197; skills **21**, 44; teams and labs 84–85
Research and Experimental Psychology 183–184, 188, 197
research assistant (RA) 28, 167, 171, 186, 197
research team 12, 25, 43–45, 52, 78, 92, 99, 114–115, 118–119, 121, 123, 150, 186, 189, 190; and labs 84–85, 87, 119
respecting yourself and others 78–82, 87; challenging interactions 79; setting boundaries 79
responsibility 12–14, 44, 62, 77, 85, 94, 98–99, 102, 112, 114, 117, 120, 127, 129–131, 137, 154, 171, 173, 181, 185, 187; conscientiousness 77; proactive, being 77, 93, 129
RIASEC theory 48; *see also* Holland, J. L.; Holland Hexagon

school certification 168, 169, 172, 200
school counseling/school counselor 11, 15, 31, 169, 196, 198, 200
school/life balance 136; integration 136–138
school psychology/school psychologists 15, 23, 29–30, 34, 149, 151, 164–166, 168–169, 184, 187, 196, 198–199
Science, Technology, Engineering, & Mathematics (STEM) 68, 96, **153**
self-awareness 8, 128
self-care as a discipline 86
Self-Directed Search 48; *see also* Holland, J. L.; Holland Hexagon; RIASEC
self-efficacy 67–68, 138
self-regulation 66
self-understanding, psychology helping in 7–9
semester plan 93, 95, 100; accountability mechanisms 227–228; creating 98–100; goals 226–227; *Semester Plan* form 99, 226–228; short-term plan 101–102; *see also* action plan; long-term plan to complete degree
service learning 148, 149
setting boundaries 79, 134; *see also* boundaries
short-term: decisions 71; plan to complete a week successfully 101–102
skills xxii–xxiii, 7, 8, 13, 21–24, 27–29, 40, 43–52, 54–55, 62–65, 67–70, 72, 78–79, 82, 84–85, 87, 91, 93–95, 102–103, 114–119, 120–121, 128, 134, 138, 150, 151, 154–156, 158, 175, 181, 189, 193–195, 198, 203

SMART goals 92–94; typical goals versus 92–93, **92**
social media 66, 86, 135, 167
Social Psychology 24, 29, 43, 167, 183, 198
social work 11–13, 28, 31, 169, 200, 201; Clinical Social Work 201; and counseling 169, 199
Society for General Psychology (SGP) 193
Society for Social and Personality Psychology (SSPP) 198
Society for the Psychological Study of Social Issues (SPSSI) 198
Society for the Teaching of Psychology (STP) 194
"soft" deadlines 96; *see also* deadlines; due dates
specialist degrees and other post-master's degrees 164–165, 168, 175, 196; *see also* specialties
specialties 12, 24, 28–31, 35, 165, 169, 193–200, 202–203; addictions counseling 200; American Board of Professional Psychology (ABPP) 194, 201; APA recognized 166, 194, 201; Applied behavior analysis (ABA) 197; Behavioral and Cognitive Psychology (BCP) 197; behavioral economics 198; behavioral psychology 197–198; to build on psychological knowledge 30–31; clinical psychology 29, **165**, 196; cognitive neuroscience 198; cognitive psychology 197–198; Council on Specialties in Professional Psychology (CoS) recognized 194, 201; couple and family **22**, 24, 202; counseling psychology 29, 169, 194, 196, 200–201; current status and trends 164; emerging 195; experimental psychology 197; forensic psychology 199; general psychology and 193–195; Industrial-Organizational (I-O) psychology 30, 167, 198; learning about, resource for 30; licensure 169, 200; neuroeconomics 198; *Occupational Outlook Handbook* as resource 30; O*Net online as resource 30, 194; organizations 78; post-doctoral 194, 203; rehabilitation psychology 198–199; research psychology 197; school psychology 30, 166, 196; selecting 170, 194–199; social psychology 24, 29, 198; social work, master's level in 169; subspecialties 194, 197, 199; substance abuse and addiction counseling 169; tracks of 197; vast array of 24, 193, 194; vocational psychology 28–30, 46, 187, 194; vocational rehabilitation 199
specialty area decision-making process recap 202–203